PRAISE FOR
The Future Is Collective

"Khonsari's experience, curiosity, sharp analysis, and fabulous storytelling bring to life incredible examples of how our organizations can get into formations to share power and bring about the culture, structure, and wins for liberation we are thirsty for."

—JENNA PETERS-GOLDEN, worker-owner and co-founder of AORTA Cooperative

"*The Future Is Collective* is not just a book—it's a movement, a call to arms for organizations and leaders to embrace a more inclusive and compassionate future."

—NICOLE WIRES, director of the Nonprofit Democracy Network

". . . a groundbreaking exploration of reimagined workplace paradigms shining a compelling light on the power and potential of collective leadership."

—MAYRA PELAGIO, former executive director of Latinos United for a New America

"This book strikes at the heart of traditional work hierarchies, proposing a transformative ethos that feels not just revolutionary but essential."

—TIRIEN STEINBACH, former associate dean for Diversity, Equity, and Inclusion at Stanford Law School

"Hierarchical workplaces repress the love and care that could transform our world. Let's build workplaces where every worker can act on their deep yearnings to care for communities and the planet. *The Future Is Collective* shows us the way."

—JANELLE ORSI, founder of Sustainable Economies Law Center

"*The Future Is Collective* brilliantly captures the zeitgeist of our times, offering a blueprint for workplaces that prioritize humanity over hierarchy. A refreshing and thought-provoking read that challenges the status quo and paves the way for meaningful change."

—EMILY GREEN, Pulitzer Prize–winning journalist

"Khonsari boldly envisions a workplace where collective leadership and equity aren't mere buzzwords but the foundational pillars of every institution. A must-read for anyone who believes in a world where work is driven by compassion and shared responsibility."

—AZADEH ZOHRABI, executive director of Berkeley Underground Scholars

"Through riveting case studies and compelling narratives, Khonsari guides us toward a new era of collaborative leadership. *The Future Is Collective* is a beacon for all those disillusioned by outdated workplace models."

—GAIL SILVERSTEIN, associate dean for experiential learning at UC Law San Francisco

"Khonsari bridges the gap between the ideal and the achievable, presenting actionable steps to transform our workspaces into hubs of inclusivity and innovation. A seminal piece."

—CURTIS YANCY, director of philanthropy

"I am so grateful to Nilou Khonsari for sharing her 'real-life-tested' experience on how to build sustainable, people-centered organizations. Her insights are not only transformative but also essential for any leader looking to shape the future of work."

—LORENA MELGAREJO, executive director of Faith In Action, Bay Area

"At a time when many workers express great dissatisfaction with the status quo and experience burnout, this book shows us ways to establish sustainable and fulfilling workplaces governed by all involved."

—ANDREW I. SCHOENHOLTZ, JD, PhD, professor from Practice at Georgetown Law and faculty director of the Human Rights Institute and the Center for Applied Legal Studies

"With many of us spending more waking hours at work than doing anything else, we need to be looking for paths and opportunities that support workers. Khonsari's book brings concrete ideas and practices, along with personal stories both positive and negative, for how we can shift our workplaces to empower workers, meet their needs, and lead to creative solutions."

—REK KWAWER, former director of operations and board member of NASCO

"*The Future Is Collective* not only challenges traditional norms but also empowers us with the tools to build workplaces where equity and shared purpose drive innovation and success."

—ZAHRA BILLOO, executive director of the Council on American-Islamic Relations, San Francisco Bay Area (CAIR-SFBA)

"This book is a powerful antidote to the cultures of power-hoarding, disenfranchisement, and marginalization that are all-too-common in our current Western industrialized society."

—RYAN MATLOW, clinical associate professor and director of community programs for the Early Life Stress and Resilience Program at Stanford School of Medicine

The Future Is Collective

EFFECTIVE WORKPLACE STRATEGIES FOR BUILDING A CULTURE OF CARE

Niloufar Khonsari

North Atlantic Books
Huichin, unceded Ohlone land
Berkeley, California

North Atlantic Books
Huichin, unceded Ohlone land
2526 Martin Luther King Jr Way
Berkeley, CA 94704 USA
www.northatlanticbooks.com

Cover art © johnjohnson13 via Getty Images
Cover design by Lauren Smith
Book design by Happenstance Type-O-Rama

Printed in Canada

The Future Is Collective: Effective Workplace Strategies for Building a Culture of Care is sponsored and published by North Atlantic Books, an educational nonprofit that collaborates with partners to develop cross-cultural perspectives; nurture holistic views of art, science, the humanities, and healing; and seed personal and global transformation by publishing work on the relationship of body, spirit, and nature.

North Atlantic Books' publications are distributed to the US trade and internationally by Penguin Random House Publishers Services. For further information, visit our website at www.northatlanticbooks.com.

Library of Congress Cataloging-in-Publication Data

Names: Khonsari, Niloufar, author.
Title: The future is collective : effective workplace strategies for
   building a culture of care / by Niloufar Khonsari.
Description: Berkeley, California : North Atlantic Books, [2025] | Includes
   bibliographical references and index.
Identifiers: LCCN 2025002444 (print) | LCCN 2025002445 (ebook) | ISBN
   9798889841975 (trade paperback) | ISBN 9798889841982 (ebook)
Subjects: LCSH: Nonprofit organizations—Management. | Political
   participation.
Classification: LCC HD62.6 .K496 2025 (print) | LCC HD62.6 (ebook) | DDC
   658/.048—dc23/eng/20250524
LC record available at https://lccn.loc.gov/2025002444
LC ebook record available at https://lccn.loc.gov/2025002445

The authorized representative in the EU for product safety and compliance is Eucomply OÜ, Pärnu mnt 139b-14, 11317 Tallinn, Estonia, hello@eucompliancepartner.com, +33757690241.

1 2 3 4 5 6 7 8 9 FRIESENS 30 29 28 27 26 25

For my daughter, Roya:

You are my greatest teacher. Your light inspires me to grow in ways I never imagined—helping me to pause, reflect, and embrace the beauty of leading with heart and vulnerability. Through you, I've discovered a deeper meaning of collective care—how it shapes the world and our everyday family moments. You've shown me the power of looking inward and leading by example.

This book is for you, so you'll always know that much of what I've learned began with you.

—*Mama*

CONTENTS

Introduction 1

1 From Revolution to Evolution 7

2 Learning to Share Power 25

3 Equity-Based Salaries 39

4 Cultivating a Culture of Care 55

5 A Structure for Our Culture 81

6 Collective Care Through Policy 101

7 Onboarding 113

8 Offboarding 125

9 Cycling Out of Executive Titles 133

10 Conflict 139

11 Funding Abundance 159

Conclusion 189

Appendices

APPENDIX A Board Resolution for Worker Self-Direction
and Distributed Authority 195

APPENDIX B Statement of Values and Principles 197

APPENDIX C Task Redistribution Chart 199

APPENDIX D Decision-Making Flowchart and Table . . . 201

APPENDIX E   Decision-Making Policy and
Gradient Voting Tool 205

APPENDIX F   Email Proposal Template 211

APPENDIX G   Handling Newly Passed Policies 213

APPENDIX H   "Life Happens" Policy 215

APPENDIX I   Job Posting 217

APPENDIX J   Detailed Job Description (Internal) 223

APPENDIX K   Candidacy Period Policy 225

APPENDIX L   Reference Checks 229

APPENDIX M   Performance Evaluation for Co-Directors . . 231

APPENDIX N   Feedback Preference Chart 245

Acknowledgments 247

How You Can Support The Future Is Collective 253

Notes 255

Index 263

About the Author 277

INTRODUCTION

Child of a Revolution

I was born in Tehran in the aftermath of war and revolution. As the Iran-Iraq War unfolded, hundreds of thousands of Iranians fled, my parents among them. They were activists, advocating for a different future, one rooted in justice and liberation, but the revolution they believed in brought another harsh regime. They sought asylum in Germany, leaving me with my grandparents in Iran as they figured out how to start over.

We were not alone in loss and struggle. Like many others, my family felt the weight of government violence. Three of my relatives were imprisoned and killed by the regime in the struggle for freedom. But what was promised as freedom instead became a system that filled more prisons and silenced more people. The trauma of our people was not just about recent events; it was compounded by harms of the 1953 US-backed coup that overthrew Iran's chance at democracy by overthrowing a democratically elected leader.

Displaced to Germany as a toddler, I grew up there with my mom before starting over again in the United States at age twelve. Even with all these changes, I was never detached from my roots. Many Iranians in the diaspora, including myself, dedicated our lives to social justice, liberation, family unity, prison abolition, and building a more just society. I had this commitment woven into the fabric of my life, along with the communal spirit at the heart of Iranian culture.

Moving across borders, I became a global citizen with a deep commitment to social justice. I lived in six countries and spoke five languages (more or less). My activism ranged from anti-war efforts to student movements, including advocating for Georgetown University to adopt a living wage policy. Later, I accepted a Fulbright Fellowship to work in Sierra Leone, where I supported lawyers and paralegals in challenging a Chinese sugarcane company that used toxic pesticides, harming both field workers and the land. In some of these spaces, I noticed a pattern: A few groups that positioned themselves as champions of social justice often ended up mirroring the same decision-making habits they criticized. I remember attending gatherings where only a few voices steered the conversation, leaving many of us feeling like we didn't matter. Decisions seemed to emerge from behind closed doors, made by a small group, rather than through an open dialogue involving everyone. This left many of us frustrated and echoed the very political dynamics we were challenging, where decisions are made in isolation, often against the will of those they impact. Through these experiences, I learned an important lesson: We can't achieve true liberation if we adopt the same practices and structures that cause harm. I saw firsthand that simply opposing what we didn't like—such as unjust wages or war—was only part of the equation.

When it came time for me to enter the job force, I felt torn between two choices: advocating for labor rights or supporting displaced people through immigration law. Each path offered a way to address injustices I'd witnessed. Then one day I had a conversation with a member of my chosen family, Helge, whom I often turn to for advice. When I shared my conflicted feelings about my career path with him, he responded gently and thoughtfully, offering a self-evident truth: "Nilou," he said, "you're a refugee."

Resilience from the Root

In 2012 I founded Pangea Legal Services, an immigrant justice organization. Our name, Pangea, was the name of the earth's original continent when it was one connected land mass, and it symbolized the unity and oneness of our global community. Alongside co-founder Marie Vincent, I established the organization's framework and helped build our foundation. From the start we were a POC (people of color)-, woman-, queer-, and immigrant-led collective, committed to uplifting communities. Between 2013 and 2023, Pangea transformed from a project funded via a small personal loan I provided and operating month to month into a robust entity with a $2.7 million operating budget and healthy reserves. It expanded from just 1.5 full-time employees to twenty-one full-time employees, along with regular contractors, interns, and law clerks. I transitioned out of Pangea in May 2023. During our time together, Pangea supported over fifty thousand people and won more than three thousand complex federal immigration cases, many of which set important legal precedents.

The team at Pangea—comprising movement lawyers, advocates, and organizers—continues to drive systems change through legal representation and community organizing. One of our proudest achievements involved establishing the first 24/7 hotline of its kind for immigrants at risk of deportation, inspiring the creation of over forty similar hotlines across the country. Our work led to the closure of three immigration detention centers and successful advocacy for legislation that ended the use of private prisons for immigrants in California. We also co-founded the Disability & Immigrant Justice Coalition, launched Project ANAR (Afghan Network for Advocacy and Resources, a program for Afghan refugees), and initiated the Asylee Legal Empowerment Project, a training program for select asylum seekers unable to find attorney representation that empowered them to defend their cases independently.

Throughout the years, Pangea faced significant hurdles, particularly around decision-making—navigating who makes which decisions and who gives input—and addressing conflicts and disagreements. Through our struggles, we gained valuable insights that shaped what some of our consultants described as "the most high-functioning" organization and governance model.

Pangea's journey exemplifies resilience. The team evolved and transformed challenges into effective structures, guides, and policies that prioritized a culture of care. At the heart of Pangea's operations was a unique and collaborative governance structure that embodied a commitment to shared leadership and collective decision-making. Staff members received equal compensation and enjoyed a four-day work week. In a notable departure from conventional practices, health benefits extended to the undocumented parents of staff. Pangea operated through a decentralized system of hubs—leadership committees where staff collaborate to develop policies, oversee projects, and manage all aspects of their work. This model fostered participation, ensuring that decision-making became a collective effort within each hub.

Major decisions impacting the organization were made by a vote by the entire team, guaranteeing that every voice gets heard. This hub system effectively distributed authority and responsibility throughout Pangea, preventing any single individual from holding all the power. Staff referred to themselves as a collective, with all members serving as co-directors.

From the outset, I aimed to ensure that Pangea embodied the same values internally that it promoted externally—an aspiration that continues to guide the organization today.

An Offering for Our Movements in Urgent Times

I am deeply inspired by the collaborative spirit of my former colleagues at Pangea and the social movements we were part of during my time there. However, there is no one-size-fits-all way to structure an organization. Just as every community has its unique tapestry of strengths and challenges, so do the ways we lead and work together. Pangea Legal Services exemplifies one effective model, showcasing collective leadership that puts people and community front and center. But what worked for us might not work for everyone else. And although our values are timeless, some things that worked for us with a smaller staff size might not work for a larger organization.

This book chronicles my journey in developing best practices at Pangea, and it lays out the main principles of collective governance: transparent and distributed decision-making, equity-based pay scales and benefits, and a culture of learning, trust, and humility. It draws on dozens of interviews, research, and best practices developed in various organizations that center a culture of care, collective governance, and liberation. It provides examples of common conflicts in workplaces and possible responses, along with tools to enhance accountability and prevent or minimize harm in organizations. Different ways to adopt and apply an abundance mindset to funding are also unpacked in later pages, and the book concludes with a vision for the future that articulates the stakes for practicing collective governance now. *The Future Is Collective* mirrors the evolution of Pangea, addressing topics that are traditionally viewed as human resources work—salaries, vacations, and benefits—and sets them in the context of liberatory culture-building, prompting us to explore the question: *What kind of culture and structure does our organization need to thrive?*

Why now?

In the summer of 2020, the national conversation around diversity, equity, and inclusion surged to the forefront. Following the murders of George Floyd and Breonna Taylor, the United States faced a profound reckoning. Business as usual was no longer an option. There was an increase in the number of Black people, Indigenous people, and women of color in executive director and management positions.[1] With their new roles came expectations to reimagine the workplace through a diversity lens, deconstruct systemic oppression, sustain ongoing programs, and navigate fundraising challenges—all while confronting mistrust and discrimination that their predecessors did not face.

In this period of sustained and compounded crises, exacerbated by a multiyear pandemic, many nonprofit organizations were reckoning with the way we work. That reckoning is still ongoing for many. According to OnePoll, 73 percent of US workers became more conscious of needing self-care in 2020.[2] According to the US Bureau of Labor Statistics, forty-seven million people in the United States voluntarily quit their jobs in 2021. That's nearly one in three of the approximately 167 million people employed at some point during that year.[3]

Nonprofit and social justice spaces were far from immune to this mass exit from the workforce, which some economists called the "Great Resignation." Adding to the general high level of stress in these spaces, a recent poll focused on community organizers also revealed high levels of burnout and turnover in the social justice nonprofit sector.[4] We can no longer keep doing this work the same way. It's time to align our organizational practices with the change we want to see in the world. As leaders in social justice, we can refuse to reform unsustainable structures and systems—and instead uproot them to create something new.

Participatory cultures and structures of care in the workplace are as diverse as the organizations themselves, ranging from single executive director leadership to multidirector models. In my research, I've had the privilege of studying a wide range of organizations and interviewing a diverse set of individuals, uncovering a wealth of effective practices. Along the way, I've connected with many inspiring voices, and I'm excited to share some of these insights with everyone involved in this important conversation.

Throughout this book, I've made a conscious effort to center the work of Black, Indigenous, and people of color (BIPOC) individuals, women, and queer people, whose wisdom and expertise are often overlooked in favor of dominant voices lacking the lived experiences of our communities. That said, *The Future Is Collective* serves as a resource for anyone—workers, students, and leaders—seeking to create meaningful changes at work. Drawing from my personal experiences and research, I hope to shed light on what it can look like to cultivate a truly collective workplace. I aim to demystify collective management by showcasing how we at Pangea translated our values into concrete policies and practices. From participatory leadership structures and decision-making processes to equitable pay scales and nonconventional benefits, this book explores practical ways to create workplaces that reflect our shared ideals. Despite our best intentions, we can often inadvertently replicate harmful structures in our organizations without noticing. This book offers practical alternatives for becoming more intentional in unlearning and dismantling conventional power dynamics that undervalue time, labor, and diverse experiences. I especially invite BIPOC workers and leaders in nonprofit and social justice sectors to engage in this conversation. Together, we can dismantle and rebuild the structures that shape our relationships and influence our world.

1

From Revolution to Evolution

My father was a revolutionary. As I was setting out to start Pangea Legal Services in 2012, we had a conversation about Iran's history, and he shared something that has stuck with me ever since. He said that lasting change requires evolution just as much as revolution—we need growth at a steady pace that can take root deeply, not just a one-time shift. I've found this to be true, both in my personal journey and in the collective work that led to the beginnings of Pangea. For real impact, we needed both vision and structure supported by steadfast, everyday action on an individual and collective scale.

The Beginning: Foundations of Collective Action

In 2011, I was a young immigration attorney in San Francisco,[*] weighed down by over $100,000 in student loans and living paycheck to paycheck in a small apartment. At that time, I had taken on three pro bono asylum cases and won

---

[*] Throughout this book, I refer to San Francisco, Berkeley, and Oakland, California, which are situated on unceded Ohlone land.

each one. Meanwhile, I made ends meet working for a couple of nonprofit organizations. One of them was the African Advocacy Network (AAN), a wonderful San Francisco–based nonprofit serving the growing diaspora of African and Afro-Caribbean immigrants. They needed attorneys for their asylum cases, and they offered me free office space and supplies in exchange for taking on some of their clients at affordable rates. It didn't take me long to realize there was a massive and increasing need for asylum and deportation defense services among immigrant populations.

Few legal nonprofits were hiring immigration attorneys then, and most of them focused on non-court legal services like helping immigrants apply for residency and citizenship. Meanwhile, the Obama administration was ramping up deportations through policies that criminalized immigrants at unprecedented rates.[*,1,2] Despite this urgent need for legal representation in court, legal nonprofits were not set up to provide it.

As a formerly undocumented immigrant to the US myself, I felt compelled to fill some of that gap in legal services. In addition to my space at the AAN, private immigration attorney Nancy Hormachea generously welcomed me to share her office. A gem of a person and a mentor, Nancy had co-founded an Iranian refugee organization called Omid Advocates for Human Rights, where I also volunteered. My days were a whirlwind—carrying massive stacks of paper files while shuttling between Nancy's office in Berkeley and the AAN office in San Francisco. In spite of all the work, I could barely afford to live in San Francisco. Eventually I moved in with my mom and stepdad for a few months, subletting my apartment during that time to save money.

Leaning on Organizers for Jesus's Freedom

In October 2012, I got an out-of-the-blue phone call from a panicked father. Immigration and Customs Enforcement (ICE) had just picked up his son,

---

* Laws like the Illegal Immigration Reform and Immigrant Responsibility Act of 1996, congressional detention bed quotas, and programs like ICE's Secure Communities meant that an estimated 478,000 people had been taken from their communities and incarcerated in immigrant detention centers across the country. As a direct result, detained people and asylum seekers were having a hard time finding attorneys to take on their cases in court. From 2009 until 2017, Congress required that thirty-four thousand immigrants be detained in US prisons on any given day. This policy was developed by the private prison industry. Although activists fought this quota and won the removal of this congressional mandate, immigrants continue to be detained in astronomical numbers that are higher than the quota.

Jesus Ruiz Diego,[3] at his job and was about to deport him to Mexico. A former client I had helped release from immigration prison a few months back had shared my number with Jesus's father.

Jesus arrived in the US with his family at just four years old, and they made a home in San Jose, California. In a community where many faced challenges like dropping out of school or dealing with incarceration and deportation, Jesus gave others hope. He became the first in his family to graduate high school—an incredible achievement! After nearly failing, he sought extra help from a teacher, attended night school, and even went to summer school. His hard work made him a role model for his younger brother and for many in his extended community.

Since Jesus had not visited Mexico, he did not have personal ties there. San Jose was truly the only home Jesus knew. Sadly, a disbarred attorney misled his family by promising them legal assistance but ultimately placed Jesus in deportation proceedings while he was still in elementary school, resulting in a deportation that would haunt him for years. After his deportation, Jesus quickly returned home to the US.

When Jesus graduated, he found a job as a sheet-metal worker, a role that demands precision, physical skill, and intellectual problem-solving. Jesus brought talent and a sense of humor to his job, consistently approaching challenges with a positive attitude. His dedication and hard work garnered his employer's respect and led to multiple promotions. His boss was among the first people to write a letter in support of Jesus's release when immigration authorities detained him.

The US and Mexican governments have an agreement that facilitates fast, same-day deportation of Mexican nationals. So unless a Mexican immigrant in California claims fear of return and wants to apply for asylum, they are almost always put on a bus and deported within a few hours. My heart raced at the thought of Jesus getting deported before I even made it to the ICE detention facility. I rushed out of the office and drove from San Francisco to San Jose, where ICE was holding Jesus. I made it to the ICE holding facility just in time to enter my appearance as Jesus's attorney, preventing his immediate deportation.

Jesus's case seemed legally impossible. The senior attorneys I turned to for help insisted that there was no legal avenue for his release from detention and no way to prevent his deportation. With nowhere else to go, I turned to undocumented organizers and political activists at FREE SF (Full Rights, Equality, and Empowerment Coalition of San Francisco) and NIYA (the National Immigrant

Youth Alliance) for support. Getting Jesus back home to his family would take a great amount of collective organizing and mobilizing efforts, as well as thinking outside of the traditional lawyer box.

When I visited Jesus at the Yuba County Jail, we spoke through two black wired phones on either side of a thick pane of glass. I told him the legal odds of prevailing were slim, but a whole community of activists was ready to fight for him. "We have allies," I said, "and they are willing to pull out all the stops for you." Jesus didn't hesitate. His face, which until then had remained stern, brightened, and his mouth widened into a smile. "I want to fight, Nilou!" he said.

Over the course of the next three months and through hundreds of hours of organizing, we launched a national public campaign. Dozens of mostly undocumented leaders and youth activists came together to lift up Jesus's humanity and illuminate the injustice of the immigration system. Among them were organizers Kiran Savage-Sangwan and Jon Rodney. Together, we made it clear that the Deferred Action for Childhood Arrivals (DACA) program* was made for people exactly like him, and the system had failed him before and was failing him again. We advocated for Jesus's release from detention to stop his deportation, and we mobilized thousands of supporters across the country along with local and national legislators. We also organized several rallies in front of the ICE detention facility in San Francisco, supported by hundreds of youth activists and allies. Over five thousand signatures petitioning for his freedom jammed up ICE's fax machine and voice-messaging system with requests to release him as we shared Jesus's story across the country and submitted his DACA application.

In the face of ICE's continued refusal to release him, Jesus didn't give up on the inside, and neither did we on the outside. Three months later, our team and Jesus won his freedom through prosecutorial discretion. This victory would not have been possible if any one person had worked on this case alone. His release came after a massive immigrant youth–led campaign. His eligibility for relief through DACA was the result of over a decade of political organizing and advocacy. Unwilling to listen to the same excuses and promises from politicians, thousands of undocumented young leaders across the country staged actions, led public campaigns, organized sit-ins in congressional offices, educated congressional representatives, protested, and

---

* DACA is a US immigration policy that allows individuals who were brought to the country as children and who meet certain criteria to receive temporary protection from deportation and work authorization. It was introduced in September 2012, one month before ICE detained Jesus.

rallied to push former president Obama to issue the executive order that could turn DACA into official policy.

Jesus's case was a key bridge to help me gradually transform my own personal shame around being undocumented in the US and having been an asylum seeker in Germany. It was an early lesson for me as an attorney to listen, learn, and build power *alongside* my clients and undocumented communities. But more than that, it was a beginning—the planting of a seed of what was possible with collective action. That seed would become Pangea.

It Started with $3,000

Within a year, my low-fee practice began to thrive, but my heavy student loan debt made it unsustainable in a private practice. I realized that transitioning to a nonprofit structure could provide significant benefits on multiple fronts. First, working for a nonprofit would qualify me for the Public Service Loan Forgiveness plan, offering potential student debt forgiveness and easing my (and my future colleagues') financial burden. Second, nonprofits are eligible for foundation and government grants, which would support the sustainability of the work by providing necessary funding and enabling us to offer reduced fees and free services to clients. This nonprofit structure could support my financial stability while also amplifying our capacity to deliver vital legal services and advocacy to those in need.

And so, with the $3,000 left from my Fulbright Fellowship award, I covered the first month's rent for an office sublet, contractor costs, and office supply expenses, laying the groundwork for what would become Pangea Legal Services. As multiple immigration and refugee crises loomed, I knew I wanted to provide crucial support for immigrants facing detention and deportation. Pangea was born out of necessity and driven by a strong commitment to social justice and to the people I saw as my extended family.

But what kind of organization would it be?

Shifting Power: Toward Collective Leadership

Even when leaders have the best intentions to run organizations in alignment with shared group values and politics, many of us fall back on a strict hierarchical model because we have been conditioned to think it is the most efficient and strategic way of meeting goals. I am no exception to this. I was raised by a working-class, immigrant, single mother who modeled hard work, which conditioned me to perform above and beyond, to go to school even if I was sick, and to compete with and outperform my peers. This conditioning is prevalent among many immigrants and BIPOC workers like me. We often feel the need to overcompensate for the manifestations of racism and negative attitudes toward foreigners in our daily lives, so we work extra hard to integrate into society in a positive light. We work hard to belong. This intensity of labor is not required to the same degree of people with race and class privilege. For years, I chased the rewards of visibility and status. Working around the clock became second nature. It was a way to build a sense of power as a femme of color. But as I began to build and grow my nonprofit organization, I realized that I was unconsciously upholding a structure that valued constant hustle over collaboration and participation. To truly lead Pangea in alignment with our values, I knew I had to do some personal work. I needed to unpack my conditioning, deconstruct the habits that reinforced conventional thinking, and rebuild my approach to work.

Most of us have little exposure to successful organizations that do things differently. Instead, we work within structures inherited from monarchies, feudal societies, the military, and colonial power structures—systems that have become accepted as the norm over time without questioning their impact. Decision-making power, responsibility, accountability, and ownership are concentrated at the top of the pyramid, diminishing as we move down. The same goes for power and wealth, which are held by a few, with the promise that hard work can lift everyone up to the top.

But this promise is flawed, if not entirely false, because the pyramid is designed to maintain its shape. What's often called trickle-down economics is actually a "trickle-*up*" reality, where those at the bottom support the wealth and power at the top. The people at the base, who generate wealth through their labor and productivity, generally do so through undergoing hardships and challenging conditions, while those at the top extract and accumulate the vast majority of the benefits and profits. This setup is designed to maximize the exploitation of the workforce and concentrate wealth and power in the hands of a few. This concentration of power and wealth is not only imbalanced at workplaces; as we've seen throughout history, it creates a disproportionate distribution of resources on a global scale.

All of these challenges are often present in conventional pyramid power structures. Although an alternative vision of a model with democratic principles might seem idealistic in our winner-takes-all society, many organizations are, at this very moment, engaging in bold experimentations with the potential to transform the fabric of our society. Wanting to weave myself into this transforming fabric, I created Pangea.

From Crisis Comes Opportunity

Many new forms of collective governance have arisen from the chaos of social unrest. During Argentina's economic crisis, for example, I personally witnessed the emergence of hundreds of new worker cooperatives, a testament to the power of collective action and shared leadership in times of upheaval.* I believe that as we face the challenges of our time, it's an opportunity to align our organizational practices with the change we want to see in the world as well as a chance to build organizations on the strong pillars of collective governance. There are many BIPOC leaders in social justice organizations we can look to for ideas and leadership on how to uproot unsustainable structures and systems to create something more viable, resilient, and transformative. Jessica Gordon Nembhard, a political economist, professor, and the author of *Collective Courage: A History of African American Cooperative Economic Thought and Practice*, describes these systems as "people-centered, member-centered, values-based" principles powered by democracy and informed by a culture of care.[4]

Early on, I envisioned how Pangea could work differently by embracing collective governance and creating spaces that prioritize collaboration and care for our communities. Centering our work on marginalized voices built a culture of trust and transparency that strengthened our collective impact. By committing to these values, as highlighted by Dr. Gordon Nembhard, we set the stage for meaningful, transformative change within our organization and the communities we served.

Building a Board Aligned with Our Vision

As I began my journey with Pangea, I approached it with a commitment to finding solutions, fueled by curiosity and energy to shape the organization into a values-driven collective. But there were challenges right from the start. In the *Nonprofit Quarterly* article "Making Economic Democracy Work: How to Practice Shared Leadership," social justice advocate Nicole Wires highlights how nonprofits aiming to democratize the workplace are often "imperfect spaces

---

* I was studying abroad in Argentina during this time. I reflect more on this experience and what I learned from cooperatives in Chapter 2.

to engage in democratic movement work," with much still to "learn, uncover, disrupt, and transform."[5] I quickly realized just how true this was. One of the first things I had to learn right away was how to establish a board and create a mission, two essential legal steps for launching a nonprofit organization in California.

Creating Pangea's mission was the easy part of the puzzle. It was a source of joy and clarity. In those early days, I was highly involved in a three-pronged approach to immigrant justice work that combined legal representation, community organizing, and policy advocacy. As a National Lawyers Guild immigration committee representative at FREE SF, I advocated for sanctuary policies and immigrant rights at San Francisco's City Hall, and I joined the American Immigration Lawyers Association in Washington, DC, to push for immigrant rights nationally.

Pangea's mission emerged naturally from this work: "to stand with immigrant communities and to provide services through direct legal representation, especially in the area of deportation defense. In addition to direct legal services, we are committed to advocating on behalf of our community through policy advocacy, education, and legal empowerment efforts."[6]

Building a board was a different story. The advice I received, summarized below, was somewhat discouraging and conflicting:

- Boards are supposed to raise money. We ask our board to contribute or commit to raising a minimum of $10,000 each.
- You need lawyers on your board.
- Avoid having lawyers; they create issues.
- Boards slow you down and drain time and resources.
- Boards create conflict and unnecessary drama.
- Boards don't do much. Sometimes they're just a checkbox, not an asset.
- Board members don't understand the mission and are too removed from operations.
- High-profile board members can help your reputation, but they may not contribute.
- Boards can be controlling, leaving you managing them instead of your work.
- Boards disengage when you need them the most.
- Boards require access to full financials, leading to potential meddling over perceived risks.

- Board members source new members from a limited network of similar profiles.
- Meetings need to be polished, which adds extra pressure on the executive director.

The top-down model of board governance is so entrenched in both the nonprofit and the for-profit sectors that it's hard to envision an alternative. In the traditional model, board members sit at the top, making strategic decisions with the executive director (ED) or CEO. The ED then communicates with staff members. Staff members, in turn, communicate back to the ED, who communicates back to the board.

This traditional chain of command, where the board holds authority over the ED and the organization's budget, reinforces the systemic challenges discussed earlier. One key issue is the limited time most boards actually contribute. While some meet as often as twelve times a year, many only gather four times, typically volunteering around sixty hours annually. Compare that to the thousands of hours staff members dedicate year-round. This creates a striking imbalance in power and decision-making authority.

Imagine a community organization where the board, meeting just a few times a year, holds the final say on critical decisions like hiring or firing senior staff. The staff, who work thousands of hours per year and thoroughly understand the organization's day-to-day needs, have little decision-making authority. For example, if a board decides to replace the ED without meaningful staff consultation, it can create confusion, disrupt team dynamics, and undermine collective leadership. This top-down decision-making undermines trust, leaving staff feeling sidelined, and ultimately weakens the organization's ability to operate in alignment with its mission and values.

Acknowledging that we often find many amazing people on boards, Vu Le, former executive director of the social justice nonprofit Rooted in Vibrant Communities and author of the blog *Nonprofit AF*, wrote a blog post that posits that "for every good board story" there are countless tales of difficult boards that micromanage staff, get caught up in operations, and prevent overall progress. He describes one board that refused to allow their organizations to publicly support Black Lives Matter because it was "too political," and another board that blocked a paid family leave policy supported by the entire staff. His conclusion is resonant: "We are talking about a structure where groups of volunteers who barely know one another, see one percent of the work, often don't reflect the communities we serve, and who may have little to no experience running nonprofits, being given vast power to supervise leadership and determine values, policies, and practices. Why did we think this weird structure would work?"[7]

Redefining Board Roles

It was clear from the start: I didn't want a conventional board structure for Pangea. I envisioned something different—something collective, flexible, and rooted in cooperative principles. I wanted a board that wasn't just overseeing the organization but was actively involved in shaping its direction, evolving as the organization grew, and supporting both the mission and the people who made it happen. Though I was unfamiliar with boards at the time, I knew I didn't want a rigid, hierarchical model. Instead, I dreamed of creating a nimble, worker-led organization, in which the board could adapt and evolve alongside Pangea.

I sought advice from established nonprofits that were rooted in collective governance. One organization that was particularly influential for me was the Sustainable Economies Law Center (also known as "the Law Center") in the San Francisco Bay Area. The Law Center provides vital legal resources—education, research, advice, and advocacy—to support grassroots economic empowerment across sectors including housing, urban agriculture, and energy. Co-founded by Janelle Orsi, a lawyer and social justice advocate, the Law Center has become a model for worker self-directed nonprofits, which they describe as "an organization in which all workers have the power to influence the realms and programs in which they work, the conditions of their workplace, their own career paths, and the direction of the organization as a whole."[8]

The Law Center's board functions differently from traditional boards. Instead of overseeing an executive leader, the board works as a smaller, integrated part of the organization and oversees a self-managing team of workers. The board president is a staff member, appointed by the team. The board's main role is to ensure that self-management principles effectively advance the nonprofit's mission, and that financial integrity is maintained. Board members take on the role of "owls," symbolizing broad vision and wisdom. There are four owls, one to oversee each of The Law Center's four key areas:

- The financial owl (treasurer) oversees finances.
- The worker governance owl oversees worker management.

- The mission owl focuses on activities and programs.
- The legal compliance owl (secretary) ensures legal adherence.

Each owl must either be knowledgeable or willing to learn about the policies and practices within their area of influence, so they can offer solutions to challenges while supporting the nonprofit's mission.

Some nonprofits have adopted this owl model in their own ways. In a Medium article titled "Resist as a Worker Self-Directed Nonprofit," author Kendra Hicks weighed in on how this model was implemented at Resist, a nonprofit that provides grants through radical philanthropy to grassroots activist organizations.[9] The Resist board includes an elder owl, a communications owl, a staff owl, a resources and redistribution owl, and a worker self-governance owl. Rather than being siloed, these owls are "in conversation with the other moving pieces within the organization." That includes the *whole* organization, with a board that "unanimously approved a board resolution that helped us forge our path towards worker self-direction." A board resolution supporting worker self-direction in a collectively led nonprofit formally commits the board to empower employees in decision-making processes.[*]

Part of that path toward worker self-direction involves always having a staff member serve on the board, typically as board chair. This is key for three reasons:

1. Board chairs do the most work—coordinating, planning, and investing time into the organization. For nonprofits that don't have funds to compensate their board members, making a staff member part of the board is an economically viable benefit for all and should be part of a job description.

2. A member of the leadership team, like an executive director, should serve on the board to bring sufficient familiarity with the staff and the overarching organizational needs. A bird's-eye view of the organization, its finances, and its growth needs is of great value in this liaison role. In addition, a staff member who doesn't hold positional power may also serve on the board, since they typically hold direct knowledge about their experience and the organizational programs. By intentionally selecting a staff member who is not in a leadership

---

[*] See appendix A, "Board Resolution for Worker Self-Direction and Distributed Authority."

role, organizations can cultivate leadership growth and development, ensuring diverse perspectives and insights are brought to the table.

3. Staff members on the board are uniquely suited to onboard new members, and to influence and maintain the organization's cultural values for the board.

Challenging Conventional Expectations

The Pangea board model initially followed a fairly conventional structure, though it differed in that we didn't rely on corporate lawyers. Over time, I realized that effective boards need to move in sync with the leadership team, adapting to the organization's needs rather than creating unnecessary barriers. A board should support and empower leadership, not act as an obstacle to progress. This is no small task, since traditional board structures don't empower staff members to participate. Meanwhile, people are complex, and relationship dynamics get complicated, so best practices and policies rooted in collectivist values that are both spacious and clear need to be put in place.

Pangea's board evolved and established policies that made our collective values real. The first step in sharing decision-making and power came when Pangea's board adopted a formal board resolution like the Law Center's, deferring greater authority and decision-making power to the staff. Sara Stephens, a former staff attorney at the Law Center and Pangea's former board member and later board chair, was instrumental in this regard, eventually helping us write bylaws and resolutions that laid down new pathways for board governance.[*]

Conventions must be challenged to make changes, starting with the most basic assumptions. "The board hires the ED. Who says?!" asks Vu Le. "The board meets once a month. Why?! The board approves the budget. Not necessarily!"[10] These practices have been ingrained as if prescribed by law, but the IRS—the federal body that governs nonprofits—and local corporations codes are quite vague about the board's duties. They merely require boards to meet the "care" and "loyalty" standards expected of a reasonable person, while also allowing flexibility for organizations to delegate duties, such as hiring or operational oversight, within their bylaws.[11]

To that end, Le suggests we "completely reimagine the board and experiment with some new structures."[12] One of those structures is a model of board

---

[*] See appendix A, "Board Resolution for Worker Self-Direction and Distributed Authority."

governance put into place by his colleague Vanessa LeBourdais, executive producer and creative director of DreamRider Productions, a children's theater nonprofit in Vancouver. LeBourdais described a board that shared power with staff and did "a lot of inner work" to remain a supportive partner to the organization as a whole. LeBourdais told Le that the model was "a little woo," to which Le replies in his article: "We need less 'Robert's Rules' and more 'woo'!"[13]

Robert's Rules, formally called "Robert's Rules of Order," are a set of parliamentary protocols written by a US Army officer in the 1800s that are still referenced for board meeting protocols to this day.[14] In the article "In Indigenous Nonprofit Governance, Values Matter More Than Tools," Rachelle Dallaire, executive director of the Indigenous Perspectives Society, writes that Robert's Rules of Order are "operationally insignificant" for many Indigenous organizations.[15] Instead, these organizations are guided by their values, mission, vision, and cultural practices. Dallaire refers to these as "indigenized" values, which prioritize principles such as "shared wisdom; protection of the land, resources and children; gratitude; humility; honour; trust; balance; love, doing well onto others; and preventing harm to others."[16] These values create a governance framework rooted in mutual respect and care, aligning closely with collective governance models.

When asked about implementing "indigenized" governance tools, Dallaire shifts the focus from tools to values, explaining that when "values which inform the practice are sound and inclusively held, the tools will not hold the power."[17] Instead, the values themselves—like inclusivity, respect, and sharing—will guide the organization's governance.

Both Dallaire's and Gordon Nembhard's insights reveal that collective governance models often thrive when they move away from rigid tools like Robert's Rules of Order and instead center on shared values. This resonates deeply with me, as Pangea's growth was closely guided by values rooted in communal care and collective priorities—principles that reflect my own Iranian cultural heritage, where the needs of the group often take precedence over individual desires.

Rooted in Community and Shared Values

Michelle Gaudet, one of Pangea's founding board members, played a key role in shaping the organization's governance model from the very beginning. With her insight and enthusiasm, she brought valuable contributions that helped establish the foundation and direction of Pangea's collective structure. Her experience at a horizontally structured nonprofit, the Community Resource Initiative (now Full Picture Justice), gave her the knowledge and insights needed to champion collective governance. Michelle's energy and belief in shared leadership had a ripple effect, helping ensure that board members understood and were trained in the principles of collective governance. She played a critical role in making sure that Pangea's governance structure reflected its values. Michelle also advised staff members on setting our salaries and creating policies and benefits consistent with our values, adding credibility and practical knowledge to our collectivist theories.

Even with Michelle on board, I made mistakes. One of them was relying too heavily on the lawyers we had on Pangea's board. Some of us lawyers tend to overanalyze and focus on liabilities, often zeroing in on risks instead of possibilities.

To that end, risk aversion got in our way in the early days after launching Pangea. I was the only full-time employee, and there were just two other board members. We didn't yet have directors and officers insurance for our board to protect them from personal liability. Although the risks to our board members were minimal at this early stage, one of our lawyer board members was seriously concerned about the lack of insurance and resigned with only a few weeks' notice. We eventually got insurance as we continued to build out Pangea's nonprofit infrastructure in the first year, which is common in the start-up phase of an organization.

When I realized that the risk aversion of most attorneys didn't align with the flexibility, bold advocacy, and nimbleness required by social justice organizations, I shifted my focus. I saw the tremendous value in recruiting board members who truly represented the community Pangea served. I sought out immigrant leaders who had personal stakes and lived experiences in the immigrant justice world as well as a willingness to take necessary risks and think creatively as we navigated our start-up phase. I also reached out to philanthropic partners and asked for contacts with people who had financial and operational expertise. This led to a hugely resourceful and immigrant-led board, including members from Hong Kong, Mexico, and El Salvador. Three of them had previously worked at a global investment firm, and they brought incredible financial skills to the table. They helped us with everything from automation charts to best practices with budgeting, multiyear financial projections, and other fiscal matters.

A vibrant new board community emerged. These folks reached out to other professional friends who brought different resources to the table, throwing us fundraisers at Michelin-star restaurants and opening multiple doors. Another meaningful addition to our board was Jesus Ruiz Diego, my former client whom we had freed from immigration detention. After his release, Jesus became an organizer with People Acting in Community Together (PACT) in San Jose, further enriching our connection to the community and our shared purpose. His presence on the board reinforced the powerful impact of our work and brought lived experience into our governance structure.

Building strong working networks didn't happen overnight; it required intentional relationship-building. I spent significant time getting to know each board member, and I met people for a glass of wine or a meal whenever and wherever possible. I even drove to Orinda, twenty miles from San Francisco, for a 5:30 a.m. meeting with a board member who started his day at 3:30 a.m. He gave me a tour of his office and walked me through his use of Excel spreadsheets and advanced formulas. These moments weren't simply social; they were investments in building personal relationships and valuable opportunities for learning and growth. They gifted me essential lessons and tools that enriched my leadership development and contributed significantly to Pangea's evolution as an organization.

At first, some people saw this relationship-building effort as a distraction, arguing I should focus more on my clients and casework. Initially I second-guessed myself, but ultimately I trusted my instincts. These connections weren't just valuable—they were critical. They helped secure the resources Pangea needed, allowed our unconventional structure to evolve smoothly, and laid the foundation for our culture of care. Relationship-building, I realized, is essential labor and should be recognized as such in job descriptions. Board members bring more than just expertise; they share in the labor of the organization, and the connections they foster are key to its growth.

When developing a board for a collectively led organization, it's important to include individuals directly connected to the mission as well as those who bring experience or commitment to shared leadership. These qualities don't always exist in the same person, but both are essential for building a balanced, effective board. Creating a liberatory board requires time, patience, and an ongoing effort to build trust and ensure fair and effective leadership.

KEY POINTS TO KEEP IN MIND WHEN STARTING A COLLECTIVE LEADERSHIP-ALIGNED BOARD:

- **Include people who are directly impacted by and connected to your mission** to ensure alignment with your goals.

- **Bring on individuals who have collective governance experience**; consider recruiting two experienced people in this area to avoid placing the burden on just one.

- **Ensure a dedicated staff member serves on your board** (alongside an ED) to effectively strengthen the connection between staff and board perspectives.

- **Recruit board members who can make bold moves and challenge the status quo.** Recruiting individuals who focus heavily on risk can limit the board's flexibility; instead, seek those who can also make bold moves to challenge conventional norms and laws that no longer serve us.

- **Limit the number of board members** to avoid complex relationship management, especially during start-up or transition phases (my ideal number of board members at Pangea was five to seven).

- **Consult your board regularly** for input and collaboration.

- **Limit the board's role to strategic guidance** and offering support within a clearly defined scope; avoid giving the board operational decision-making authority.

- **Clarify the board's authority** to avoid confusion and ensure effective governance.

- **Have a conflict resolution or mediation plan** in place to address disagreements between the board and staff and prevent organizational conflicts.

- **Understand that as your organization evolves, so will your board.** You may find the need to include more expertise in certain areas or board members who are willing and able to speak about the organization's mission and impact at public events.

As I reflect on those early days—the late-night strategy calls, the adrenaline of last-minute court filings, and the joy of winning Jesus's release—I see that it wasn't just about legal victories. It was about discovering the power of collective action. We weren't just fighting for one person's freedom; we were up against an entire system that sought to divide and exploit. In every rally, every meeting, every petition, there was an undeniable sense of community, shared purpose, and solidarity. This was the beginning of something far bigger than any one of us could achieve alone. The foundation of Pangea Legal Services was laid by people working together for a vision of justice that was rooted in care, trust, and deep accountability to each other.

Just as we advocated together for Jesus's freedom, we knew our internal structure had to reflect the same commitment to care, shared power, and collaboration. The question then became: How would we continue structuring the organization to embody these values fully? The progress we had already made in embracing shared leadership and horizontal structures—and the impact of aligning our values with our practices—reaffirmed our belief in participatory leadership, both in our community work and within the organization. To truly live these values, we were motivated to keep pushing beyond conventional models and make sure that power was not just shared in theory, but integrated into how we operated every day.

Actionable Takeaways

Select diverse board members. Choose board members who reflect the demographics of the community served by the nonprofit. These individuals bring a rich understanding of the mission and are often motivated to think creatively, take risks, and collaborate with like-minded peers.

Include staff on the board. Bridge the gap between the board and staff by including a staff member, potentially as board chair. This economically viable strategy ensures that the board benefits from the staff member's deeper understanding of organizational needs and culture, enhancing many collective processes.

Invest in relationship-building. Dedicate time to develop meaningful relationships with board members. Building these connections fosters a culture of care and directly supports the smooth operation of the organization.

Consider the "owl" model. Integrate the board into the organization using the owl model, which assigns specific roles (e.g., financial owl, communications owl) to board members. This approach encourages collaboration and ensures that board members work closely with the collective.

Leverage flexibility in governance. Recognize that many traditional board functions, like hiring an executive director, are not strictly required by legal codes. Use this legal ambiguity as an opportunity for creative experimentation in forming the board and defining its roles and structure.

2

Learning to Share Power

By the fall of 2013, Pangea had grown successfully enough that I was able to officially hire our first full-time employee other than myself: Marie Vincent, a co-founder of Pangea. We first met while volunteering at a legal clinic where we prepared immigration applications for DACA-eligible youth. Fluent in English, Spanish, and French, Marie was a French immigrant and recent law school graduate eager to network. We had worked together on the case of a French-speaking Algerian (of Amazigh origin) asylum seeker. Our connection was immediate. Due to our complementary strengths and shared values, Marie was the ideal partner with whom to launch the organization.

At that point, our board consisted of three members, including myself. In addition to being Pangea's executive director, I was also running and chairing our board. I delegated work to the board, asked for advice, and led our conversations. Though I sought feedback and input from the board and many outside partners, friends, and community—all the time, on everything—I was still the sole and final decision-maker. As Pangea brought on new people, sharing leadership effectively would require a significant amount of time and a genuine collective effort. I would also have to confront my ego.

A Cooperative Alternative: Lessons from Argentina

Eleven years earlier, as a college student in 2002, I was immersed in activism and organizing for various social justice causes. I took to the streets to protest the wars in Iraq and Afghanistan. I rallied against the International Monetary Fund (IMF) and the World Bank's short-term loans that devastated communities by cutting public benefits and social programs down to the bone. I also joined efforts to secure a living wage for immigrant workers subcontracted by my university. However, despite all this activism, I had never experienced a system where power wasn't held over others. Until Alberto.

In the early 2000s, something extraordinary happened in Argentina: over three hundred abandoned factories sprang back to life.[*,1] This was not by chance, but through the long-term sustained effort of the workers that reclaimed them. They didn't just reopen the doors; they became their own bosses, creating workplaces rooted in dignity, shared leadership, and care.

This was hard to imagine because in 2001 Argentina's economy crashed—hard. After decades of US-backed military dictatorship, the government, under pressure from the IMF, sold off public assets like utilities and oil to foreign corporations. It also took on massive loans that required harsh budget cuts, deregulation, and a fixed dollar-peso exchange rate, which made basic goods unaffordable for many. These neoliberal policies sank the country into debt, skyrocketed unemployment, and slashed public services. In a desperate attempt to stop money from leaving the country during the collapse, the Argentinian government froze all bank accounts.

Overnight, banks locked their doors to customers, causing people to smash ATMs and break bank doors in attempts to access their savings. Factories around Buenos Aires closed up shop without notice. Thousands of workers in the garment business, the glass industry, and many other sectors were abruptly unemployed. Over fifty percent of Argentines suddenly lived below the official poverty line, including seven out of every ten children. The country was in shambles, and the government and financial systems were more focused on tending to the interests of foreign investors and wealthy business owners than to citizens. Those in power made things worse by arresting protesting workers and violently disrupting organized actions.

---

* The recovered factories movement started in the late 1990s and gained momentum after the economic crisis in the early 2000s.

But over time, something remarkable happened. Workers began self-organizing to reclaim their workplaces and set them up as cooperatives. They recuperated hundreds of businesses, shops, and factories, restoring thousands of jobs in the process. In the beginning, businesses struggled to survive in the face of government resistance, legal battles, and ongoing bank closures, but they persisted. As the number of recovered factory cooperatives grew, a network developed around sharing financial, legal, and other resources.

I arrived at the University of Buenos Aires amid this economic and social resistance to study international politics and economics as part of my education at Georgetown University. I lived with a host family and took the Subte, a public transit system, to the university, where I studied with renowned social justice leader Adolfo Pérez Esquivel, who won the Nobel Peace Prize for his work against the country's military dictatorship.

Not long after beginning my studies, I met Alberto,[‡] a garment factory worker who had lost his job following the economic crash. As a result, his family had lost their car and all their bank savings. Alberto started meeting with his former colleagues to talk about other factories that were being restarted by workers. Soon they restarted the garment factory where they had worked. Within months of the reopening, the police appeared to confiscate equipment on behalf of the former factory owners. Neighborhood assemblies and people from the local community showed up in defense of the workers. Outnumbering the police, they established a blockade, set tires on fire, and prevented the police from entering the factory. The police eventually gave up and left.

When I visited the factory, the workers were still in a battle with the state for legal ownership of their workplace. One day, Alberto took me along to a management meeting. Fifteen workers sat on folding chairs in a circle next to conveyor belts and industrial-sized rolls of fabric. They represented the range of labor required to run the factory, from sewing machine operators to administrative staff. Everyone wore jeans and comfortable clothes; there were no uniforms or three-piece suits to be found. As they discussed the factory's future, their treatment of each other was humane and dignified.

Later, Alberto and I sat in a quiet, glass-walled cafe on a busy street lively with people going about their affairs. Over delicious *alfajores*, a traditional

---

‡ To protect the privacy and confidentiality of individuals and organizations, some names have been changed throughout this book. Additionally, certain stories have been merged to represent the experiences of two or more individuals within one narrative. These name changes and combined stories are marked with a double dagger (‡) upon their first reference in each chapter.

Argentine pastry with two cookies and sweet milk caramel in the middle, I asked him about the struggles and upsides of the worker cooperatives. His answers flowed so fast I could barely keep up: he and his co-workers made decisions by consensus, rotated leadership roles, and distributed the company's revenues based on people's needs and family size rather than seniority or educational attainment. The meeting I had witnessed, he said, was a part of their collective management structure. "People work better when they have a say," added Alberto. "The old bosses weren't as efficient as we are, even though we spend a lot of time coordinating and discussing."

Alberto went on to say that he and his co-workers placed no importance on titles, individual gain, or status. Rather, they focused on people's needs and their collective well-being. Teams didn't need to be hierarchical and follow a strict chain of command to be sustainable and operational. The cooperatives operated at high efficiency, centered their values and humanity, and worked their way into financial stability, even amid an economic disaster.

This system of shared leadership inspired me. It defied the strict disciplinarian models of authority that many of us have experienced through our upbringing, education systems, workplaces, and state structures. Here was a living example of what collective governance and social justice looked like in practice, not in the far-off future but in the here and now.

For the first time in my life, I witnessed the power of thoughtful, mutually respectful, and incredibly humane professional relationships. Witnessing Alberto's garment co-op meeting left a lasting impression on me. What I'd glimpsed in Argentina was a different way forward—a transparent, equitable, and more values-aligned model for organizing in the social justice space. Not top-down but circular, and ultimately more liberating for all. It was truly collective governance in action.

I felt a spark go off in my core.

It all seemed so intuitive.

But it wasn't.

Unpacking Power: Challenging Inherited Hierarchies

I had been conditioned to accept the chain-of-command systems of authority and organizational structures specifically designed to maintain power at the top—the ones Alberto warned me about. A traditional chain of command in the workplace originates from military systems, where decisions are passed down from top-ranking officers to lower ranks.[2] This model emphasizes obedience and control, often leaving little room for input from those at the bottom. In this setup, managers or leaders make the calls, and employees are expected to follow without much room for discussion.

Chain-of-command systems usually lead to a pyramidal organizational structure. For-profit corporations are typically built with top-down pyramidal structures, but, as I was learning, so are nonprofits. Unfortunately, many of us have inherited conventional hierarchical models by default rather than intentional design.

The Challenges of Pyramid Power

In practical terms, a few key characteristics of the pyramid power structure include the following:

- **Bottleneck effect:** When decision-making is concentrated in the hands of just a few people, it can lead to those at the top delegating only a few tasks to their colleagues and being overwhelmed with responsibilities. This often causes those at the top to overlook or not address important issues. Since decision-making is entrusted to a few, there is little trust in other staff's decision-making, and they are unable to move forward without top-level approval.

- **Exploitation and extraction:** These models often produce power, wealth, and status for a few in power at the expense of the majority of workers. The workers who produce value and contribute the most to the organization's day-to-day operations are left disempowered.

- **Exclusion and collective disempowerment:** Because strictly hierarchical organizations depend so heavily on direction from the few at the top, they don't benefit from the collective wisdom, skills, and experiences of the great majority of the organization's members or employees who are structurally disempowered. Most people affected by the consequences of major organizational decisions either don't get to provide feedback or vote on a policy, or they don't get any information about the policy at all, including major decisions and policies like benefits, salaries, deliverables to funders, and professional development opportunities.

At one of my previous workplaces, there was a clear example of how power concentrated at the top creates a bottleneck. My boss made all the decisions but was so busy that it was almost impossible to get their attention. Even when my colleagues and I had ideas that could help our organization, we couldn't act on them because everything required approval that rarely came. This bottleneck effect left the team stuck and disempowered, unable to move forward. There was no transparency about important decisions that affected all of us; for example, when three of our seven colleagues got fired in a span of six months, no one knew how or why. This pyramid structure of concentrated power and decision-making at the top, excluded us from key decisions, left us out of conversations that directly affected us, and disempowered us. It showed me how harmful these models can be for the majority at the bottom.

In Farsi, we have a proverb that says, "'Who did you learn this goodness from?' The person answered, 'From those who don't have it.'" Our language flows with a wisdom and simplicity that is embodied in our actions. When something is wrong, we do right. When there is injustice, we seek justice. I knew I didn't want to recreate the dynamic of my previous workplace. I wanted to do better.

Introducing Collective Governance

My inspiration for Pangea's governance structure stemmed from Argentina's worker cooperatives, which emphasized shared resources, co-leadership, and worker-leaders like Alberto. This type of structure is known by many names: collective governance, shared leadership, worker-led, co-governance, participatory governance, horizontal leadership, worker self-directed, and more. While organizations may use similar terms, each defines its structure in its own way. Dozens, perhaps hundreds, of words and phrases can describe methods to decentralize power and strive toward equity or equality.

On the preceding page are some common terms associated with collective governance or collective leadership. Throughout this book, terms like *collective governance, collectivism,* and *participatory democracy* will be used interchangeably to frame various aspects of this concept. The goal is not to focus on specific terminology but to inspire a broader vision of shared power and collaborative structures. What is most important is that teams develop clarity and alignment in their vision, culture, and day-to-day operations. This book is here to guide groups in taking meaningful steps toward that goal.

It's important to remember that even hierarchical organizations can adopt collective practices and share leadership in meaningful ways. Conversely, some groups that call themselves collective or horizontal may function in a top-down manner, showing that labels alone don't guarantee equity or inclusivity. What truly matters is not the label we use but how we put these principles into practice. The real impact comes from the processes we create and how we engage with one another.

Roots of Collective Governance

Whatever we call it, collective governance has old roots in liberatory social movements and ancestral lineages of BIPOC individuals working toward justice. In the 1950s and '60s, American activist Ella Baker was putting participatory democracy and collective leadership on our cultural map. A key figure in the civil rights movement, Baker significantly shaped the practice of participatory democracy long before it gained widespread recognition. Her philosophy centered on the power of collective action, based on the belief that people working together—rather than following a single charismatic leader—was the path to true change.

While the concept of participatory democracy often gets attributed to student activists in the 1960s, Baker's work was pivotal in advancing these ideas. Baker championed the idea that everyone should have a voice and play an active role in decision-making, not just those at the top. Her grassroots approach sought to minimize hierarchy, ensuring direct involvement from the people most impacted by injustice. She believed in the power of people working together to make decisions, rather than relying on a single leader. She was a champion of the idea that everyone should have a voice and play a part in shaping the direction of movements. Her grassroots approach emphasized minimizing hierarchy and fostering direct, collective involvement in decision-making. As Carol Mueller highlights in the *Ella Baker Black Studies Reader,*

Baker's philosophy was foundational to the Student Nonviolent Coordinating Committee and other movements, advocating for decentralized, group-centered leadership over charismatic, hierarchical models.[3] This commitment to empowering individuals to act collectively on their own behalf transformed the landscape of social justice activism in America.

Ella Baker's advocacy for decentralized leadership connects profoundly with broader traditions of collective action and mutual support. Her commitment is mirrored in the values of African American collectives, which have cultivated a culture of mutuality for centuries. In her book *Collective Courage*, Dr. Gordon Nembhard highlights how African Americans have long relied on values of mutual aid and fraternal organizations.[4] Dating back to the Civil War, African Americans pooled their resources and built cooperative ownership models rooted in survival and collective empowerment. These values, like those found in some Indigenous governance models, continue to shape cooperative organizations today.

Similarly, in 1956 in the Basque region of Spain, Spanish priest and activist Jose Maria Arizmendiarrieta founded a worker cooperative in the town of Mondragon that essentially organized the entire town based on collective governance. Over the years, Mondragon grew into one of the world's largest networks of worker-owned cooperatives, with businesses spanning industries such as aerospace, elevators, bicycles, and wind turbines. The cooperative operates with salary caps for executives and equal voting for worker-owners on key decisions, and it shares resources across co-ops during tough periods.[5] During times of economic challenge, workers voted to temporarily reduce all their salaries or hours to preserve jobs. The *New Yorker* highlighted how Mondragon has thrived for nearly seventy years: "Its persistence suggests that there are fairer and more sustainable ways of doing business. . . . The collective has a unique history, and its density powers a rare feedback loop in which cooperative values shape institutions, which then reinforce the same values, spiraling outward to define an entire way of life. Mondragon is an inspiring and successful experiment."[6]

But the values-based collective spirit that informs these organizational paradigms has its roots *even further back in time*. All of these systems and practices that are now being heralded as "new" and "revolutionary" are not new. They overlap significantly with older frameworks but are being repackaged with modern terms. For example, holacracy, a term for collective governance championed by tech entrepreneur Brian Robertson, draws heavily from sociocracy. Sociocracy is a governance system based on equal, consent-based decision-making. Rather than crediting a single founder, it draws on influences from earlier movements, particularly the thought of early twentieth-century Quaker activist Kees Boeke and the book *Sociocracy: The Organization of Decision-Making*, written by Dutch engineer Gerard Endenburg.[7] Inspired by cybernetics, this system reflects patterns and feedback loops found in nature, making decision-making as dynamic and responsive as ecosystems themselves. And this wisdom inherent in the natural world—from fractals to seasons to the intelligent and interconnected network under every tree on earth—has been practiced, honored, and transmitted on many levels by Indigenous people for thousands of years.

Indigenous Wisdom

Indigenous people around the world have long been at the forefront of participatory and collective governance. Yet in a society that is driven by self-promotion, novelty, and trying to be first, Indigenous ways and wisdom are often overlooked or marginalized. For example, in *Reinventing Organizations: A Guide to Creating Organizations Inspired by the Next Stage in Human Consciousness*, Frédéric Laloux introduces the "Teal Revolution" as a groundbreaking framework for collective governance.[8] Yet Indigenous communities have modeled collective decision-making, shared leadership, and care for one another long before modern management theories emerged. As Jessica Prentice points out in her 2016 article "The Most Dangerous Notion in 'Reinventing Organizations,'" this oversight is not uncommon.[9] She contrasts Laloux's ideas with those explored in *Tending the Wild* by M. Kat Anderson, which details the sophisticated land management systems of Native Americans in California. These Indigenous practices, rooted in stewardship, interdependence, and community care, were highly effective during continuous use over centuries. Early settlers, however, failed to recognize the wisdom in these systems and imposed their own, often destructive, approaches to land and governance.

In *Braiding Sweetgrass*, Robin Wall Kimmerer illuminates how deep the Indigenous roots of collective governance are, drawing on her Potawatomi heritage.[10] She explains that Indigenous governance is grounded in reciprocity and respect for the natural world, where decision-making is rooted in interdependence and mutual care. Much like the "Honorable Harvest," which emphasizes balance and respect, these systems prioritize the collective well-being of all living beings, including the environment and future generations. These values create collective structures that are inclusive, thoughtful, and committed to sustainability and collective well-being.

Similar to the Indigenous wisdom of the Potawatomi people that empha-sizes interconnection and reciprocity, my own Iranian roots taught me the importance of community and collective well-being. Decisions and support flowed through the community with an understanding that our well-being was interdependent. This deep sense of connection, passed down through genera-tions and across borders, continued to surface for me over time, and I wanted to explore how I could contribute to fostering this interconnected care in a broader context.

Pay Equity in Practice: Aligning Salaries with Shared Values

"Why do you want to be paid $1,000 more than Marie?" our founding board member, Michelle, asked me.

It was a simple but profound question: if I wanted to create a truly collec-tively led organization, why *wouldn't* I onboard Marie at the same salary level as mine?

I was poised to hire Marie as Pangea's second full-time employee when I pro-posed to Michelle that I be paid $1,000 more a year than Marie. By then Marie had been working part time on contract for Pangea for as long as I had. She had studied accounting in college, had great instincts for restricting spending, was realistic about taking on new projects and seeing them through to completion, was meticulous about timely bill payments and record keeping, and was super organized. Her strengths and interests in these areas far surpassed mine. In fact, we were opposites: I had piles of papers on my desk that I planned to get to one day, my electronic files were all saved under different formats and names for each client, and I had many big, beautiful visions for connecting our clients, organizing projects, and spending our revenue. Marie was already indispens-able, with vital organizational skills that weren't my strength.

Before she joined full time, Marie was interviewing at other jobs for full-time positions, and I was constantly worried she would leave. Within the first few years at Pangea, in addition to working as an immigration lawyer, Marie had taken on the role of bookkeeper, was overseeing accounting, and was responsible for all matters related to expenses and bills. Luckily, she was still available by the time Pangea officially offered her a full-time position in the fall of 2013.

Still, in addition to Michelle's question about why I should be paid $1,000 more than Marie to start, another question overlaid it: Why *shouldn't* I be paid $1,000 more than Marie from the start? After all, I had worked long and hard to attain visibility and recognition. I had two years more experience as a practicing attorney than Marie, had reviewed and supported her in asylum case work, and had connected her with community organizers. I was the primary external face of the organization. In those early days, I held many roles as Pangea's board chair, executive director, and sole full-time staff attorney. I had created Pangea's mission, vision, and website, networked with partners, researched insurance plans, and coordinated with many players in our ecosystem. Didn't that qualify me for a higher salary, even if it was only $1,000 more a year?

From a young age, I was taught that I had to work harder than others to be valued. Competitive systems in the US reinforced the idea that my worth had to be proven through external achievements, whether it was a school award, praise from an immigration judge, or a higher salary. The focus was always on rising above, not working together with others; on doing more, faster, and better, rather than finding joy, taking care, and working collectively.

This competitive conditioning is common in the United States, especially among immigrants and BIPOC leaders, partly due to the pressures imposed on us by almost every system we spend most of our time in, from school to internships to places of work. It's isolating and rewards individualism and material gain rather than collective well-being. Despite the collectivist nature of my Iranian roots, these individualistic pressures of US culture still permeated my life.

Michelle's question made me reflect deeply and raised new concerns: Should we really pay more for my experiences or expertise? If so, how do we compare this with Marie's skills? How can we redefine merit and compensation in a way that acknowledges the significant disparities between those with privilege and those without?

Ultimately Michelle's question helped me reconcile my ego with my values and the values I wanted Pangea to uphold: collectivism, care, joy, and community. Earning $1,000 more a year did not serve those values, but rather the values of the systems I had been steeped in my whole life. I had every intention of being nonhierarchical in my approach to building Pangea, but in practice and skills I was not there yet. I was lucky to be supported by people with strong values who held me accountable. I had chosen Michelle as a founding board member in part because of her experience at the collectively governed Community Resource Initiative. Her organization had salary caps and less than a 1.2 percent salary difference between the highest-paid and lowest-paid worker. Speaking from the perspective of a worker who was paid on the lower end of the scale in her organization at the time, Michelle recognized that a salary difference of $1,000 per year might seem trivial in isolation.

However, she realized that even small pay gaps could create a sense of unfairness and division, affecting morale, especially in a small team. Michelle felt that addressing these small but meaningful discrepancies was essential for creating a truly fair and supportive workplace, and she advocated against creating a pay gap between me and Marie. Ultimately, each organization must make its own decisions around compensation, but approaching these choices with intention and a willingness to question conventional norms is essential in collective structures.

Michelle reminded me of my conversation with Alberto, which underscored the challenge I wanted to address early in Pangea's life: creating a fair salary structure in a multifaceted landscape. After a lot of reflection and discussion, I chose to set a flat salary for everyone in the organization. This meant that Marie, myself, and all our full-time staff members had the same pay. This salary structure worked well for us for several years.

With the salary question answered, Marie and I moved into a new, dedicated Pangea office in San Francisco near the immigration court. Marie sent out flyers announcing our new address, and together we focused on countless details involved in Pangea's growth.

Actionable Takeaways

Recruit diverse strengths. Bring on team members whose strengths complement your own. Avoid the tendency to hire people similar to yourself; in my experience with Marie, our contrasting strengths created a powerful partnership.

Delegate decision-making with clarity. Start sharing power by delegating significant areas of work in manageable portions. Let both the individual and the team know that the person in the role has final decision-making authority in that area, reducing bottlenecks and fostering trust.

Build systems of accountability. Establish relationships with advisors, board members, or trusted colleagues who can hold you accountable to the values of equity, collaboration, and shared power. Choose people who are willing to ask hard questions and provide honest feedback to help you stay aligned with your learning goals.

Recognize inherited systems. Acknowledge that traditional systems of obedience and control may still unconsciously influence your organization. Explore what works and what doesn't, recognizing that even hierarchical organizations can incorporate meaningful collective practices.

Consider salary equity. Explore salary structures, such as setting defined ranges between the highest and lowest earners, or even implementing equal salaries across the team.

3

Equity-Based Salaries

Money, as it turns out, is a highly sensitive issue. Compensation affects every worker's life significantly and is usually the largest expense in an organization's budget. It touches on deep emotions, including self-worth, security, and dignity. It connects to our personal and family histories with money, shaping how we navigate security, provide for our loved ones, and uphold our sense of dignity. Those personal histories, family histories, and values had informed Pangea's compensation structure.

When we hired our first law fellow, Joe,‡ I learned another hard lesson about compensation and communication. Joe was a young white man with great enthusiasm about joining Pangea. After our interview, Marie and I decided he'd be a good fit and offered him the same salary as us: $40,000. Rather than accepting the offer, he sent back a detailed email negotiating for a higher salary, explaining why he was worth it. For a moment I was taken aback. How could this law fellow feel confident negotiating for a salary higher than mine or Marie's? There was a lot to unpack here.

Compensation in Context

When considering compensation, it's important to first ground our awareness in the structural racism and historical factors that have shaped inequality.

Our starting points in life and the financial challenges we face differ widely. Although everyone encounters some form of hardship or harm at some point in their lives, certain groups like BIPOC, women, gender-nonconforming people, people with disabilities, and immigrants often face additional layers of difficulty. This extra burden, rooted in historical and cultural injustices, has been imposed on these groups for centuries. In the report "Systemic Racism and the Gender Pay Gap: A Supplement to the Simple Truth," the American Association of University Women explores the history of the gender and racial wage gaps that are closely linked to the history of labor and compensation. The report states: "From depriving Black women of wages while they toiled under the system of slavery and its aftermath, to creating lasting disparities in health, education, safety, and opportunity for Native women through land theft, to the legal and cultural limitations on women's ability to earn money, our nation's story is replete with discrimination and its consequences. Exploitation of and theft from women of color fueled America's economic growth, and those crimes continue to reverberate in women's lives today."[1]

Recognizing the uneven starting points faced by BIPOC communities today is a valuable initial step. BIPOC communities and other marginalized groups have been systematically denied opportunities to build and maintain wealth through a series of discriminatory policies and practices rooted in pyramidal systems of domination. Here's a brief timeline created by Harmonize, a worker-owned cooperative that provides organizational consulting,* that highlights key events in the history of the oppression of marginalized communities in the United States:

1500s–present: Theft of Indigenous land

1787: Slavery enshrined in the US Constitution

1830: Indian Removal Act

1880s: Further Indian removal policies

1882: Chinese Exclusion Act

1880s–1950s: Jim Crow laws

1924: Immigration Act; Border Patrol established

---

* This historical timeline and the Employment, Insurance, and Wealth Trend data on the proceeding pages was provided by Harmonize as part of a presentation on equitable salaries for Pangea Legal Services on March 30, 2022.

1935: Federal Housing Administration's redlining practices

1942–45: Japanese American internment

1944: G.I. Bill benefits mostly for white veterans

1965: Immigration quotas enforced

1970s–present: Mass incarceration

2007: Subprime mortgage crisis

2020: COVID-19 pandemic

These historical injustices are not remnants of the past; they are the roots of today's economic disparities faced by BIPOC workers. The income data below, from the United States Census Bureau,[*,2] exposes stark income inequalities, underscoring the persistence of systemic racism in this country:

MEDIAN US HOUSEHOLD INCOME BY RACE

White: $89,000

Latinx: $66,000

Black: $56,000

This means that, on average, White households earn over 59 percent more than Black households and 35 percent more than Latinx households. According to a study by the Urban Institute,[3] in 1983 white families had three times the wealth of Black families. By 2022, that gap widened even more, with white families holding more than four times the wealth of Black families. This means while white families' wealth keeps growing, Black families fall even further behind.

In the same presentation by the Harmonize cooperative, additional disparities in income and wealth by race were clearly illustrated:

WEALTH GAP:

- White households have over five times the wealth of Latinx households and nearly eight times that of Black households.
- For every dollar of wealth held by a white man, a white woman has fifty-four cents, a Black woman has one cent, and a Latinx woman has less than one cent.

---

* These income numbers have been rounded to the nearest thousand.

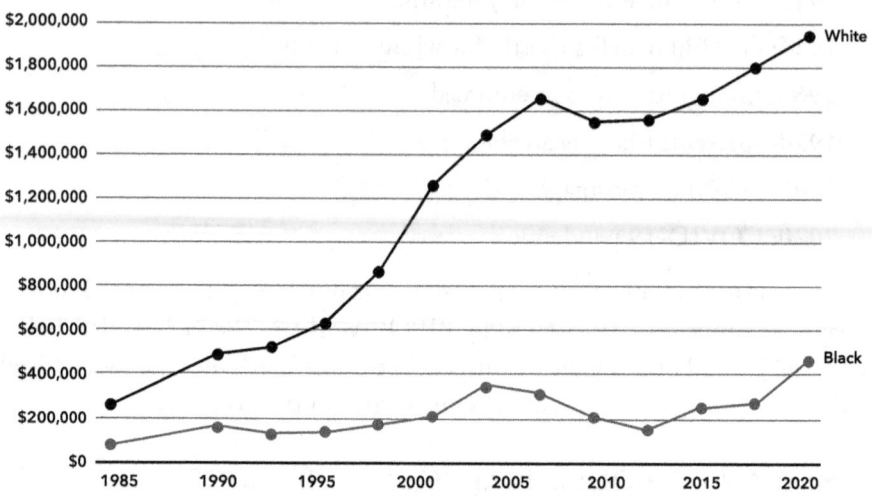

Average Family Wealth among People Born Between 1943 and 1951, by Race, 1983-2022

Source: Urban Institute calculations from the Survey of Consumer Finances 1983-2022.
Notes: 2022 dollars. The Hispanic sample size is too small to show. Age is the head of household's age. In 2022, these people were ages 71 to 79, and in 1983, they were ages 32 to 40. We used inflation adjustment factors from *Changes in U.S. Family Finances from 2019 to 2022: Evidence from the Survey of Consumer Finances.*

Stark inequality: from 1983 to 2022, white families' wealth soared past $1.8 million, while Black families were left behind at just over $400,000—illustrating a widening racial wealth gap.

EMPLOYMENT AND INSURANCE:

- Trans people of color are four times more likely to be unemployed than the general US population.
- One in five Indigenous people are uninsured.

WEALTH TRENDS:

- Black families' wealth has dropped by over 50 percent in the last thirty years, while white families' wealth has increased.
- The top 1 percent of Americans own 40 percent of the nation's wealth, leaving the remaining 99 percent with a shrinking share.

These disparities are particularly acute in the United States, partly because, contrary to other Global North countries, the US does not provide universal health care, high-quality public education, high-quality public housing, or universal childcare. These four essential needs have become increasingly unaffordable privileges as the sectors that provide them have rapidly privatized over the years. As a result, workers are highly dependent on their employers to meet their basic needs and uphold their livelihoods, with BIPOC and immigrants experiencing the most significant impact.

These figures reveal the profound inequities of our harsh system—one that I saw every day through the experiences of my immigrant and undocumented worker clients. For them, even securing a job that pays a living wage—a rare possibility—could be just the beginning of an ongoing struggle. When Maya,‡ one of my undocumented immigrant clients, finally found a job that offered her a glimmer of hope, her situation quickly unraveled as she faced a series of small but relentless setbacks. A sudden family hospitalization forced her into a tangled mess of health care paperwork, leaving her with $20,000 in medical debt and searching for help.*,[4] A single parking ticket snowballed into her car being towed and impounded, adding thousands more to her debt and leaving her without a way to get around. Missing a rent payment led to a chain reaction of late fees and eviction notices, pushing her further into financial trouble. Living paycheck to paycheck, she had to miss work to deal with these challenges, putting her job at risk. While others might have been able to handle these obstacles with enough time, money, or support, for Maya these disruptions were more than just setbacks; they intensified her struggle and kept her stuck in a cycle of instability and hardship. James Baldwin summed it up in one line from *Nobody Knows My Name*: "Anyone who has ever struggled with poverty knows how extremely expensive it is to be poor."[5]

Maya's struggles reveal the critical need for all workplaces to approach compensation with intention and thoughtfulness. Her story also underscores why equitable pay and supportive practices are essential for navigating the complexities and invisible factors that impact workers, especially those from marginalized backgrounds. Although we may not be able to rectify all historical and ongoing injustices in our efforts to create liberatory compensation strategies, acknowledging these disparities is a vital step toward preventing their continuation. Once we recognize and strive to prevent these injustices, the next question we ask ourselves may be: how can we refine compensation practices to address or partially remedy these historical injustices and their ongoing impact?

While there are no easy answers, our flat salary structure was our attempt at one.

---

* The majority of US citizens also cannot pay their medical bills or other emergency bills.

Educational Roadblocks

The inequities surrounding compensation become even more complex when we factor in that education is often a key to earning a higher salary or even a basic living wage. But even the cost of education continues to rise. Education can open doors to countless opportunities, but what happens when we can't afford it?

The article "Who Got Rich off the Student Debt Crisis?," published in *Reveal News*, explores how student loans have become profit centers for Wall Street and the federal government. "Step by step, Congress has enacted one law after another to make student debt the worst kind of debt for Americans—and the best kind for banks and debt collectors." Citing Senator Elizabeth Warren's characterization of this state of affairs as "obscene," the article adds that the student debt crisis has become "a microcosm of America—a tale of the haves and have-nots. Students who attend the richest schools often have less debt than students who graduate from state colleges. Students from low- or moderate-income families who attend for-profit schools usually take on the heaviest debt load of all."[6] This sharp contrast made me reflect on my own complex privilege as an immigrant.

It wasn't until I was in my twenties that I fully understood how fortunate I was to have access to student loans to pay for my costly university education. My mother's abundance mindset and relentless hard work were privileges in themselves, shaping my own approach to challenges and opportunities. Despite her positive outlook, we didn't have financial or class privilege growing up. As a single mother, she worked three jobs simultaneously when we first arrived in the US just to make ends meet. Once, when I was in middle school, she scolded me for spending too much on a brownie. We were too proud to apply for free lunch or reveal that we were undocumented. Later, through marriage, we gained citizenship and some security, but this shift left me feeling conflicted once I was at Pangea. How could I hold these nuanced experiences or talk about them in the face of the financial hardships experienced by my clients and colleagues? I struggled with the contrast between my newfound ease and the financial difficulties faced by my colleagues and clients. I often wondered how to address these complex inequities while still prioritizing my own basic needs for housing, health insurance, and food.

In "The Nonprofit Industrial Complex and Trans Resistance," Rickke Mananzala and Dean Spade address some of the inequalities caused by educational roadblocks.[7] They highlight how the most well-funded nonprofits often mirror private-sector pay scales, with executive directors earning significantly more than lower-level employees. This pay gap is often tied to educational privilege, which disproportionately benefits white employees from privileged backgrounds while leaving employees of color and those without access to higher education underpaid. The result is an inequitable distribution of resources that reinforces systemic inequalities within organizations,[8] something we wanted to avoid at Pangea.

So, what to do about our law fellow, Joe, who was requesting a salary higher than our flat rate? Daisy Auger-Dominguez, an author and consultant on issues of diversity, equity, and inclusion, addresses these issues in her book *Inclusion Revolution: The Essential Guide to Dismantling Racial Inequity in the Workplace.* She writes that while men are groomed for leadership from birth, "Women and BIPOC are gaslighted into being grateful for being begrudgingly allowed into spaces where white men assume they don't belong, and are rarely groomed for leadership."[9] At first I defaulted to this line of thinking about our fellow, but then I quickly realized that I hadn't shared anything with him about our values or our flat salary structure during our interviews. In fact, I hadn't even mentioned Pangea's salary structure in our job posting. While there might have been elements of privilege involved, his actions were actually in line with what all employees are expected to do in a nontransparent salary negotiation process: advocating for a higher salary.

This was a simple but significant wake-up call about the importance of not only establishing intentional recruitment and onboarding practices (more on that later) but also proactively sharing about our collective structure with all future interns, fellows, and staff from the first point of contact, and to continue reinforcing it throughout their employment. Receptionists and attorneys alike would join at the same flat salary structure, and this very unconventional strategy would need to be contextualized for everyone because we were all part of the same ecosystem.

We were creating the model for it as we went, inspired by existing frameworks but still figuring out how to apply them to our unique context.

Salary Needs May Evolve, and That's Okay

I know from experience that the idea of equal salaries might raise concerns or even fear among some leaders and funders. In fact, as Pangea grew, it eventually became apparent that the "same pay for all" approach was no longer the best fit for the organization's needs. A flat salary structure isn't right for every organization or at every stage of an organization's development. Many organizations could benefit from a tiered salary structure with reasonable salary caps, like the system in place at Full Picture Justice (formerly Community Resource Initiative), with a percentage cap on the gap between the highest-paid and lowest-paid employee.

A flat salary system can become challenging when it comes to retaining experienced staff, as it doesn't always align with market rates for those who have gained skills and expertise over the years. Balancing market realities with equity, merit, and values is crucial. For example, at Pangea, I later advocated for a tiered salary system to offer higher pay for attorneys, especially after we lost three senior attorneys, one of whom left for a forty thousand dollar pay raise elsewhere. While our flat salary approach worked well in the early years, when everyone had similar levels of experience and age, shifting to a tiered system would have better addressed the needs of experienced staff and improved our recruitment and retention efforts.

Shifting the way we think about compensation can be scary. However, embracing democratic leadership and collective governance means that we need to rethink how we define and measure merit in terms of compensation. To build truly effective organizations that address the injustices we aim to correct, we must first acknowledge and confront those very injustices. While there is no universal solution, we need to lead by example and genuinely practice what we promote.

In the typical workplace, salaries are often based on conventional merits like education, work experience, and an individual's ability to self-advocate for a higher salary. In corporations and nonprofit organizations alike, there is little if any transparency where salaries are concerned. Salary information is generally not shared with all staff, especially the top-tier salaries, and there are no salary maximums or minimums. Recognizing and questioning these practices are the first steps to designing something different.

Unfortunately, many nonprofit organizations have inherited traditional compensation structures as a matter of custom rather than intentional design. These structures are perpetuated by an overemphasis on appealing to funders, a scarcity mindset, short-term vision, a pressure to overwork, and a belief that leadership has to conform to a specific mold. Even when socially conscious leaders have the best intentions to run our organizations in alignment with our values and politics, many of us default to conventional salary tiers because we have been conditioned to think they are the most efficient and strategic way of operating, and because we have little or no exposure to successful organizations doing things differently.

How can we start redefining merit and creating equitable salary structures? Social justice nonprofits and worker cooperatives are exploring innovative approaches to address these challenges. Organizations like Harmonize are leading the way by offering tools to help organizations think about compensating for historical disenfranchisement and the often-overlooked emotional labor that can lead to burnout. Recognizing that discussions about salaries can be highly sensitive, Harmonize suggests framing the purposes of compensation through these four categories:

1. **Needs:** This involves considering the basic cost of living to ensure that all employees can meet their essential needs. This includes housing, food, health care, and other necessary expenses so organizations can adjust salaries to align with local living costs.

2. **Deserve:** This category assesses the type of work performed and the level of experience required. It recognizes that different roles and amounts of experience should be reflected in compensation, valuing the skills and expertise each employee brings to the organization.

3. **Reparation:** This acknowledges historical economic exclusion and its lasting effects. Compensation in this category aims to address and mitigate the impact of past injustices, offering equitable pay that takes into account systemic disadvantages experienced by marginalized groups.

4. **Benefit to the organization:** This considers factors like employee retention and the need to compete with market rates for specialized skills. It helps ensure that salaries are structured to maintain a skilled workforce and align with industry standards while remaining equitable.

Being clear about what an organization's compensation structure is attempting to address can help focus the group's conversation and shape the resulting salary structure.

Harmonize also proposes practical strategies like the "Bonus Bucket Experiment," which involves distributing one-time bonuses from a predefined pool of funds based on the categories above, and determining raise allocations by using multiple salary bands with a scoring system for the four categories listed above. These approaches aim to balance fairness with practical considerations in salary management.

Transparency and Trust

Contrary to prevailing practices in the labor marketplace (and much to our funders' surprise), several employees took a pay cut to come work at Pangea because they were personally aligned with the values of collective governance and had a strong belief in participatory democracy. This type of values-based alignment comes easier when organizations are in a start-up phase, when staff members are roughly the same age or have approximately the same amount of work experience, and when information is shared on a regular, systematic basis. Transparency is key.

When Pangea was a small team of ten, we had ongoing, open salary conversations about our varying personal financial backgrounds. One colleague shared that their parents were undocumented and worked in factories seven days a week. That colleague's salary from Pangea was more than their parents had ever made combined. A formerly undocumented staff member shared that their mother was always financially dependent on a partner, so it was important for the colleague to have financial independence as an individual. An undocumented staff member shared that their Pangea salary and their credit score helped them purchase a house together with their undocumented family members. On the other side of the spectrum, a different staff member described how their parents were paid a great deal working in the university system and took long vacations in the summers. These conversations facilitated understanding, connection, and care among the staff, strengthening our commitment to equitable compensation policies.

Fostering a culture of open communication about compensation requires skillful navigation of complex and highly personal topics. These conversations can easily stir emotions and, if not handled thoughtfully, may lead to competition for resources rather than a collective effort to achieve equitable outcomes. It's essential that we approach these discussions with empathy and a shared commitment to understanding each other's unique financial backgrounds, building trust and strengthening our collective commitment to equity.

These open conversations helped us build trust, deepen empathy for each other's unique financial journeys, and reaffirm our commitment to equity in all aspects of our work. This same values-driven approach also shaped how we thought about hiring, focusing on lived experience as much as formal education.

Redefining Merit

Every role in a collectively led organization is essential, but not every role requires a college degree. At Pangea, what we truly valued was lived experience.

Immigrants and undocumented workers brought a wealth of wisdom, emotional intelligence, resourcefulness, proactiveness, and hands-on experience with the very systems that our clients were moving through. So, over time we established intentional recruitment practices that accounted for lived experience in lieu of (or as a supplement to) traditional education. One way we did that was by aligning ourselves with organizations committed to developing the skills and leadership of the kinds of organizers, paralegals, movement lawyers, and social justice practitioners we wanted to hire.

For example, we established a relationship with the New York University (NYU) Immigrant Rights Clinic, where we connected to Luis Angel, a recent DACA recipient. He was a student there and joined our staff as a law fellow in 2015; later he became one of the first undocumented attorneys in the US. As a youth activist, Luis Angel organized hundreds of undocumented youth in the Bay Area before law school, navigated the immigration system (and helped many of his relatives do the same), and paid his way through school as a dishwasher. Through his relationships, he eventually brought on board five more values-aligned attorneys from the NYU program.

We also developed a relationship with fellows from the city of San Francisco's DACA internship program. We met prospective fellows, interns, and staff through collaborations with other organizations and programs that shared our purpose through clinics, workshops, and shared work. Luis Angel came on at the same salary level as me and everyone else at Pangea.

Another incredible addition to our team was Jesus. After his release from immigration prison, he began working as an organizer at PACT. He later joined Pangea's board of directors, where he played a crucial role in shaping the direction of our strategic plans, including the intentional expansion of Pangea's organizing capacity. His strategic vision was instrumental in guiding our growth, which led to Pangea hiring him as one of our full-time immigrant justice organizers. Jesus's depth of lived experience far exceeded what he could have gained through formal education alone.

Esperanza was another shining example of how invaluable lived experience can be. Although she came on board without a formal degree, her experience with navigating the immigration system for her own family gave her a unique perspective. She had led the process of her three siblings and parents applying for immigration status, a journey that taught her more than any textbook could. Starting out as our front desk receptionist, Esperanza went above and beyond her role. When clients returned after their legal cases were resolved, she took it upon herself to assist them further. She taught herself how to recover bond money from ICE and even organized an entire team of high school students to fill the courtroom in support of a child whose mother was detained. She spearheaded a national letter-writing campaign with these students. Though she had never been formally trained as an organizer, her instincts, intelligence, and proactive nature proved far more effective than conventional training, demonstrating the powerful impact of lived experience.

Had we followed a conventional pay scale rooted in the attainment of formal education, Luis Angel would have earned the most, followed by Jesus, and Esperanza (an Indigenous-Latina woman) would have been the lowest paid. Despite their immense lived experience and deep community connections, all three would have been paid less than me and other attorneys, several of whom were white US citizens. By upholding equal pay across all staff regardless of education level and role, we acknowledged the significance of each staff member's experience, honoring the value and wisdom we all brought to our team.

Another way we redefined traditional merit was by removing the requirement that paralegals must have a certificate or degree, because the emphasis placed on formal educational credentials often overshadows the value of practical experience and skills. Along similar lines, at the Law Center, Janelle Orsi and Chris Tittle wanted to create pathways for people to become lawyers at their nonprofit without paying hundreds of thousands of dollars to go to law school. California law provides an alternative route to legal practice through apprenticeship, allowing individuals to learn from licensed attorneys without formal schooling.[10] To achieve this, the Law Center developed a four-year mentorship program that enables aspiring lawyers to work alongside experienced lawyers in a hands-on apprenticeship. The program still requires achieving key milestones and passing the bar exam, but it's an example of how breaking away from traditional systems and conventional notions of merit can be done through innovative, out-of-the-box thinking.

Compensation Pathways and Practice

Pangea's alternative pathways to compensation would not come easily. We knew we would need to create protocols and practices for processing internalized biases, external systemic challenges, and diverse opinions on an ongoing basis. We were still working against entrenched biases around conventional compensation systems. By the time Pangea had grown to a staff of twenty-one, people outside our organization had repeatedly challenged our flat salary structure with questions and statements like these:

- Why are your salaries the same?
- An ED has to be paid more than other staff.
- But you're the one who doesn't sleep at night; why aren't you compensated more?
- You have more experience and responsibility, so why isn't that reflected in your salary?
- The buck stops with you. That's why you should be paid more.
- My board decides my ED salary, and they just increased it, so I didn't have anything to do with it. Why don't you do the same?
- You'll never retain good attorneys with a flat salary structure. How do you expect to retain people?

These were reasonable questions, especially given the norms of traditional organizations and work systems. However, our critics didn't always understand that we were challenging the very assumptions their questions were based on. These assumptions included fixed ideas about board roles, the notion that the executive director is the only one working tirelessly behind the scenes, the idea that the executive director is solely responsible for everything, and the belief that good attorneys, particularly newer ones, weren't willing to make pay adjustments to align with their values.

As Pangea grew and the responsibility on my shoulders began to spread to my colleagues, we shared a collective and intentional effort to diffuse authority, decision-making, and execution power across all members of the staff. We had systems in place to dialogue about salaries and compensation issues. But back in 2013, when Michelle asked me why I should make $1,000 more than Marie, I was still at the beginning of my journey. Marie and I both started with a flat salary of $40,000 in 2013, and by the time I transitioned out of Pangea in 2023, we were all earning $80,000.

We recognized that our salaries were below market rate, but with a small organizational budget, our first goal was simply to ensure everyone earned a living wage in San Francisco. In 2013, the living wage was around $50,000 for an adult with no dependents. Our initial focus was on reaching this benchmark before considering any broader compensation changes. Each year, we held an open team conversation to reassess our flat salaries and explore alternatives like salary tiers. However, after each discussion, we collectively decided to maintain the flat salary structure, reaffirming our commitment to our shared values.

Actionable Takeaways

Acknowledge socioeconomic barriers that applicants face. Salary systems often emphasize work experience and expertise without accounting for how socioeconomic background affects access to these qualifications. BIPOC women, LGBTQ+ people, immigrants, and people with disabilities often face unique challenges that place them lower on the salary scale. However, they can bring valuable, unconventional gifts—like relational care work, creative solutions, and expertise gained from lived experiences—that are essential but often undervalued in compensation decisions. Acknowledging these barriers and intentionally deciding whether to remedy them is an essential step in equitable compensation considerations. Consider compensating for invisible labor and relational care work by providing either a bonus pool or a higher salary. At Pangea, we made space every year during our annual compensation discussions to openly share and acknowledge our varied access to wealth, as well as our personal histories and relationships with money.

Question beliefs about money. Developing a salary system that prioritizes collective well-being over individual gain invites a nuanced reflection upon our own experiences and biases regarding money. This exploration of underlying beliefs encourages a richer understanding of equitable compensation. In some of our early compensation discussions at Pangea, we created space to openly share our personal views on money, our roles, and the emotions tied to these topics. These conversations helped us better understand each other and guided how we approached compensation decisions as a collective.

Implement salary structures with limits. Value nuance in discussions and considerations, but also value simplicity when putting equitable salaries in place. Create a clear salary system with defined levels and set minimums based on a living wage and regional cost of living. Take into account market rates for certain positions and roles, as well as the cost of living in areas where staff live. Consider the entire compensation package, including factors like health insurance, professional development opportunities, and other benefits.

Value lived experience. The US education system creates disparities in access, affecting who can gain work experience and expertise. Hiring practices that prioritize lived experience as much as formal education can be highly effective.

Learn from social justice organizations. Focus on values that are important to your workplace and are connected to your work and mission. Some organizations successfully incorporate mediating factors—like staff undergoing direct systemic impact or having significant financial needs—into their salary structures alongside work experience. Others promote financial transparency to better address the unique needs of their staff. We considered both at Pangea.

Be transparent about compensation. Many people might not be familiar with how collectively governed organizations operate. Clearly explaining your structures and salary practices to potential employees from the start, and continuing transparent conversations with current staff, ensures everyone understands what to expect. Reinforcing these discussions throughout the team builds trust and alignment around compensation decisions. At Pangea we communicated about our values, collective structure, and compensation with all staff transparently and from the start, including in our job postings. (See appendix I, "Job Posting," for details.) It was easy for us because everyone's salary was the same. Some tiered organizations provide internal salary databases accessible to all staff, allowing employees to see role-based salary ranges, benefits packages, and other compensation data.

4

Cultivating a Culture of Care

Living Our Values Daily

When a culture of care aligns with thoughtful structures, it does more than influence behavior; it creates meaningful rituals and systems that nurture growth, connection, and a commitment to shared purpose. Recruiting our law fellow, Joe,[‡] was an important lesson in how to communicate our values of collective governance. I had written a set of internal principles for Pangea's culture and shared them with staff and interns, but we hadn't developed them collectively or formalized them into shared guidelines. It became clear that we needed to embed these principles into our team's daily practices and organizational structure.

As we deepened our understanding of collective governance, we realized that building a culture of care required more than just principles on paper; it demanded intentional relationship-building, setting boundaries, and acknowledging the emotional labor involved in this work. To create a truly supportive environment, we needed to align our values with daily practices, ensuring that our emotional well-being and the collective care we envision were embedded into every aspect of our organizational structure.

Echoing Audre Lorde's wisdom, as social justice practitioners we often operate within the spaces where the personal meets the political.[1] Because the personal is inherently political, it is also heavy with collective historical struggles. This interconnectedness underscores the importance of nurturing our emotional capacity without compromising our own mental health. If we don't support our well-being in the movement over the long haul, both workers and the purpose of our work suffer; so too does the very culture of care we seek to establish. "If we are not intentional about our culture, it will be formed from the conditioned tendencies and habits that we have learned through capitalism, white supremacy, patriarchy, and the resulting traumas that come from such violence," writes organizer Sammie Ablaza Wills, the former executive director of Lavender Phoenix (formerly known as Asian Pacific Islander Equality—Northern California). In their article "Right-Sized Belonging: Six Practices for Organizers" in *Convergence*, Ablaza Wills notes that it is not enough to rely on culture built from tradition; as our conditions change, "we must be able to truly examine ourselves, see our weaknesses, and implement practices that make our movements worthwhile and irresistible."[2]

Culture and structure are not easy to change, but like the pillars of a building they provide support that keeps everything standing when the ground is shaky. Creating structure around our culture of care is absolutely necessary for social justice workers. It creates a space where we can uplift one another, especially during difficult times.

With the support of coaches and expert facilitators, Pangea refined and strengthened its practices to nurture our team's emotional health. It wasn't a straightforward path, but every time we made progress it brought a deeper sense of care and connection to the work.

Building a Team and Trust Together

In liberatory organizations, building a culture of care is essential for everyone's growth and transformation. It brings to life what we truly value and guides us in shaping policies and roles that create a more supportive workplace. Although dedicating time and resources to this work can be challenging, the first step is being intentional about relationship-building.

This commitment to cultivating a culture of care begins with strong relationships, which are the heart of our collectively led organizations. By nurturing meaningful connections with our colleagues, we spark trust and collaboration, the core of our collective well-being. A thriving culture of care encompasses role clarity, accountability, recognition of emotional labor, and boundaries, as well as the ways we communicate and celebrate each other's contributions. As we move forward, it's important to nurture these connections and build a supportive environment, recognizing that we can face challenges, learn from them, and grow together.

I asked Rek Kwawer, the former director of operations at the North American Students of Cooperation (NASCO), to tell me about staff members' early experiences with NASCO'S collective management structure. NASCO is a unionized nonprofit organization formed in 1968 that supports the growth of housing cooperatives and other cooperative models across campuses in North America and Canada. The organization represents over 3,500 housing cooperative members and provides vital resources such as financing, loans, and organizational design to help these co-ops thrive. In 2012 NASCO transitioned from a hierarchical structure to democratic governance. All staff and leadership are now unionized, and the organization is run collectively, with the board of directors serving as the management team.

Kwawer replied, "There was always an element of personal check-in. I'd ask: 'How are you? What's going on in your life?' It was an opportunity to get to know more about what was happening for people. Building strong relationships with people is important so that there's trust; with trust, you can have honest and even hard conversations with people. You can say, 'Okay, I know this is gonna be hard for you to hear, but I need to say it. I know that you know where I'm coming from.' That person will hear it better. Relationship-building is really important." Kwawer's emphasis on personal check-ins at NASCO highlights how genuine relationship-building creates the trust needed for candid and sometimes difficult conversations. By focusing on people beyond their roles, NASCO shows how connection strengthens collective work.

At Pangea, I cared about my colleagues' well-being and wanted to know how they were doing beyond work. Before jumping into tasks, I'd ask about their lives—their joys, struggles, and experiences. Even during busy work check-ins with long lists of cases, I always made space for personal conversations first. It wasn't planned or strategic; it just felt natural and aligned with our collective leadership values, where building genuine relationships is key to nurturing a supportive environment. Over time, this informal practice became structured. We integrated a guide into our check-ins that included personal well-being questions, such as "On a scale of 1 to 10, how is your overall well-being at work?" and "On a scale of 1 to 10, how much stress are you experiencing?" This allowed space for personal check-ins and a shared understanding of each other's well-being.

Our organizations are ecosystems, and the relationships we forge within them are deeply interconnected. But it's easy to lose sight of these interconnections when we're so intensely focused on our individual tasks that we can't see how they fit into the larger body.

Balancing Care and Boundaries

I worked to nurture a culture of care that, in its own way, echoed the warm, communal essence of Iranian culture, even if this outcome was more a result of my personal approach than a deliberate intention. In Iranian culture, collective needs and desires are often placed above those of the individual. My guests and my community, the thinking goes, are of the highest priority. I have to offer my community everything I have, even if it means I have nothing left—even if the community's request was unexpected. This generosity thrives in a culture that values reciprocity.

I remember a time when my grandmother, Maryam, had prepared a special jeweled rice dish and bought sweet treats for the evening's guests. When some additional cousins showed up unexpectedly a few hours beforehand, she offered them everything we had and made a run for the store to replenish the treats before the next round of guests came. Before she ate herself, she made sure everyone else had already eaten or had seconds before she even took a bite.

Offering abundance to others is about hospitality and care—the essence of home. This mindset assumes that we will place the well-being of others before our own. I carried this same commitment to relationship-building into Pangea, helping to foster a strong sense of trust within our team and community. This emphasis on personal connection is vital for nurturing a culture of care in social justice nonprofits.

But if this self-sacrificing ethos of care is combined with the US culture of individualism and overwork, where more is always considered better, it can become a form of overextending oneself to the point of blurring boundaries and ignoring one's own needs. This shadow manifested in my leadership. My lack of desire to draw boundaries with my work—and my desire to work hard through every vacation—felt like the right thing to do. I'd send emails at all hours of the night and on weekends. I agreed to lead projects that I later learned would also impact my colleagues' workloads and override their boundaries. I did much of this because I was conditioned to equate overwork with my value. I also believed that sacrificing my own needs was the ultimate expression of care and commitment, a belief shaped by both cultural expectations and my desire to prove my worth. I felt that I had to prove myself as a femme of color because the default message of the culture at large was *You're not good enough*. I was operating in a system rooted in people at the top benefiting from the work of people at the bottom. And of course I also didn't realize that, as in any ecosystem, my work habits had an impact on everyone, just as an ache in one small part of a limb impacts the whole body—a truth beautifully expressed by the Iranian poet Saadi, who wrote that the human family is interconnected like the limbs of a single being.[3] I needed boundaries.

In her book *Set Boundaries, Find Peace*, author Nedra Glover Tawwab writes that boundary issues in the workplace look like this:[4]

- Doing work for others
- Being asked about personal issues
- Taking on more than you can handle
- Not delegating
- Working without pay
- Not taking advantage of vacation days
- Saying yes to tasks you can't responsibly complete
- Engaging in stressful interactions
- Working during downtime
- Doing jobs intended for more than one person
- Not taking needed time off

Tawwab says many people don't realize when they cross someone else's boundaries because boundaries aren't a matter of common sense; they're learned behaviors. In a workplace, these boundaries are influenced by HR rules, the overall work culture, and the expectations set by management. When employees are worried about job security, it becomes even tougher for them to stand up for their limits. This pressure can push them to overextend themselves in an effort to be viewed as good employees.

Challenging the Urgency Trap

Despite our commitment to creating a culture of care at Pangea, a few of us were also creating a culture of urgency. The nature of the emotional labor we were doing only intensified this sense of urgency. In hindsight, I now understand why, as we were growing, my colleagues sat me down and told me that they wanted me to take an offline vacation—no emails or other work-related tasks. At the time, however, I felt patronized. I thought, *I don't need a vacation. I support you in taking one, but I need to focus on my detained clients and help reunite families, coordinate with organizers to launch a public campaign, secure a new source of funding, be present for my coalition meetings, and do other life-nurturing work. This is what I want.* And I really *did* want that.

I didn't read the subtext of my colleagues' input in that moment, which was this: *Please do this not only for yourself, but also for us. Please model a healthier, more boundaried leadership style for us because we have a hard time believing and following what you say when you're not doing it.* What my colleagues really wanted was for me to help everyone participate in a true culture of care by modeling care for myself.

But I did not model what I said and what I wanted for my peers because I actively did *not* want boundaries between my personal life and my work life. Working around the clock and beyond the industry standard had become second nature to me. Working hard and giving my all was a way to show my love and care for others. This conditioning is prevalent among many marginalized workers. For instance, researchers from UNC-Chapel Hill and Michigan State University conducted a study that identified an overachieving mindset prevalent among Black women, which they call the "superwoman schema."[5] The researchers interviewed women who reported taking on so many tasks and so much work that they felt extremely overwhelmed, and they admitted that this way of living created unnecessary struggles, emotional drain, and burnout. Other study participants said they felt obligated to meet the needs of others. This intensity of labor is not similarly required of people with privilege related to race, class, gender, or physical ability.

At Pangea, these dynamics were unfolding beneath the surface until my colleagues began to speak up. Celine, a dedicated Pangea attorney, worked tirelessly for both our clients and the team. Although she showed me great respect, she noticed how my lack of boundaries was affecting the whole organization. Celine sat me down to tell me she wanted a better work-life balance for herself, and she felt that this shift could benefit everyone. But I needed support.

It was Ambri Pukhraj—a worker co-owner at the Cheese Board Collective who would later have a key role at Pangea—who led me to the right expert facilitator. Ambri told me the Cheese Board Collective had hired kiran nigam to help them service and deepen their already rich culture of care and connection. I was curious and immediately reached out to kiran.

kiran is the co-founder of a worker-owned consulting cooperative called the Anti-Oppression Resource and Training Alliance (AORTA). A brilliant facilitator with broad experience working in cooperatives with shared decision-making processes and collective governance structures, kiran ended up facilitating Pangea's second board and staff retreat, with remarkable results. Having a wise, impartial individual with leadership skills guide us through the retreat process was generative and efficient. We got to know each other better both interpersonally and in the context of our roles at Pangea. I was able to step back and let go of the reins, rather than talking more and dominating the retreat. kiran modeled collective power by gently guardrailing me so others could openly express their opinions, feelings, and questions. They also modeled distributed authority and shared power this way, paving the way for other people to take ownership in areas I might have been inclined to manage. After being in control for so long, with my hands in every slice of the pie, I was learning how to take collective work from theory to practice while simultaneously becoming aware of the culture of urgency and stress I was creating.

kiran also helped us expand and elevate the principles I'd written on my own to the level of collective operational values that we called our Points of Unity. These thirteen key statements boldly defined and articulated Pangea's shared values, forming the guiding framework that continues to serve as the organization's central doctrine to this day.*

Developing our Points of Unity was a process. In conjunction with kiran's facilitation, Celine had conducted a full-team survey of work-life balance and boundaries, with questions that explored what people enjoyed doing outside of work, how much they managed to do that while working at Pangea, whether they felt comfortable expressing their need or wish for fewer hours at Pangea, and what their actual versus ideal weekly working hours were. The survey made it clear that we all had different expectations and desires. Some of us, myself included, felt that this work was our purpose and our priority, but there was still a unanimous desire to have more time for loved ones and activities outside of work, which wasn't happening at the time.

The survey results inspired us to incorporate wellness into all stages of our development. Two of Pangea's Points of Unity reflected our commitment to wellness. Years later, we would include wellness in our strategic plan objectives and continue to talk about it openly and frequently. In the meantime,

---

* See appendix B, "Statement of Values and Principles."

we created a Task Redistribution Chart* that helped everyone understand and visualize the scope of our collective work—or the Pangea ecosystem—ranging from detailed administrative tasks to sweeping legal efforts. We could also lean on the chart as our roles evolved, when conflicts arose, and when we reached growth edges. The Task Redistribution Chart and our Points of Unity helped us set and hold boundaries collectively.†

A significant takeaway from this ongoing growth was a big-picture under-standing of three key practices that are fundamental to creating a culture of care: setting and holding boundaries, valuing emotional labor, and co-creating clear expectations.

Setting and Holding Boundaries

As we were learning, when authority and responsibility are shared in democrat-ically managed workplaces or collectives where there is no single boss, boundar-ies become crucial to promote health and balance as well as to prevent conflict and resentment. The American Psychological Association defines a "boundary" as a psychological demarcation that protects the integrity of an individual or group or that helps the person or group set realistic limits on participation in a relationship or activity.[6] In the workplace, boundaries help to maintain our integrity as individuals and as teams. They offer us clarity in building healthy relationships with our work and our co-workers by establishing conditions for engagement. But setting and holding boundaries in the workplace require emotional work and take practice.

As I began to recognize and tend to my old wounds, I also became more attuned to the needs of my colleagues and the broader community. I realized that prioritizing needs outside of work is more than a personal responsibility; it's a collective one. For example, when I have the necessary support and resources at work, I'm able to complete tasks within my work hours. If something doesn't get done, we approach it as a team to find a solution together so I can still tend to my needs outside of work. When we take care of ourselves together, we're better equipped to support our teams and carry out our mission effectively. This shift in perspective was transformative both for me and for Pangea.

---

* Celine created the original chart after surveying the team and asking folks to fill in their roles.

† See appendix C, "Task Redistribution Chart."

Rather than seeing boundaries as limitations, I learned to view them as essential tools for cultivating a healthy organizational culture. Boundaries create space for genuine collaboration and creativity. When we feel secure in our roles and know we can take time off without guilt, we are more likely to do our best work. This sense of security allows us to bring our whole selves to work, strengthening our collective impact.

It's essential to redefine what it means to feel that the work is "enough"—not as endless busyness but as a commitment to well-being. By establishing a culture of balance and encouraging ourselves to say no more intentionally and unapologetically, we challenged the pervasive overwork that often characterizes nonprofit organizations. This shift not only helped us create healthier boundaries but also allowed us to say yes to our priorities—those aligned with our mission and Points of Unity. In a field where clients like Jesus face urgent threats such as detention or deportation every day, this balance was essential. Restoring energy and spirit is crucial; we want to keep our passion for social justice alive rather than letting it be drained by external demands. By nurturing boundaries within a culture of care, we enhance our individual health as well as the vitality of our organizations and the communities we serve, reminding ourselves that our work is about thriving together, not just surviving. Although this shift in perspective and practice is challenging, acknowledging the likelihood that unpredictable obstacles will arise—and setting aside space to address them when they do—can create a healthier work environment.

As leaders, when we prioritize our well-being, we also model this behavior for our colleagues. We can show that caring for our needs is just as important as caring for our communities. Simply saying no to taking on new tasks before our workload becomes unmanageable is one way to do this. Every layer—ourselves as individuals, our co-workers, and the communities we serve—is interconnected. By taking steps to care for ourselves, we uplift our spirits and create the conditions for our colleagues to feel empowered to do the same.

Roshni Sampath, co-executive director of Rooted in Vibrant Communities (RVC), shared with me how RVC's employees care for themselves and create healthy boundaries internally. RVC is a nonprofit organization that cultivates leaders and communities of color. It is an example of a high-functioning workplace that collectively supports boundary setting and role shifting, frequently through a collective decision-making process. "At RVC, the roles that you inhabit really determine your decision-making power," Roshni said. "We talk about our jobs as a collection of different roles. When moving to our shared executive leadership structure, we dug into which roles were high in emotional labor, pressure, and urgency. We tried to determine: What burns people out? We put every role down and treated them like dominoes, switching around the tiles as we tried to get people involved in things that energize them." Through their role-mapping exercises, RVC's leadership tackles practical challenges like burnout and overextension in a grounded way. This approach highlights how intentional adjustments to roles can create a supportive, balanced environment for everyone involved.

It is important to acknowledge here that our relationship to work is intimately related to the circumstances of our upbringing. It is everyone's responsibility to understand those differences; but those who have the privilege or power to either uphold or change damaging systems should actively work toward greater balance for everyone.

Boundaries as an Act of Care

A few years before I transitioned out of Pangea, I started to set firmer boundaries around my time and energy. I went from doing the work of multiple full-time staff members to reducing my responsibilities to that of just one full-time staff member. Making myself unavailable on weekends, requesting advance notice when colleagues needed me to review documents, and prioritizing more vacation time became essential practices.

Surprisingly, instead of facing resistance, a noticeable shift occurred. My colleagues began treating me differently. For the first time, I felt truly valued and appreciated. Even though I was doing less than I had before, I received more praise and recognition. As I started valuing my time and setting boundaries, I noticed that my colleagues began to mirror this respect back to me. They no longer assumed I would always be available. When I was flexible and made time for something on short notice despite my stated boundary, there was a genuine sense of respect and gratitude—something I hadn't experienced when I was always accessible. One colleague even told me, "I admire how you advocate for yourself, Nilou." These were some of the unexpected but powerful outcomes of setting boundaries.

I also felt the impact at home. I was more present, more at peace, and more connected with my family. Setting boundaries didn't make me rigid or distant. Instead, it helped me show up as my full self both at work and in my personal life. This experience taught me that drawing boundaries isn't just about self-preservation; it's about creating space for mutual respect and deeper connection with others, both in the workplace and beyond.

The development of my boundaries required three key elements. First, I needed a strong will to set boundaries—a resolve that naturally strengthened after becoming a parent and that I further nurtured through therapy and coaching. Second, Pangea's collective efforts, including a substantial fellowship award, provided us the resources to hire additional staff, such as a coordinator who could take on responsibilities I had previously managed. Finally, the collective structure we established, with intentional task redistribution meetings every six months, allowed me to gradually delegate my workload. While the delegation of my workload to other staff members wasn't a perfect science, it served as an important structural support.

This raises an important question: How can we truly prioritize boundaries without adequate resourcing? We need to recognize that our system is inherently flawed; nonprofits often do public-sector work funded by government contracts at rates far lower than government-level compensation. While we often don't have the resources to hire the staffing we need, we can begin with a strong sense of will and determination. By establishing long-term goals and co-creating values that uphold our commitment to balance, we can lay the foundation for the boundaries we aspire to so we can implement them when resources become available.

In collectively led organizations, we often work together with an entrepreneurial spirit, driven by our shared passions and goals. This enthusiasm can sometimes lead us to feel like we need to be available all the time, pushing our limits and compromising our well-being. It's important to remember that we have the autonomy to set our own boundaries.

Below are some strategies for establishing and maintaining workplace boundaries.

Practical Tips for Leaders Developing Well-Boundaried Organizations

Communicate Boundaries

- **Be explicit and affirming.** Clearly state your boundaries and invite others to state theirs. Acknowledge the diversity in needs early on, and find ways to affirm boundaries. For example, openly share when you need uninterrupted focus time, or set expectations for response times on emails.

Model Boundaries

- **Lead by example.** Adhere to your own boundaries. For instance, avoid sending emails after hours. Rek Kwawer of NASCO shared, "One of the boundaries we established was to use separate phones for work and personal calls, or to create a dedicated Google Voice number for work. This encouraged everyone to turn off their work devices when they were off the clock."

Recognize That Boundaries Change

- **Reassess regularly.** Boundaries evolve with life circumstances. After I became a parent in 2018, my boundaries and priorities shifted. In 2022, with coaching from Sheena Wadhawan, I prioritized attending my daughter's day care gathering at four p.m., even when it conflicted with a recurring work meeting. I asked three colleagues who would be impacted by moving this meeting to change the time. Previously, I would have shown up late or missed my child's event. With a new perspective, and Pangea's written Points of Unity supporting our wellness as individuals, I learned to create boundaries that aligned with my reality.

Celebrate Boundaries

- **Acknowledge achievements.** At Pangea, each staff member shared their vacation plans via email, checking our responsibilities and coordinating with colleagues to delegate tasks. Once these steps were completed, we didn't need to seek approval. Instead, we announced our time off in an all-team email and tracked it in a shared chart, allowing everyone to take vacation when they wanted while maintaining trust and accountability. When others received these vacation-plan emails, we celebrated their time away and sent notes of encouragement.

Practical Tips for Establishing Workplace Boundaries[7]

Boundaries in the Office

- **Set clear working hours.** Define the hours when you are available and avoid working outside of them unless necessary.

- **Take lunch breaks.** Avoid eating at your desk; take time to enjoy your meal without distractions.

- **Minimize distractions.** Limit personal calls and texts during work hours so as to not distract others.

- **Communicate about your workload.** Inform your colleagues if your workload becomes unmanageable.

- **Don't work if you're sick.** Take time off to heal.

- **Stick to focused time.** Protect blocks of time on your calendar for focused work (e.g., no meetings or emails on Thursdays from ten a.m. to one p.m.).

Boundaries Away from the Office

- **Use your vacation days.** Over 40 percent of US workers don't take all their paid time off.[8] Make it a priority!

- **Limit after-hours communication.** Avoid checking work emails or going into the office during your time off.

- **Limit stress talk.** To avoid reactivating anxiety and overwhelm, be mindful of talking about work-related stress. Reserve these conversations for designated supportive spaces.

- **Set automatic out-of-office responses.** Set automatic email and voicemail replies directing inquiries to a colleague during your absence.

- **Delegate tasks.** Identify tasks that others can handle to reduce your workload.

Boundaries are essential for protecting both our individual and collective integrity, especially in organizations with shared leadership; but they don't have to be rigid. Flexibility within those boundaries allows us to maintain balance while still showing up for ourselves and each other. When we create space for our limits and honor the diverse needs of our peers, we cultivate an environment where we can thrive collectively. According to Prentis Hemphill, co-founder of the Embodiment Institute, "Boundaries are the distance at which I can love you and me simultaneously."[9] Hemphill's words indicate that boundaries are about more than self-protection; they are about creating the space where mutual care and respect can flourish. By supporting one another in setting boundaries, we embrace our own evolution while also contributing to the creation of a more liberated and joyful community.

Valuing Emotional Labor

According to Penn State's Workplace Emotional Labor and Diversity Lab, emotional labor involves regulating or managing emotional expressions with others as part of one's professional work role.[10] Emotional labor is necessary to achieve professional goals and conform to work role requirements. Like physical labor, it requires effort, but it is often unseen and therefore underacknowledged, ingraining itself into an organization's culture.

Emotional labor is one of the most complex aspects of organizational dynamics, particularly in the context of social justice work. Pangea's staff and clients—migrants and asylum seekers—are often in the thick of enduring, surviving, and fighting systemic harm. These challenges are all too familiar to organizations across social justice sectors working with communities on the front lines. When we, as advocates, engage in emotional labor such as holding space for a client who is on the brink of potential deportation and permanent separation from their families and communities, we listen to their stories as they process their feelings in the face of huge stakes. We try to regulate our own emotions as we find strategies that will support them in the short term and connect them to broader movements for systemic change in the long term. Being in direct contact with people during times of high need or crisis requires emotional labor.

At Pangea, for example, we were constantly balancing large immigration caseloads with high-stakes policy advocacy. Our work extended beyond the office, taking us to the heart of political action in Sacramento and Washington, DC. We were coordinating closely with organizers, supporting community-led campaigns, and each of us was often doing the work of multiple people. In this environment, finding the space to focus on internal practices of care was difficult.

We also perform emotional labor when we visit a prison where people are held in inhumane conditions; when we have to file a report or complaint to address a health access violation while we're working on an immigration case; or when we listen to an asylum client retell the story of traumatic gender-based violence in their country of origin during a court hearing, then immediately sit down for a staff meeting to discuss our budget for the next fiscal year. The sense of injustice and unfairness that we see in every system, and the community struggles and pain that service workers hold and process daily, involve significant emotional labor. Over time, without the proper acknowledgment or support, it all takes a heavy toll.

Secondary trauma is also an implicit part of work for most people in the social justice field. For those of us who are also directly impacted by the same or similar forms of oppression as the communities we work with, the impact can be even more pronounced. Though not all workers recognize it in other fields, it's common knowledge in the world of therapy that people need to take care of themselves and build recovery and healing time into their work lives. We need to understand how our own personal histories and emotional responses influence our work, often in subtle ways. At the same time, we need to prioritize finding resources and time to nurture our own healing. Although there is a growing call for self-care in our work, many social justice practitioners appreciate this less due to our commitment to the work. And we need our community and work structures to support us in our care work. It took me years of intentional practice, introspection, and the support of colleagues and thoughtful structures to grasp the extent of emotional labor required of us in the social justice movement. One formative experience that helped me achieve this realization was working with a client named Irani.

"The Violence Brought Me"

Irani is an indigenous Guatemalan who fled to the United States to seek asylum after surviving enormous racial and economic harm in his home country. After being beaten bloody and left for dead in Guatemala, Irani spent months recovering in hiding, afraid of being found again and this time killed. He decided to walk north to the United States, but as soon as he arrived, he was only met with more of the same abuse. In an op-ed published by BuzzFeed, Irani described his first encounter with American officials:

> In Spanish, one officer warned me they would shoot to kill if I attempted to run. Then they forced me to my knees and ripped off my shirt, looking for tattoos I didn't have. I had been forced to my knees on small rocks by my teachers as a student in Guatemala. My teachers in Guatemala accused me of being inferior and made me feel like I didn't belong for being brown and Indigenous in a Ladino school. The American officers spat at me, called me a bitch, and accused me of bringing violence to their country. I didn't bring the violence, I cried. The violence brought me.[11]

After US immigration officers forced Irani to his knees and humiliated him, they took him into a prison that felt like a refrigerator. He was locked in this cage for the next six months. Initially, he was in there together with another thirty migrants, all of whom had to sleep on the freezing floors. No one explained to Irani why he was in this cage and for how long he had to stay there. He learned from the guards that the cold temperatures were intended to punish migrants like Irani and force them to self-deport. After about a month in the shared cell, Irani was moved to a bigger prison facility that was still cold but had bunk beds, showers, and basic hygiene products. He stayed there for the next five months. He refused to sign his deportation papers, despite repeated pressure by the guards and despite the rotten food and chemical-tasting water.

By the time I met Irani, he had survived six months of detention in inhumane conditions before being released on a bond payment of $7,500 raised by his wife and community members. He was living in a small shared room in San Francisco. He was happy to be reunited with his wife and children but scared of being degraded and detained again—or worse, deported. Irani had a very strong asylum case but a hostile immigration judge: Cory Picton. This was the same judge who, just a month later, said to me, "It's okay to smile, counsel," before another asylum hearing. My client Martha,‡ who is also brown, black-haired, and female, was sitting quietly next to me in the sterile courtroom, nervous and afraid. Judge Picton had the power to decide that morning whether Martha would stay in the US and be put on a path to citizenship or whether she would be deported and sent on a path to sexual abuse, torture, and possible death in Guatemala. The immigration judge and ICE attorney—both white, able-bodied, cisgender men, both with government salaries that were tens of thousands of dollars higher than mine—joked with each other minutes before our high-stakes, life-and-death asylum hearing. When Judge Picton suggested that I smile, I responded, "Would you ask a male attorney to smile, judge?" We won Martha's case that day, but the underlying injustice of that experience stays with me.

In Irani's case, however, despite all the evidence in our favor, Judge Picton did not grant him asylum on the day of his hearing. He cross-examined Irani, doing the job of the ICE attorney, and he refused to issue a decision. During the course of my representation, I had multiple conversations with Irani about the system and the court process. I reflected back to him the power of his story and the positive impact that sharing it could have. He then agreed to work with one of our interns to write the op-ed that we published with BuzzFeed. I spoke with Irani about the judge's low rate of granting asylum and the benefits of having community supporters, especially in a context like this, where the system is not our ally. We have to bring our own. Media, legislators, family, friends, and other court observers all make for powerful allies. In Irani's case, only about ten attorneys who were new to asylum law practice came to observe the hearing. They came to support Irani but primarily to learn.

The judge's failure to grant asylum indicated that he intended to deny and deport Irani; he just didn't want to deny in front of a room full of observers. I had seen this from other judges before. Given that Irani's case was so clear-cut and heavily supported by case law, I knew that if we had to appeal his case, we had a high chance of success. However, one of the most difficult things to appeal is a denial based on credibility. The appellate courts generally defer to the immigration judge on negative findings of credibility because courts of appeals only review the record on paper. They don't get a chance to reexamine the client directly.

While Irani's case was being resolved, I didn't sleep for weeks because I wasn't going to wait to mobilize more resources until the judge made a decision. I pushed ahead and contacted every attorney who had attended the hearing and asked them to write a letter stating their observations of Irani's testimony, including his candor, his genuineness, the consistency in his story, and anything else that stood out or was particularly compelling to them. I attached the four letters I got to my written closing argument and filed them with the court. This was not customary for immigration lawyers to do, nor had I seen it done before; but I needed to do whatever I could.

My intention was to put appellate courts on notice that the immigration judge was only one officer of the law in the courtroom that day, and there were multiple other legal officers—attorneys—who witnessed the same case and made sworn statements about it under penalty of perjury. After reviewing our submissions, the judge ruled in Irani's favor. We won his case without having to appeal. While we can't know for sure, I firmly believe the informal court witnesses and their letters influenced the outcome.

Irani's case highlights how community participation, the creation of care-centered organizations, and the emotional labor involved in asylum court cases can be powerful forces for change. There are many more ways that Pangea advocates consistently employed participatory power-building strategies: we presented on legal education panels with clients; we empowered clients to speak at community events and rallies to share their stories and make calls to action; we connected them to community groups and media for interviews, op-eds, and talks; and we coordinated meetings with clients and elected leaders and legislators to advocate for immigrant-friendly policy changes.

The work was especially emotionally demanding for me. Making space for reflection, connection, and care during the representation of clients like Irani, who moved me deeply, was an ongoing lesson for me about how to practice law and social justice in the context of a high-urgency system.

My family was in Iran in 1953 when the CIA helped overthrow the country's democratically elected prime minister, Mohammad Mossadegh. Mossadegh had nationalized Iran's oil industry to protect its resources from foreign control. After the coup, the shah (king) of Iran was restored to power with support from the US and the UK. The shah's regime benefited from strong ties with foreign powers and led to increased wealth for a small elite, while many Iranians experienced significant hardships.

My parents and other relatives actively opposed the monarchy, advocating for a democratic and more participatory Iran. The replacement of the shah led to the rise of another repressive regime: the Islamic Republic. The US government then sought to undermine Iran's new regime by supporting Saddam Hussein's Iraq, including funding its bombing campaign during the eight-year Iran-Iraq War. One of my aunts was killed in that war. Bombings shook our home and shattered our windows. For safety, we slept in the basement of my grandparents' house.

Many of my relatives were scattered all over the world, displaced by forces beyond their control. We weren't looking for a better life and a good education, like many immigrants often say with proud smiles. The reality is that US imperialism brought us here. The same reality was true for Irani and nearly every single one of my clients. I carried that truth in my core.

The emotional labor of advocating for people facing life-altering situations like mine or Irani's is immense, as are the wounds we absorb or activate from their stories and from our own encounters with unjust systems like courtrooms. In this work, introspection, self-care, and community care are not just nice-to-haves—they are essential for sustaining ourselves and our movements.

Whether we're challenging unjust systems, filing complaints about inhumane prison conditions, or listening to clients recount traumatic experiences, emotional labor is a constant part of the job. It's not limited to the work itself; it's about the weight we carry, both from our clients' stories and from our own experiences that sometimes mirror those of our clients. When we talk about collective care, we have to include the emotional labor that comes with this work. Supporting each other through it, acknowledging the impact, and finding time to heal are critical for sustaining ourselves and our movements. Taking care of our emotional well-being is more than self-care; it's community care, and it's how we keep going.

A Supportive Structure for Emotional Labor

Organizations can address emotional labor in their work by recognizing and actively supporting the effort required to perform tasks that place significant demands on their teams. Roshni Sampath emphasized the importance of making a list of "high emotional labor, high pressure, and urgent work which included conflict management, financial transactions, fundraising and legal compliance work." At Pangea, this work included internal responsibilities like human resources, fundraising, and finance, as well as intense client and program work driven by external systems with strict deadlines. Creating space for support and setting boundaries around these areas of work often lead to more sustainable leadership, improving retention and strengthening the well-being of both individuals and the collective.[12]

In line with the Task Redistribution Chart, another invaluable practice is designating someone to oversee the well-being of individual staff members and the organization as a whole. This person proactively facilitates transformative conversations when needed and makes sure the pace and scope of work do not exceed the organization's capacity to manage it.

Collectively led organizations like Movement Generation, a nonprofit dedicated to the liberation and restoration of land, labor, and culture, have implemented this practice by designating someone to oversee emotional well-being at retreats and meetings. This function can rotate among people, but it's good to have it clearly designated. Some organizations give it a title like vibes watcher, bird's-eye-view coordinator, emotional labor leader, director of culture and people, or another name that fits their context. Structural support—such as appropriate compensation, workload adjustment, and recognition—reinforces the importance of this role and prevents the people who take it on from being overburdened.

Emotional labor leaders are essential in shaping an organization's emotional well-being and cohesion. They nurture individual relationships, help teams bond, and create closeness and warmth. They know the talents of each team member and can call upon them on behalf of the collective. In collectively run organizations, they act as the glue that holds the team together during hard conversations, difficult decision-making processes, and conflict. For example, if a staff member expresses stress about a project during a meeting, an emotional labor leader might follow up afterward, check in on the colleague's well-being, and coordinate solutions such as redistributing tasks or adjusting deadlines. Despite their invaluable contributions, an emotional labor leader's work is often unnoticed and undervalued, leaving them vulnerable to burnout.

At Pangea, we came to recognize the importance of this work, so we hired a coach to support both leadership and staff in managing the emotional dynamics of the workplace. This step was key in addressing the emotional toll that comes with conflict management, stress, and building a positive, participatory work environment. Before we had the resources for professional help, I would have taken a more proactive approach: identifying team members with strong emotional intelligence and providing them with training for these roles.

Research shows that the emotional labor of staff in workplaces is comparable to the work of front-line service workers who have to deliver "service with a smile."[13] This kind of work often lacks formal recognition or boundaries and continues long after work hours. To address this, organizations can structurally integrate emotional labor into job descriptions, allocating specific time and resources for these tasks. This may involve redistributing other responsibilities to balance workloads more equitably.

In addition to creating structures of care for all staff, it is especially important to support the default emotional labor leaders on our teams—often women and gender-expansive people of color. These individuals frequently build and sustain care structures for their teams but rarely receive the same level of care in return. This imbalance highlights the need for reciprocal care and safeguards. For example, organizations can designate a dedicated person or team specifically tasked with supporting the well-being of emotional labor leaders. This could involve regular check-ins, offering access to external coaching or therapy, redistributing their workload, or simply creating spaces where they feel valued or cared for, just as they do for others.

Co-Create Clear Expectations

For people to succeed in the workplace, they need to have clear expectations, especially in a workplace that is collectively governed. Without a shared understanding of the specific roles and responsibilities within an organization—and without policies in place to keep everyone accountable to those roles—we set ourselves up for disappointment and heartache.

Co-workers can sometimes show up in ways that are misaligned with or harmful to the organization's values. Many have dealt with co-workers who consistently miss the mark by missing important deadlines, getting defensive when receiving feedback, submitting lower-quality work, or contributing far less than their peers, leaving others to pick up the slack. Unfortunately, it's common for organizations to lack processes and structures that help co-workers have a clear sense of their role and the structures in place to help them stay accountable to their responsibilities.

Co-creating clear expectations and policies that support staff accountability can be a transformative and liberating act of care. Far from being oppressive or punitive, clear expectations can provide transparency, grounding, and even a sense of safety. They are a structural support not only for staff but also for the community and the organization. Still, setting and meeting work expectations in a collectively governed workplace require a very different frame of mind than working under a conventional hierarchy.

Many of us who have worked in hierarchical organizations have experienced the impersonal, punitive, top-down nature of these policies and structures. Under a conventional hierarchy, managers are responsible for setting and communicating work expectations, and it is the employees' responsibility to meet them. Processes like hiring, supervision, and termination are usually the responsibility of one person or a small group of people who are often guided by the perceived threat of discrimination lawsuits, and who emphasize confidential written records rather than care-centered interactions. When an employee is perceived as being unable to meet expectations, it is usually the responsibility of one or a few people at the top to make the decision to fire them behind closed doors. There is seldom room for curiosity, support, accountability, opportunity, or healing from potential harm that may have been done.

Lack of intentionality even occurs in anti-oppression organizations and collectives.

Things are good when everyone is fulfilling their role or appears to be, but situations can deteriorate when the facade of high performance is lifted or when one person is perceived as not adequately fulfilling their role. Resentment then starts to build among staff, leading them to question everything: the organization itself, its structure, the leadership, and whether there is any shared understanding or transparency at all. This may be especially true when staff are all being paid the same.

At Pangea, without clarity or structure, things didn't always run smoothly; instead they sometimes led to confusion, frustration, and unfairness. These challenges showed us that collective governance needed intentional systems of accountability. By working together to set clear expectations and creating supportive supervision, we built a workplace where accountability was a shared responsibility, rather than a burden placed on any one individual or group. This responsibility was distributed among the supervisor and three to five peers, each holding varying levels of power in the organization, ensuring it was carried collaboratively and democratically. In addition to improving workflows, this was about honoring the trust and energy every person brought into the collective.

To begin with, our supervision system was not top-down; it was circular. Every staff member, including the most senior leaders, had a supervisor who cared for their well-being, supported their accountability, and helped ensure nothing fell through the cracks.[*] For instance, my supervisor, Bianca, taught me how to use my calendar more effectively, sharing best practices for time management—a lifelong skill I still use today. Our recurring agenda usually looked like this:

1. Status check (both):

    a. On a scale of 1–10, how is your overall well-being at work?

    b. On a scale of 1–10, how much stress are you experiencing?

2. Thought partnership (fifteen minutes)

3. Work review (Bianca to ask about deadlines) (ten minutes)

4. Feedback (ten minutes)

5. Wayfinding; support; goal setting (fifteen minutes, quarterly)

6. Closing (two minutes)

    a. How was this check-in for you?

Our supervision system was about accountability. It was about supporting each other's well-being and helping each other succeed in our roles and responsibilities.

We also organized collective work sessions when patterns emerged of certain important but non-urgent tasks being left undone. For example, when we moved offices and needed to update records for hundreds of clients, supervisors coordinated with our Legal Services Hub (described further in the next chapter) to organize "mandatory parties." During these sessions, staff came together for several hours to collaboratively update client records. This shared accountability helped lighten the load and ensured that critical work stayed on track.

Although we rarely relied on formal accountability processes like performance improvement plans (PIPs), they were important and necessary in certain

---

[*] We developed this structure for supervision with support from our organizational consultant, Sheena Wadhawan.

situations. Unlike the traditional top-down, hierarchical approach that often used PIPs as a last step before termination, we used PIPs with the clear intention of supporting staff to genuinely improve and succeed. Supervisors offered follow-through support, checking in at key milestones, to help staff meet these goals. For those facing challenges, the accountability system became an opportunity for growth with a strong structure of care.

These systems also relied on transparency to make sure accountability was manageable and sustainable. We implemented streamlined work management systems (including charts, case lists, and uniform tracking systems) that everyone used. This meant that if someone was out sick or unavailable, anyone else could step in and continue their work seamlessly. This practice reinforced collective accountability, ensuring the organization remained functional and responsive no matter the circumstances.

Our accountability was about meeting expectations and achieving organizational goals as well as building relationships, systems, and habits that allowed everyone to thrive. At its core, accountability acted as a boundary—offering clarity, structure, and mutual agreements that helped protect both individual well-being and the health of the collective. Supervision, collaborative work sessions, and transparent processes were all ways to reflect our core values of care, equity, and shared responsibility. By investing in these systems, we created a culture where accountability strengthened the collective, much like healthy soil nourishing plants, allowing them to grow and flourish together.

Actionable Takeaways

Build strong relationships. Strong relationships are vital in any workplace because they impact both individual and collective well-being. Creating intentional spaces and spending time to build meaningful connections with colleagues help create a supportive environment where trust and collaboration can thrive.

Co-create clear expectations. Establish and share clear expectations within the team to foster a sense of predictability and accountability.

Establish and communicate boundaries. Set and respect clear boundaries to avoid feelings of guilt and maintain alignment with values. Start by identifying your core organizational principles and the limits needed to uphold them. Acknowledge that cultural and social expectations can influence how people manage work and personal life, and understand that immigrants and BIPOC may face additional challenges related to overwork. Ensure regular check-ins among your colleagues to discuss boundaries, and encourage open dialogue about needs and expectations. Make these boundaries explicit.

Use tools for healthy boundaries and relationships. Implement practical tools like a Task Redistribution Chart (see appendix C) to clarify responsibilities and support boundary management. Consider organizing retreats facilitated by an impartial third party, distributing surveys to learn about personal boundaries, and integrating wellness considerations into your strategic plan.

Embrace emotional and personal growth. Acknowledge the importance of doing personal, internal work to build self-awareness. Whether through study, somatic practices, therapy, meditation, or other methods, this inner work is essential for systems of collective care. Encourage integrating emotional and personal development into your team's culture, and create space for open dialogue around these practices.

Affirm and celebrate boundaries. Clearly communicate and model your own boundaries to maintain both personal and team integrity. Encourage and celebrate the setting of boundaries, such as taking time off, to reinforce their importance and the organization's collective values.

Implement key practices for a culture of care. Allocate time and resources for emotional labor, especially in demanding fields like social justice. Model and communicate your own boundaries, celebrate when others take time off, and co-create clear role expectations to prevent burnout.

Allocate resources for emotional labor. Emotional labor, especially in fields like social justice, is significant and needs to be recognized. It's important to allocate time and resources to manage the emotional aspects of the work, because neglecting them can lead to secondary trauma and burnout.

Designate a leader for relational work. Create at least one role focused on emotional and relational well-being, such as a director of culture and people. This role should nurture connection and address conflicts promptly and effectively. And there should always be a second desig-nated person to reciprocate this work for the main designated person. The size and structure of this role will depend on the organization's needs.

Recognize the impact of high-pressure roles. One way to address the challenges inherent in high-pressure roles is to implement a role-mapping system and create a space for redistributing responsi-bilities. This approach can help identify tasks that may contribute to burnout and create space for role sharing, allowing team members to engage in work that feels more manageable and energizing. The key is to strive for balance, sharing high-pressure tasks in a way that sup-ports both individual and collective well-being.

Design systems for shared accountability. Create intentional struc-tures that distribute accountability among a small group—such as a supervisor and three to five peers—with varying levels of responsibility and organizational roles. Use circular supervision to ensure that every-one, including senior leaders, has someone supporting their well-being and accountability. Incorporate practices like collaborative check-ins and shared task tracking to promote transparency and teamwork, making accountability a collective effort rather than a single manager's burden.

5

A Structure
for Our Culture

By 2017, despite our successes in building a strong culture, fostering relationships, and doing impactful work, Pangea was in emergency response mode. Without a structure to support the culture we wanted to cultivate and sustain, tensions did more than just brew; they escalated. We hired and fired people in ways that created harm, with no transparent process or healing practices in place to repair broken bonds of trust. We operated with the misconception that having a flat salary structure meant that everyone should and would work at the same fast pace. We invited staff to share what they wanted or needed, and they invariably expressed a desire for higher salaries. Instead of creating a safe space for these important conversations, I inadvertently dismissed their concerns, making them feel uncomfortable for voicing their needs. I didn't realize how much support I needed during that time. As I took on more responsibilities, I felt increasingly overwhelmed. Juggling a heavy caseload with my management duties made it difficult for me to give my team the attention and care they needed. In trying to do everything at once, I made the situation worse and missed an opportunity to address my colleagues' concerns.

In a traditional hierarchical organization, I might have just left. But I stayed because I valued our work and my colleagues, and I knew we were creating something important. We had good intentions but no formal system of governance.

Our growing pains were becoming too great to ignore. We were overworked and heading for a crisis point. The yellow flags, which many collectively governed nonprofits experience, included stress, fatigue, short fuses, resentment, impatience, lack of organizational cohesion, and an erosion of trust. This crisis pushed Pangea to truly grow up and reckon with our growing edges. Donald Trump—a figure that fueled harm and division—had just been elected president of the United States, and decades of social justice advocacy and safeguards were beginning to unravel before our eyes. Asylum law and refugee rights processes were being dismantled, and the president was appointing anti-immigrant leaders and judges across the country, detaining and deporting immigrants at a devastating rate.

In the midst of this crisis, Pangea had to make a choice quickly: Do we grow rapidly, expand services, and accept new philanthropic and government dollars that were suddenly available, or not? The tendency in these cases is to pivot—to grow when money is available and take opportunities when they come, even if an organization is not positioned to take on the additional work. At Pangea we had developed a five-year strategic plan with our consultant, kiran nigam, but we did not yet realize how useful it would be when put to the test during this moment of crisis.

The previous year had been a big year for us because that was when we launched our Universal Representation campaign—an effort to create a public defender program for all immigrants in detention or involved in deportation proceedings and civil immigration cases. This bold initiative was transformative in its vision and impact. We stuck to our strategic plan and brought on more attorneys who could represent immigrants in prison and stop deportations. By early 2016, I started mobilizing with prison abolition advocates Grisel Ruiz and Clara Long. Clara and I flew to New York, where a coalition of advocates had built out the first and only state-funded program to represent detained immigrants. We interviewed many individuals who led and contributed to that program, including staffers with nonprofits, university professors, public officials in the mayor's office, and a federal judge. We came back home and dove into action, presenting our proposals to county governments, funders, and partner organizations. We joined forces with partners throughout California to drive a statewide effort and press our advocacy in Sacramento. We brought formerly detained Pangea clients to testify at the state capitol and San Francisco City Hall, grounding our cause in the powerful voices that informed it.

Despite our efforts, progress felt painfully slow. Weeks turned into months, with little response. Then everything changed with Donald Trump's election.

Suddenly, millions of dollars in funding became available. Requests for our proposals flooded in, and we secured the support we needed—and then some.

But as new opportunities for additional funding piled up, we faced a critical moment. We chose not to expand our staff beyond our planned growth, even with the tempting offers before us. Our decision was guided by two key principles: 1) staying true to our strategic plan, which laid out our staff growth and project direction, and 2) recognizing that rapid growth can strain both culture and structure. We were determined to grow thoughtfully and sustainably, keeping our values and vision at the forefront.

We also recognized that new staff at Pangea needed at least a year to get acclimatized to the organization, even if they came on board with some amount of values alignment or interest in collective governance. If we grew too fast by bringing on too many folks at once without paying attention to the cultural dynamics and adjusting the infrastructure accordingly, little by little the work of collective culture-building could be compromised. This is particularly the case when an organization has more new people than old-timers. Established norms that take significant time to create—often after dismantling harmful habits—can easily be overshadowed by a sudden influx of new staff. This shift risks altering the organization's collectivist culture and can lead to unforeseen complications. Long-standing team members may feel fatigued and overwhelmed by the demands of onboarding too many new colleagues at once, while new staff might miss out on the attention and training they need to thrive. This cycle can create a downward spiral, threatening the strong foundation built over time and potentially undermining it in just a matter of days.

This has happened to many nonprofits. When responding to large external needs, many organizations and social justice movements have inadvertently created internal havoc by taking whatever funding came in the door with little discernment, losing sight of the long game. By 2017, this was widespread among nonprofits. Many organizations became unsteady and disconnected from their core values because the mindset shifted to one of rapid expansion. The thinking went: *Okay, let's do as much as we can. Let's grind.*

The People's Organization,‡ for example, ballooned in size overnight. They doubled their number of staff, took on hundreds of thousands of dollars in philanthropic funds, and received over $2 million in state funds, along with large volumes of deliverables to represent high-needs community members. Their staff was overworked, underpaid, and emotionally and physically overwhelmed by high-pressure, labor-intensive casework. Their leadership modeled zero rest and demanded that staff step it up, work harder, and respond to crises faster. For several years the teams worked hard under pressure and continued to grow, hiring new staff. Then, suddenly the People's Organization experienced a blowout—a mass exodus and high turnover.

Organizers know well that the biggest moments of crisis are also the biggest moments for opportunity—to mobilize, politicize, engage, act, and grow. The key is preparation and planning for such moments, because they are cyclical. They can happen on a large scale or a small, individual scale. For example, my former client Jesus was inspired to get involved in social justice work after facing a significant crisis during his incarceration and imminent deportation, a pivotal moment that spurred his politicization and transformed him into a powerful organizer. This is an example of how a moment of crisis can become an opportunity to mobilize a powerful response toward collective action.

Organizers understand that while moments of crisis can serve as powerful catalysts for mobilization and present opportunities for change, these moments are also often fleeting. Real, lasting change requires sustained, continuous action—showing up day after day, holding ongoing one-on-one meetings, and fostering a collective understanding of the ultimate goal. At Pangea, we were careful about creating new staff positions and building resources we couldn't financially sustain over the long term. We created programs, hotlines, and Migra Watch (a program modeled after Cop Watch, to document illegal ICE actions and protect neighbors) for allies and impacted folks.* But rather than housing these efforts at Pangea, we collaborated in a coalition of organizations to run them. It was clear to us that structural change and growth had to be incremental, sustained, and consistently reinforced by culture. But we were not immune to growing pains. Our work still frequently pushed the limit of our organizational capacities. Our client Rosa‡ was a case in point.

When ICE agents barged into Rosa's home and ripped her away from her nine-month-old nursing baby, they gave her two options: She could secure a passport for her baby so she could take her on the plane with her when she was deported to Brazil, or she could stay imprisoned and separated from her baby, husband, family, and community indefinitely to fight her losing case. "Unfortunately, that's the law," said the officers who detained her. Her previous attorney echoed the same two cruel options.

A few days after Rosa was detained, her husband called me. His voice was strained, heavy with the weight of their reality. Rosa's attorney had previously

---

* To learn more about Migra Watch go to https://www.pangealegal.org/rapidresponsenetworks

fought her case and finally exhausted all the legal avenues, so he was now helping her prepare for the inevitable—ensuring her baby could board the deportation plane with her. The attorney's advice followed the limits of the law: Rosa could reunite with her baby and leave prison quickly, but it meant leaving behind her husband, her church, her community, and the life she'd built in the US over the past eight years. It felt like the system had taken more than her freedom; it had suddenly dismantled her world. Still, in her husband's voice there was a quiet resilience, a flicker of hope that kept them moving forward. I knew deep down Rosa's story wasn't over, and there had to be another way—we just hadn't found it yet.

In years of organizing and litigating in support of clients to push beyond the confines of the law, we had learned that challenging cases require us to think of the law as one of many tools to achieve our client's safety and well-being. This was articulated in points 7 and 8 of Pangea's Points of Unity (see appendix B):

7. The law is a living document. Its flaws do not constrict us. We use it strategically to ask boldly for the best for our community.

8. We are positive and solution oriented. We value fresh attitudes, innovation, and creativity. We challenge conventional thinking in order to redefine what is possible.

Coordinating Rosa's case was an around-the-clock effort. Sleepless nights were spent filing urgent legal motions, building a campaign, and collaborating with advocates. I immediately filed a stay of deportation to pause Rosa's deportation process. Because Rosa was deeply involved in her church community and was in the process of becoming a pastor, I connected with Rev. Deborah Lee and other leaders of the Interfaith Movement for Human Integrity. Together, we made phone calls and reached out to journalists who could amplify Rosa's story. After Rosa was in prison for a week, her twenty-pound baby had lost a whole pound because he was not nursing. When we highlighted Rosa's story in the media, even the chief counsel for the Department of Homeland Security in Texas agreed to join a motion to reopen Rosa's deportation order. This gave her another chance at asylum and had the effect of canceling her expedited deportation process. ICE released Rosa after ten days in prison, immediately after the media contacted ICE to inquire about her case.

My role was to not only fight for Rosa's release but to contribute to a larger movement aimed at ending deportations and building thriving communities. For Rosa's situation, we shared everything with the community, coordinating with organizers and media outlets to make sure her story wasn't just a legal case but a rallying point for others facing similar struggles. When people see that organizing combined with legal efforts can make an impact, it creates a ripple effect. They start asking, "How do I plug in?" By organizing and using multiple strategies, Pangea prevailed on Rosa's behalf.

Pangea's incredible staff rose to the occasion time after time, one campaign after another, but it came at a price. What should have been a healthy workflow gradually became a grind that began to erode morale, contradicting our values. In fact, there was not just a contradiction between our work and our values; there was a significant gap. As we wrote in our tenth Point of Unity, we had committed to value our team's individual and collective well-being and support the "mechanisms to support well-roundedness and our team's mental, physical, and spiritual health." But we had no such mechanisms in place. We still lacked clear job descriptions, onboarding and offboarding policies, and a formal, collectively determined decision-making system.

Most organizational problems often stem from decisions made at the organizational system level, including those related to recruiting and hiring, workloads, and accountability processes. For an organization aiming to grow and improve in serving its purpose, establishing intentional systems for organizational development and problem-solving that effectively balance workloads and ensure equitable experiences for all staff members is key.

In Pangea's case, without an organizational structure in place to balance our workloads and address the differing experiences of long-term staff and newer arrivals, we faced significant challenges. In conventional hierarchically structured organizations, it's generally understood that management staff have more work and more decision-making power, and entry-level staff have less work and less decision-making power. In a collectivist organization committed to democratic management, where all staff were paid the same, this imbalance also existed but created significant friction.

We were not alone in this predicament. Many collectively governed social justice nonprofits I've encountered have shared similar experiences, where serious tensions can escalate into volatile conflicts, ultimately weakening or even dismantling the organization. As Maurice Mitchell points out, many new organizations and activists become cynical or drop out due to "interpersonal conflict gone awry" or the "exceptional dynamics of a broken environment or a movement that's lost its way. A 'bad supervisor,' a 'toxic workplace,' a 'messy movement space,' or a 'problematic person with privilege' are just some of the refrains echoed from all corners of our movements." While individuals point fingers at each other and battle lines are drawn, "identity and position are misused to create a doom loop that can lead to unnecessary ruptures of our political vehicles and the shuttering of vital movement spaces."[1]

These organizational gaps, with their structural or cultural shortcomings, create negative ripples across whole teams and entire organizations. To prevent these gaps from widening and negatively impacting our social justice purpose and communities, it's essential to proactively address and bridge them.

The Three Big Structural Gaps

In my experience with nonprofit organizations, the most prevalent structural gaps that impede culture are overwork, lack of transparency, and workplace inequity. These issues do more than create draining work environments; they also undermine the greater purpose of social change organizations.

One sign of overwork is a high worker turnover rate. When staff members are overworked and disconnected from decision-making power, they may experience inequity and leave the organization. As a result, organizations have trouble retaining workers over long periods of time. High turnover rates are expensive for organizations, impacting finances as well as emotional labor and overall capacity. This often occurs in tandem with problematic (or nonexistent) termination policies that undermine trust and erode morale.

It is essential for staff members who have influence, whether through their roles or their experience, to pay attention and tend to these growing edges. In Pangea's case, I was part of the problem. I was deeply shaped by my own experiences and background, which led me to adopt a very directive approach. When staff members voiced their frustrations, I responded in ways that felt overly hierarchical to the team. As tensions escalated to uncomfortable levels, I once again sought help from kiran nigam, our facilitator and consultant.

This time, kiran took us on a whole different journey that led to an entirely new stage in Pangea's development. By then we had grown to a staff of ten. Rather than diving into problem-solving mode, kiran created a safe space for staff to share their individual perspectives. Much of it can be summed up by what one staff member said: "I'm relatively new at Pangea and was told that I can express my needs, but when I asked for a higher salary because the cost of living in the Bay Area is high, my concern wasn't welcomed. I was told to take time to better understand the organization, recognize what had been accomplished, and increase my caseload before requesting more. That made me feel dismissed for speaking up, as if my concerns were unwarranted. I've been telling all my friends about our horizontal model and love that our salaries are equal, but in practice I feel like there is a lot of hierarchy, and I don't get a say in organizational decisions."

Initially, I felt defensive, knowing how much effort Pangea had put into building a horizontal structure and centering values. But with time, I could also see the truth in my colleague's perspective. Holding space for both my reality and theirs wasn't easy, but it was essential to our growth and understanding.

kiran held space for everyone to express themselves. At the end of that facilitation process kiran made a suggestion that was both hugely impactful and strikingly obvious: We needed to design an actual working collective governance structure for Pangea, one that addressed power redistribution head-on and recognized the many forms of labor we perform in the workplace. Instead of relying solely on a collective culture and equal salaries, we had to create structures and systems to support this culture. From this spark of insight came the first iteration of our hub structure, a committee-based system of governance that became the foundation for every policy and practice, guiding the growth and development of the entire organization from that point forward.[2]

A Circle-Based Hub System

The hub system we introduced following our retreat with kiran was a game-changer. It gave us a robust, adaptable framework that elevated our organizational structure to new heights. We designed multiple "hubs," each hub like the hub of a wheel, with spokes extending outward; each spoke of the wheel represented a key function. This wheel-like structure supported our growth and strengthened the core of our workflow by ensuring all parts were interconnected. As Pangea expanded, our hubs worked together in harmony, keeping the wheels turning and the organization moving forward. This system allowed us to manage growth, streamline processes, and stay rooted in our core values.

In many respects, the circle-based hub system of governance mirrors structures found in nature. adrienne maree brown, a writer, activist, and facilitator, has been an influential voice in shaping this line of thinking. Her work on emergent strategy, influenced by the visionary writings of Octavia Butler and her ability to envision alternative, just futures, has evolved into "strategies for organizers building movements for justice and liberation that leverage relatively simple interactions to create complex patterns, systems, and transformations."[3] brown looks intently at nature to find these complex patterns, systems, and dynamics. She cites the collective work and sustainability of ants; the shared leadership, adaptability, and synchronized movement of starlings; the regenerative resilience of the dandelion; the fractal-like fluid dynamics of the wavicle; and the intelligent, interconnected network of mycelia beneath the soil.

These interactions go beyond symbolism. They are essential practices for building the structures and systems that foster a true culture of care. As brown says, they are "ways for humans to practice being in right relationship to our home and each other, to practice complexity, and grow a compelling future together through relatively simple interactions. Emergent strategy is how we intentionally change in ways that grow our capacity to embody the just and liberated worlds we long for."[4] Through these relatively simple but intentional interactions, we can foster the deep, regenerative practices needed to build resilient, adaptive organizations rooted in equity and collective well-being.

Vivien Sansour, founder of the Palestine Heirloom Seed Library, spoke to a similar emergent strategy in an interview in the Substack newsletter *Good Mud.* "In our love for seeds, our commitment to the land and living beings, we are creating another world," she said. "This is the beauty and power of it, and it's important that we keep pushing in this work because we're creating a model— big or small—for an alternative."[5] Sansour's work shows that by investing in foundational elements like seeds, relationships, and practices, we model alternatives that challenge exploitative systems. Both brown and Sansour remind us that intentional care, in even the smallest of acts, can lay the groundwork for a larger transformative impact.

The Art of Flocking

Focusing on work structure can be tough, especially when we recognize our role within an interconnected ecosystem. Our efforts are influenced by a world that is often filled with turbulence that feels unpredictable. A beautiful example from nature is the way geese fly together in a *V* formation during migration, covering thousands of miles each day despite challenging weather. Their flight formation is crucial: The lead goose reduces air resistance for those following, enabling the group to travel about 70 percent farther together than they could alone. The goose in front isn't a permanent leader; the geese take turns, with each leader shifting to the back when they're tired and encouraging others in front. This rotation helps them collaborate in creating a draft they all can use, exemplifying true collective effort. Remarkably, no goose is left behind; they often stay by the side of a sick or injured mate or chick, even as winter approaches and others fly south. When birds fly together, they fly farther and with greater ease. Similarly, when we collaborate, we build resilience and strength. As adrienne maree brown and others in collective leadership emphasize, this is "the art of flocking."[6]

The hub structure kiran proposed was a way for Pangea to flock together and reflected the principles of sociocracy referenced in chapter 1. Sociocracy is a governance system characterized by interconnected circles, with each circle responsible for specific areas while collaborating on broader decision-making.[7] Sociocracy takes its cues from nature, which is intrinsically tied to cycles and circles. Many precolonial Indigenous cultures, like the Muscogee Nation (now located in Oklahoma), structured their governance democratically and collectively, preventing anyone from accumulating too much power.[8] This form of governance mirrors natural patterns of interconnectedness, where each circle operates autonomously within its domain while contributing to collective decisions, promoting both efficiency and inclusive participation. The circle as a structure for collective life finds powerful expression in the governance and decision-making models of Indigenous communities past and present.

Circles in Governance

"The circle is the most basic element of democracy," says writer and educator Ann Linnea in a video about her book *The Circle Way: A Leader in Every Chair*.[9] In discussing talking circles, she names the value of rotating leadership, shared responsibility, fairness, integrity, and empathy and respect for others. The First Nations Pedagogy Online project, a sweeping body of resources compiled by curriculum development specialists June Kaminski and Sylvia Currie, describes "talking circles" or "circle talks" as a foundational communications approach to First Nations pedagogy.[10] Talking circles began with First Nations leaders as a way to ensure that everyone in a tribal council was heard in a respectful fashion. Among many other things, the First Nations Pedagogy Online Project presents a step-by-step approach to these circle talks, which honor the connection to nature. "First Nations people observed that the circle is a dominant system in nature and has come to represent wholeness, completion, and the cycles of life (including the cycle of human communication)," Kaminski writes, adding that the model is "very adaptive to any circle of people who need to discuss topics and make decisions together."[11] Circles—or hubs, in the case of Pangea—can be used in any organization.

Redesigning the Engine

The circle-based hub system we introduced during our retreat with kiran was both practical and intuitive. The structure worked like a wheel. Each hub represented a key area of work, functioning like a specialized committee or circle. The spokes were the individuals working in that area, making it clear who is responsible for decisions, accountability, and ownership over policies and practices. Most decisions were made within hubs, which typically consisted of two to five people. Some decisions that impacted all staff were made by the full team. For those, a designated hub took the lead and followed a detailed protocol, including multiple layers of staff feedback, to ensure thorough and considerate implementation of new policies.

To facilitate this structure, many organizations use tools like DARCI* and MOCHA† to bring clarity and transparency to the process, defining roles and decision-making power and outlining task management responsibilities. Similarly, in Pangea's hub system, decision-making power was about who gets to make important choices and set policies for each part of the organization. Responsibility meant the obligation to handle specific tasks and make sure they were carried out effectively. Accountability was being answerable for what happens as a result of those decisions and making sure the organization's goals are achieved. Ownership meant taking charge and being deeply committed to managing and improving that area.

Deliberate design and transparency are what sets this system apart. Unlike traditional hierarchical structures, this system is intentionally crafted to cultivate shared leadership and ownership. It adapts as the organization grows, to ensure that leadership and accountability are distributed and accessible.

During Pangea's retreat, kiran guided us through a comprehensive process to define our organizational hub structure. Through that process we established eight primary hubs, each one crucial to our operations:[12]

1. **Governance:** Manages organizational rules that govern how Pangea operates; ensures that Pangea processes and policies meet organizational goals; creates and manages connections between hubs.

---

* DARCI is a decision-making framework that clarifies roles by designating who's **Deciding**, who's **Accountable**, who's **Responsible** for doing the work, and who's **Consulted** or **Informed**. This tool ensures everyone knows their role, improving accountability and transparency in decision-making.

† MOCHA is a framework that helps define roles in projects by assigning the roles of **Manager, Owner, Consulted, Helped,** and **Approver**. It facilitates effective collaboration and decision-making by providing a structure to define who leads, supports, and approves a project.

2. **Operations** (internally referred to as Function Junction or "FuJu"):
   Oversees general and daily business operations; ensures that the
   organization functions as smoothly as possible to support the
   provision of high-quality services.

3. **Human Resources:** Implements benefits, team wellness, and team
   life cycle recruitment and retention.

4. **Finance:** Manages and oversees Pangea's expenses, budget, accounting, and taxes.

5. **Income:** Oversees and maintains diversified cash flows rooted in organizational values, our budget, Pangea's needs, and team needs.

6. **Communications:** Responsible for ensuring positive messaging in line
   with our Points of Unity, mission, and vision; displaying our achievements; and disseminating information about Pangea's work and values.

7. **Community Empowerment and Policy Advocacy:** Elevates stories from impacted community members to shift the immigrant
   narrative, educate the larger population on systemic human rights
   abuses and inequities that immigrant community members face,
   and galvanize support for pro-immigrant policies across the region,
   state, and country.

8. **Legal Services:** Creates and updates internal resources and best
   practices related to consultations, legal representation, case accep-
   tance priorities, and caseload management.

Decision-making policies in any workplace should be iterative; they should
evolve and adapt with the needs of the organization and its people. At Pangea,
we created a table to clearly show where decision-making authority resided—
whether with individual employees, hubs, or the full team—and what factors
needed to be considered when making those decisions.* Another way of looking at the table was through three key questions:

1. What decisions can each individual employee make on their own?

2. What decisions can hubs (or those with authority delegated by
   hubs) make on their own?

3. What decisions must be made by the full team?

---

* See appendix D, "Decision-Making Flowchart and Table."

To keep our organizational wheels turning smoothly, we ensured that each hub included one seasoned member with institutional knowledge and one newer team member. This setup brought specialized expertise to the forefront while also creating a safety net. Just like spokes in a wheel work together to support the ride, having multiple voices ensured that knowledge was shared and accessible, allowing the organization to keep moving forward even if someone was absent. This distribution of expertise facilitated a more even flow of power throughout the organization and distributed the weight of high-pressure responsibilities.

We also created a voting scale of 1 through 8 to lay onto this decision-making matrix, with 1 being enthusiastic support and 8 representing a block.[*] If more than 25 percent of our members voted to block a policy, that policy or proposal did not pass. Through trying out our decision-making process, we also learned that we wanted to move forward on decisions with enthusiastic support; so we adopted a modified consensus process that required 51 percent of the team to vote a 4 or higher for a decision to pass.[†] Some decisions, like hiring and firing, were decided by a simple yes-no vote, per the recommendation of our consultant, kiran nigam. These voting scales allowed colleagues to be heard while challenging staff to name what improvements or changes to a policy they would want to see, which ultimately helped strengthen policies before we finalized them.

Here is how Pangea's modified consensus process might look in practice, with seven employees voting on a proposal to change the organization's vacation policy:

- Three people vote 1 (enthusiastic support).
- Two people vote 4 (moderate support).
- One person votes 6 (some concerns).
- One person votes 8 (block).

Since only one person out of seven voted to block the proposal (an 8), the blocking vote doesn't reach the 25 percent threshold required to fully block the decision (which would require two people in this case).

Now, to determine if the proposal passes, we would look at whether 51 percent of the team voted 4 or higher. In this case, five out of seven (71%) voted 4 or higher, so the proposal would pass.

---

[*] See appendix D, "Decision-Making Flowchart and Table."

[†] See appendix E, "Decision-Making Policy and Gradient Voting Tool."

Everyone who voted less than a 1 (enthusiastic support) would be asked to provide feedback on what their concerns are and what improvements they'd like to see. This input could help refine the policy before it is finalized, further strengthening the final decision.

Process
Strive for consensus; if >25 percent is an 8, can't move forward; no individual can block
Quorum
75 percent of decision-makers; abstentions count toward quorum; extended leaves do not count

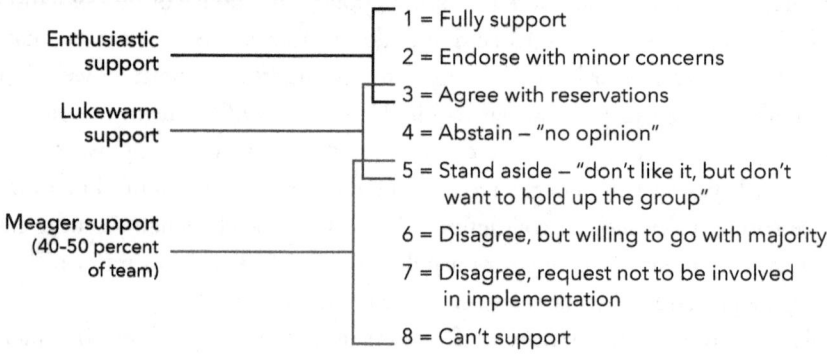

CONSENSUS SCALE

Enthusiastic support
Lukewarm support
Meager support (40-50 percent of team)

1 = Fully support
2 = Endorse with minor concerns
3 = Agree with reservations
4 = Abstain – "no opinion"
5 = Stand aside – "don't like it, but don't want to hold up the group"
6 = Disagree, but willing to go with majority
7 = Disagree, request not to be involved in implementation
8 = Can't support

Ambiguous support: all over the scale

Another commonly used tool is the fist-to-five decision-making method, a consensus-building tool to gauge team members' support for a proposal or decision. It allows participants to express their level of agreement or concern in a simple and visual way:

Fist: Represents strong disagreement or a complete veto.

One finger: Indicates significant concerns or reservations.

Two fingers: Shows moderate concern but overall support.

Three fingers: Signals general agreement with minor reservations.

Four fingers: Demonstrates strong support with no major concerns.

Five fingers: Represents full support and no reservations.

Similar to the 1–8 gradient, this method helps teams quickly assess where they stand on an issue and can facilitate discussion and decision-making by highlighting areas of agreement and disagreement.

In any organization practicing distributed leadership, clarity around decision-making processes is particularly important. Without clear structures in place, groups can get bogged down by confusion, delayed decisions, or unresolved conflicts. Or sometimes organizations might find themselves making decisions that don't truly reflect individual preferences because team members hesitate to voice their true opinions, leading to choices that aren't fully supported, which may cause issues down the line. When everyone understands how decisions are made—whether through consensus, consent, advice, voting, or another method—that shared understanding fosters trust, accountability, and efficiency. Especially in social justice collectives, where values and mission are deeply intertwined with the work, having a clear decision-making process supports us in aligning our actions with those values even as we're meeting deadlines and achieving organizational goals.

Here's a breakdown of the most common decision-making methods I've seen used in shared leadership settings, along with examples of how they function in practice, and tools to gauge support within those methods:

- **Consensus:** In a consensus process, everyone has to fully agree before a decision is finalized. This method is about inclusivity, making sure that every voice is heard and that decisions reflect the collective will. For example, when deciding whether to launch a new community advocacy campaign, the entire team would need to agree on the plan. Discussions could last a long time until all concerns are addressed and resolved. While this process supports collaboration and invites every voice to be considered, it can be time-consuming. Consensus works best when decisions are values-driven, such as when deciding on major organizational shifts or policies that require full commitment. It's ideal for smaller, values-driven groups where collective commitment is key, but it can feel heavy for fast-moving projects.

- **Consent:** Rooted in sociocracy, consent allows decisions to move forward as long as there are no strong "reasoned objections," a term commonly used to describe concerns grounded in logic and relevance to the group's goals. Consent doesn't require everyone to fully agree, but it allows the group to proceed unless someone has a serious concern. Consent requires training to implement effectively, as it can be confused with consensus. In the same advocacy campaign example, any team members who had strong reasons not to move ahead would say so. If one person has minor concerns but no one objects strongly, the decision moves forward. This method balances inclusivity with efficiency. It's quicker than consensus and helps the group stay agile, but it might not always build the same deep alignment because not everyone has to agree entirely. It is especially useful when time is tight or when absolute agreement isn't necessary. However, because the threshold for objections is so high, decisions can pass without robust support, and there is a risk of overlooking minor concerns that may resurface later, resulting in less overall commitment from the group.

- **Majority or supermajority voting:** In majority or supermajority voting, decisions move forward based on a set percentage of votes, either a simple majority or a larger supermajority threshold. In a majority model, over half the votes are required to pass a decision; in a supermajority, it may be two-thirds or more. For example, if a worker collective of twenty members is deciding on whether to invest in new equipment, and eleven members vote in favor, the decision passes with a simple majority. Teams may use this for straightforward, lower-stakes decisions, making it quick and efficient. While this model allows for quick decision-making, it can inadvertently overlook minority opinions, potentially leaving some participants feeling excluded or disconnected from the process.

- **Advice process:** In the advice process, any individual can make a decision, but they first have to consult with those impacted and those with relevant expertise. This method, highlighted in the book *Reinventing Organizations*, decentralizes decision-making and empowers an individual to make the call after seeking input from others.[13] For example, one person on the team could lead the campaign decision but would first ask for advice from colleagues who have relevant expertise and those impacted by the decision. The advice process supports a sense of ownership, enhances autonomy, and accelerates decision-making, while also ensuring that important perspectives are taken into account. It is particularly effective when specialized knowledge is important and accountability is clearly defined. However, there is a risk that essential expertise may be overlooked or that feedback could be disregarded, which can undermine the effectiveness of the decision-making process.

- **Gradient voting:** In gradient voting, members express their stance on a scale (e.g., 1 to 8) instead of a simple yes or no, which captures the nuances of their opinions. For instance, when deciding on the advocacy campaign, each team member rates their position, with a 1 signaling strong opposition and an 8 indicating full support. The decision moves forward if the majority (or supermajority, depending on the rule) of votes fall in favor, allowing for nuance in opinions. This process is great for quickly gauging where the group stands and identifying areas of resistance, allowing decisions to move forward without waiting for full alignment. However, it can lead to ambiguity if the numbers aren't discussed further, as the range of opinions might still leave underlying issues unaddressed.

Each approach serves unique needs. For significant decisions where values are at stake, **consensus** can be necessary to ensure full buy-in. For instance, applying for funding that has strings attached might call for consensus with a more thorough gradient voting process or advice process, as these decisions could affect the entire team and would require careful consideration of the implications. **Consent**, on the other hand, allows decisions to move forward as long as there are no strong objections, making it valuable when time is of the essence, as for a grant application. **Majority or supermajority** voting with a straightforward yes/no decision works well when deciding on hiring or firing, for example, as these decisions often require clarity and a clear mandate with a short turnaround. In my experience, **gradient voting** has been an effective tool for most decisions. It allows teams to quickly assess the range of opinions and move forward without needing full agreement. The **advice process** has been ideal for empowering individuals while ensuring collaboration.

Having a default method is helpful, but organizations should also remain flexible enough to adapt to specific needs. No matter which decision-making method we choose, it's essential to incorporate feedback from team members, especially dissenting voices. This helps employees feel heard and valued, and it can help strengthen the overall decision. Ultimately, the goal is to create an environment where decision-making processes are both inclusive and efficient.

The challenges in each of the decision-making processes and voting mechanisms discussed above can be addressed by using flexible, adaptable tools that encourage broad participation. Mixing different approaches, like including feedback rounds and adapting based on the team's needs, can help create a process that feels right for the group. This is similar to Pangea's modified consensus approach, which used gradient voting to strike a balance between consensus and efficiency. Combining different methods and tools often leads to the right balance of participation, efficiency, and clarity.

Key Considerations for Developing a Distributed Decision-Making System

The process of developing a distributed authority structure may involve taking the following steps:

- Create an inventory of current decision-making areas. What do people in our organization do individually? In committees?

  - In what areas do staff have final decision-making authority?

  - In what areas do staff have execution authority within an existing policy or practice?

  - What can we notice about the existing structure and roles?

  - Are there certain people or identities that hold certain responsibilities? Who is overrepresented? Who is underrepresented?

- Discuss as a team what models of other organizations we might like.

  - Consider interviewing other groups that are values aligned.

  - Consider interviewing related nonprofits.

  - Consider interviewing worker cooperatives.

- Define key terms like *authority, responsibility, implementation, execution,* and *ownership.*

- Evaluate your collective need for efficiency versus full-team involvement.

  - Do we want to be involved in every decision at every level?

  - Are there certain topics where we want to be involved at every level?

  - Are there certain things where we'd want full delegation to another person or team?

- Create a pilot structure and try on a distributed authority structure.

- Schedule a periodic check-up, for example every six months. Do an annual review thereafter. In the first check-up, questions that may be asked are

  - Do these thematic groupings for hubs or committees feel like what we want?

  - Do we want to rename them?

- What is each hub doing?
- Do we need more authority within a hub?
- Do we need more authority in the large group?
- Does the membership make sense?
- How frequently should roles rotate?
- What roles would benefit from continuity?

Reflecting on Pangea's journey, it's clear that dedication and passion drove the organization forward. However, as is the case with many nonprofits, the absence of a structured support system sometimes hindered progress. Recognizing this gap presented an opportunity for Pangea to develop a robust and highly effective hub structure, aligning its culture and operations to better serve its mission. By acknowledging structural challenges and embracing intentional frameworks, organizations can transform collective energy into sustainable growth, harmonizing culture and structure.

Actionable Takeaways

Start by developing intentional culture principles. Recognize that an organization's culture is deeply connected to its structure. Document your cultural principles that reflect your collective values and guide how people interact and contribute.

Take inventory of current decision-making structures. What kinds of decisions are made at your organization? How are these decisions reached? Who makes what kind of decisions? Who is consulted and how? What does your current decision-making structure and culture say about the values of your organization? Where is the decision-making structure out of alignment with your organization's values? Document existing processes.

Establish clear decision-making processes. Define the decision-making methods your organization will use, such as consensus, consent, advice process, or gradient voting, and identify a default method. This clarity helps avoid confusion and delays, ensuring everyone understands how decisions will be made and promoting accountability within the team.

Encourage diverse feedback. Regardless of the decision-making method chosen, actively seek feedback from all team members, especially dissenting voices. This practice not only supports a participatory culture and respect but also enriches the decision-making process by incorporating varied perspectives, which can lead to more thoughtful and effective outcomes.

Embrace iterative practices. Consider implementing an exploratory phase for new decision-making methods. Use this time to gather feedback and assess how well the approach aligns with your organization's goals and values. Schedule periodic check-ins to adjust and refine the process so you can stay responsive to your organization's needs.

6

Collective Care Through Policy

Organizational Integrity: From Onboarding to Offboarding

Leonie[‡] had just moved into the role of manager at a large social justice organization. It was an exciting leap that also felt daunting. But as she settled in, her world was shaken by her mother's sudden health decline. After multiple surgeries, Leonie's mother lost a lot of weight, and her memory started to fade. Having lost her other mom to dementia the year before, Leonie knew how precious her remaining time with her mother was.

To balance her new responsibilities and family needs, Leonie stopped staying late at the office and began leaving to care for her mother promptly at five p.m. By using her vacation days for doctor's appointments and to provide extra support to her mother, she hoped to strike a balance. But as time passed, exhaustion set in. Leonie felt increasingly isolated, her energy was drained, and her connections to her colleagues diminished. The emotional weight of caregiving, coupled with the relentless pressures of work, became overwhelming.

Finally, Leonie gathered the courage to ask her supervisor for a formal reduction in her hours, hoping to leave at three p.m. every day. But her supervisor directed her to HR, and the process there was frustratingly slow. HR seemed more concerned about legal protocols than addressing Leonie's urgent needs.

The wait was painful. Guilt and stress followed Leonie wherever she went. Just as she reached her breaking point and threatened to quit, HR finally began to move. They demanded detailed documentation of her situation before approving her request for reduced hours. Although she finally got the time she needed to care for her mother, the process left Leonie feeling alone and frustrated. She was disillusioned that the organization's rules had overshadowed the compassion she desperately needed during such a tough time. This is important because so often in our efforts to avoid organizational harm through legal and HR bureaucracy, we impose a delay that causes greater harm.

Leonie's experience highlights the disconnect between policy and compassion, showing how delayed processes and poor communication can affect those in urgent need. We'll explore this gap further below, focusing on how timely responses and empathetic systems can transform the way organizations support their staff in critical moments.

When Policies Reflect Values

In a collectivist organization with a vibrant culture of care and an operational structure to support it, Leonie's story could have unfolded differently. At Pangea, we aimed to meet challenges with intentional changes that centered the well-being of our team. For example, during an acute time of loss, transition, and grief in my life, I knew I needed some time off to navigate the challenges I was facing. I was part of Pangea's HR Hub, and we had been talking about creating a sabbatical policy to help with situations like mine. Even though we had started working on the policy, it wasn't ready yet. As months went by, I came to a breaking point. When I reached out for help and asked for a partially paid three-month personal leave, colleagues from HR Hub listened and quickly stepped in to suggest a special exception for my situation. This idea led to some important conversations among the staff about how such an exception would work and why we didn't have a policy in place for everyone already. This push led us to later create our Life Happens policy,* designed to handle unique personal situations that aren't covered by standard policies.

---

* See appendix H, "'Life Happens' Policy."

The Life Happens policy acknowledges that there are times of personal crisis that merit a one-time exception to an existing HR policy. Some of the exceptions that have been granted to Pangea staff include

- Requests to work remotely (before a remote work policy for all staff existed)
- Request to retroactively use accrued vacation/sick time that the person forgot to request in advance of going on parental leave
- Request to have dependent spouse health insurance covered at 50 percent for one month instead of 5 percent, due to an HR communication error (this was before Pangea's dependents policy was updated to cover all dependents at 50 percent)
- Request to work every weekday but Wednesday because childcare fell through; missing important legal team meetings over a period of time
- Request to use 8.5 vacation days in advance of accruing them
- Request to work remotely for two weeks prior to becoming a co-director due to a gap in housing; working from family's house in another region (all staff are voted on to become co-directors after nine months of candidacy, after which they are eligible to apply for the remote work policy)
- Request to work part time for six months for reduced salary and benefits

As more team members needed extended leave, we created Pangea's Reasonable Accommodations policy to provide clearer support for personal leaves. This leave experience got me through a rough patch while helping to shape a more compassionate approach to handling personal challenges within our organization.

As we encountered additional staff needs, we leaned into our Points of Unity and organizational hub structure to implement policies that supported relational tending, which is a natural expression of a culture of care. Organizations like the worker-owned cooperative AORTA help movements cultivate cultures of care and collective governance. With years of experience across various justice issues, organizations like these play a crucial role in helping other organizations align their practices with their values, emphasizing interdependence and solidarity. In describing its culture of care, AORTA says "the way we care for relationships in our group or organization, is a reflection of our political values. It is the day-to-day practices in our organization that express our values of interdependence and solidarity."[1]

With the hub system in place at Pangea, we began to lay the groundwork for intentional policies with organizational integrity at every stage of operations, from the start of the recruitment process through onboarding and onward to offboarding. Authority flowed from the full team to hubs, and individuals within each hub had the authority to carry out tasks and make decisions in accordance with those policies. Within this ecosystem of distributed power, our process for making most decisions took place in hubs composed of two to four staff members. A few major decisions involved all staff and the following steps:

1. A hub brings an idea or proposal to the full staff.

2. The team responds and gives feedback.

3. The hub incorporates feedback into a proposal or conducts further research.

4. As needed, the hub follows up with individuals on their feedback. A hub member is designated to prioritize check-ins with individuals who are directly impacted by the proposal (e.g., to keep them updated before the full team is presented with an updated proposal, ask for their input individually, inform them of next steps and the timeline for follow-up, and to answer questions they may have).

5. If necessary, the hub writes up a question-and-answer list to address main questions and concerns.

6. The hub updates the proposal and presents it to the team for a vote (sometimes there is more discussion and then a vote the next time).

7. All staff vote on the proposal using the gradients of agreement.

Policies are developed and voted on in accordance with these steps. The policies developed in this way are not just administrative in nature; they are also developed in response to the pressing personal needs of staff, and they help us right-size workloads as we juggle intense competing priorities. For example, in 2014 Pangea instituted an optional four-day workweek with 80 percent pay. Years later when I gave birth to my child, I opted into this reduced salary in exchange for the extra day off. The trade-off worked for my family in a two-income household, but when I separated from my partner and transitioned into single parenthood with a $70,000 salary (or $58,000 at 80 percent) in the Bay Area, I suddenly found myself under a tremendous amount of financial stress. Although I had support, the uncertainty about how long it would last made my anxiety grow. I could not go back to a five-day workweek because I needed more time with my toddler during the week, since she would be living with her other parent during part of the weekend. While I was worried about balancing my responsibilities at work and providing for my family, I also believed that others shouldn't face the same difficult situation. It felt unfair that parents like me were only receiving 80 percent of their salary despite continuing to contribute significant value to the organization, even with reduced hours. To address this, I asked for help, and Pangea's Human Resources Hub took action. They went through many steps to explore the potential policy, and while I was on my Life Happens leave, they voted to expand the four-day workweek to all staff, *keeping the full-time salary intact.*

My colleagues' response to my request for help was overwhelmingly supportive, and they set out to figure out and decide together what would constitute our workweek. Pangea's HR Hub went through the steps above and conducted a survey of all staff to explore needs, desires, and potential avenues to implement an expanded four-day workweek policy for some or all staff. They carefully considered factors such as workload, grant deliverables, vacation policies, and other organizational needs that intersected with our operations. While not every detail was finalized before launching the pilot—for instance, workload was revisited a year later during our strategic planning retreat, and we later refined how to communicate office closures to partners—consensus emerged.

After reviewing all the options, the team collectively supported a four-day workweek for all staff, rather than just a subset. What started as a solution to support me as a single parent turned out to be a valuable and desired policy for the entire team. The HR Hub planned to experiment with two implementation strategies over the course of four months: one where individual staff chose their own day off between Tuesday and Thursday, and a second one where all staff took off Fridays and the office was closed to the public. After the four months, we evaluated the experiments and learned that a uniform four-day workweek created a period of collective rest, allowed for consistent messaging with partners, and reduced the pressure to be available in person and over email. So we voted to close the office on Fridays and make the policy permanent.

As we transitioned to a four-day workweek, we worked to balance productivity with well-being. Expectations shifted to reflect a more sustainable approach to workload, valuing rest and mental health. This new focus on balance was later built into our five-year strategic plan, paving the way for long-term sustainability and a more vibrant and supportive work culture.

Benefits for Undocumented Parents

In a conventional hierarchical organization, when "life happens," there is usually no effective system in place to support an employee. The results are challenging, as was the case with Leonie. By contrast, the culture of care supported by hub structures and policies at Pangea helped us serve staff members in unique ways that met our team's needs. When a colleague requested that the organization consider expanding our health benefits to include spouses as dependents, for example, we began to identify the need to account for the particular challenges that some of our undocumented colleagues and their families faced with health care as well. We considered the context of one staff member who had recently footed a medical bill of $10,000 for their parent. Despite years of labor and tax contributions to the state and federal governments, their parent was not eligible for full medical coverage from the state of California. Like many children of undocumented immigrants, my colleague was their parents' main line of support, and they took on expenses not covered by the state.

Pangea needed to acknowledge the reality that immigrant staff often have a higher cost of living than staff with US citizen dependents and families. We resolved that our benefits policy needed to take this reality into account, which set things in motion. The HR Hub began by researching ways to extend benefits to undocumented dependents, starting with negotiations to expand the definition of "dependents" with our insurance provider. When those efforts fell short, we recognized a conflict within our HR Hub. Some members, particularly those with racial and citizenship privilege, hesitated to commit the extra effort needed to create a nonstandard policy, citing external barriers and the legal work required for compliance. Without consensus in the hub, we decided to pause and revisit the issue at another time. Later in the year, we brought it up again as part of our annual compensation conversation with the full team, where there was enthusiastic support for the policy. This collective support motivated our HR Hub members to look beyond the limitations of exclusionary laws and reject the idea that we had to accept the status quo. We understood that systems and laws often overlook families with undocumented members, so we decided to take an educated risk and get creative.

In seeking input from the team, the HR Hub opened up the conversation to all members as part of our annual compensation discussion. We all deliberated on whether and how to implement a health benefit for undocumented loved ones. If there was support, how expansively would we define "dependents" for this benefit? How many people would use it, and who would qualify for it under the broadest definition? How many people would support a benefit of $5,000 per year versus $3,000 per year? Would it cover up to two loved ones, or three? It became clear that staff members were in strong support of a policy that benefited staff with undocumented loved ones and that was aligned with our vision of a dignified and free world for immigrants and refugees.

Through careful deliberation we came to alignment on key issues. The HR Hub gathered the learnings, researched the legal questions, and developed language for a policy that offered $10,000 in equitable salary to staff for up to two undocumented parents per year for medical expenses. Everyone on the team had an opportunity to review the policy, ask questions, and give feedback. The policy was then refined and finalized for a vote. It passed and was implemented. In the process, we learned the following:

- There was strong support for the development of this policy.
  - Out of fifteen total staff, all fifteen stated they believed this policy would contribute to equity, and all ten of the staff who commented further in writing expressed strong support for the policy.
  - All staff who said they themselves would not benefit from the policy strongly supported it regardless.
- Most supported the higher amount for the benefit.
- Most supported offering this for up to two loved ones as opposed to three.
- To staff, this benefit was as important as our other health and child-dependent benefits.
- Staff voiced opposition to extending this policy to friends or loved ones who were not financial dependents of staff.

The HR Hub members who initially expressed hesitation about the challenges were inspired by the broader team's enthusiasm and commitment, which motivated them to put in the extra effort and research needed to make the policy a reality. With strong collective support, we empowered the HR Hub to take the lead in implementing the details. Without that consensus, the HR Hub might have chosen to conserve resources and let the policy go. But in pushing forward together, we proved that creative solutions were possible, even in the face of systemic barriers.

What we learned from this process was both humbling and valuable. Despite Pangea's focus on advocating creatively and beyond the bounds of the law for undocumented immigrant clients, we realized we could still miss obvious gaps when it came to our own staff and undocumented families. It was a reminder that even when we're immersed in a specific area of expertise, wider input remains invaluable. By bringing in more perspectives, we gain insights that might not be obvious from our individual viewpoints, leading to more well-rounded and equitable decisions reflective of the group's collective wisdom.

While budget constraints and fixed costs are a reality in any organization, we can shape compensation discussions in a way that reflects our collective values and counters scarcity thinking. At Pangea, we saw this play out during our efforts to develop a health benefit for undocumented parents, which began as a daunting challenge but turned into a meaningful opportunity for equity and connection. One framing may be: *We have $50,000 in our budget for salaries and benefits. Where and how should we prioritize allocating it?* Or we might ask staff to rank priorities for benefits. But the trade-off mentality—i.e., if you take this benefit, you can't have that benefit—is a scarcity mindset that's not particularly constructive; it's neither generative nor forward-thinking.

Instead, we approached our undocumented parent policy by embracing shared values and asking the team: *What's most important to us? What can we create together to support staff equitably?* This reframing opened the door to new possibilities, moving us beyond limitations and toward values-aligned action and growth.

Teams of Twelve

A policy that Pangea didn't have but that we considered was to create intentional teams of twelve or fewer people. Until our team reached about ten staff members in size, information and work seemed to flow naturally. Relationships formed with ease, and care was a seamless part of our daily operations. I had the capacity to connect directly to check in with and support my colleagues, and coordinating tasks felt manageable. However, as we grew larger, those natural systems of connection started to feel strained. Things that used to feel simple became more complicated. Some friendships deepened, and new staff plugged into these connections, but it was harder to ensure that everyone felt truly connected. It also became challenging for any one person—like me—to maintain relationships with all staff and provide the care and support I had been able to offer when our team was smaller. Without a clear structure in place, it was difficult to keep care and collaboration as strong as they had been.

Looking back, I now realize that what we were missing was the intentionality and follow-through needed to structure our team sizes effectively. At the time, we didn't fully understand how much structure and intentionality were needed to maintain the care and connection we valued as our team grew. It's something we've come to realize in hindsight: how critical it is to create systems that support relationships and collaboration in a larger organization.

Dividing a larger organization into smaller teams of ten to twelve people could have helped Pangea keep those connections strong. Smaller teams make it easier to build trust, collaborate deeply, and create a sense of belonging where everyone feels supported and empowered to participate fully in decision-making. Creating spaces and policies for these smaller groups to collaborate, both for work and informally, creates the kind of relationships that are foundational to an effective, caring workplace.

The effectiveness of this approach is well-documented. A Harvard Business School case study on Buurtzorg, a home-care nursing organization in the Netherlands, shares an effective example of how this model works in practice, showing how the autonomous and intentional size of team structures can strengthen relationships and improve the quality of care.[2] Buurtzorg's model is built around self-managing teams of up to twelve people. Each team operates autonomously, taking full responsibility for its own group of clients. These small teams make their own decisions, solve problems together, and form deep, supportive relationships. It's a structure that has transformed both their workplace and the lives of the people they care for.

The impact of Buurtzorg's structure is remarkable: Their client satisfaction ratings are 30 percent higher than the average ratings for similar organizations. In addition, staff absenteeism, business overhead, required hours of care per client, and staff turnover are one-third to two-thirds lower. What especially stands out is how Buurtzorg grew their organization. Even as they expanded to over ten thousand staff members organized into about nine hundred teams across the Netherlands, they managed to preserve their culture of care and connection. Instead of becoming more bureaucratic, they continued to add small, self-managing teams, each operating as a tight-knit group. These teams meet regularly to support one another, brainstorm solutions, and share feedback, keeping care and accountability alive and thriving. The entire organization is supported by just fifty administrative staff and two directors—no middle managers. This model allows teams to make decisions independently and keeps management decentralized, helping each group to stay focused on their clients and each other. By creating intentional structures that prioritize care, relationships, and distributed decision-making, Buurtzorg shows that even in a large organization, we can maintain intimacy and connections without giving up high performance. Scaling doesn't have to mean sacrificing relationships; instead, intentional structural design can create workplaces where teams thrive, and organizations remain both effective and deeply human.

For Pangea, creating intentional, self-managing teams like Buurtzorg's could have allowed us to more effectively maintain the care and connection that were so central to our culture, even as we grew. It's a reminder that growth doesn't have to dilute what makes an organization unique. With the right structures and policies in place, growth can amplify care and deepen relationships, creating a culture that uplifts everyone involved.

Actionable Takeaways

Create policies that adapt to life's unpredictability. When staff face personal crises, have flexible policies that accommodate their needs without bureaucratic delays. Establishing dynamic policies like Pangea's Life Happens policy to address unique personal circumstances that may not be covered by standard HR rules may be one way to achieve that. Prioritize compassion and empathy over strict protocols, ensuring that employees feel supported during challenging times.

Engage the whole team in certain areas of decision-making and evaluation. Make major decisions, like benefits policies or strategic changes, through collaborative processes with everyone's input. Regularly gather feedback from all team members on new and existing policies, and adapt your policies to reflect the collective wisdom and needs of the organization.

Acknowledge gaps and address systemic inequities. Even as experts, it's easy to miss key issues, especially when external systems—like government policies or institutional failures—impact some people more than others. Bringing in diverse voices, including external experts, can help identify and address these gaps. Consider how your workplace can compensate for systemic failings by creating policies and benefits that support equity. Just as we challenge societal inequities in our mission-driven work, we can ensure that our internal workplace practices also help alleviate these disparities where feasible.

Embrace the abundance inherent in collective work. Shift away from a trade-off mentality that limits possibilities. Instead of framing decisions as either-or, create a container, and ask your team to rank their priorities within that container.

Organize teams of up to twelve for intentional care. As your team grows, consider creating small, self-managing teams of ten to twelve people to foster trust, participatory decision-making, and a sense of belonging. Use Buurtzorg's model as a guide: Empower teams of twelve to make independent decisions and take responsibility for their work while staying connected to the organization's mission.

7

Onboarding

As Pangea grew, it felt like I was tending to a lively garden, trying to support each new team member and help them thrive. We were doing our best to recruit with an equity focus, and though we didn't have a formal onboarding process yet, I personally introduced every new staff member to Pangea's values and our approach to collective governance, which was key to understanding our culture.

With hubs supporting collective decision-making and the distribution of power to all staff, we were able to create robust policies for intentional onboarding that started at the very first stage of a staff member's relationship to Pangea: recruitment. I had already learned the hard way about the importance of putting these policies in place in 2013 when we hired our first law fellow, Joe,‡ without telling him about our flat salary structure. With our growing team, the HR Hub was now responsible for overseeing what we called the "life cycle" of an employee at Pangea. This ranged from recruitment, onboarding, and retention to off-boarding and farewell celebrations.

When organizations are recruiting, they often rely on assumptions about what should go into a job posting or description. For years, we followed the standard templates used by our nonprofit peers. It wasn't until we received training from our consultant kiran that we made subtle but meaningful changes, creating postings and descriptions that were deliberate, intentional, and more transparent.[*] We wanted the impact of our recruitment process to be equitable and to invite candidates aligned with our values. Through further research and expert consultation, we developed new recruiting practices and standards, which featured these characteristics:

- Transparency about our flat salary structure and benefits, ensuring candidates knew our pay model up front.

- Clear communication about our collective governance and Points of Unity, so recruits understood our values and collaborative decision-making process.

- Setting expectations early about participation as a collective member, including work beyond specific roles, like organizational management and administration.

- Differentiating between "required" and "preferred" qualifications. We found that long lists of required qualifications often discouraged highly capable candidates—especially women of color—who might under-value their abilities, while disproportionately appealing to overconfident candidates. By separating essential qualifications from skills that could be learned on the job, we attracted a broader and more diverse range of candidates with the lived experiences and perspectives essential to our mission. For example, if a bachelor's degree wasn't necessary for the role, we didn't even list it as a bonus qualification. This change widened our candidate pool and aligned with our commitment to equitable hiring practices.

Recruiting the Right Team

Once the recruitment process performed its function effectively—incorporating the detailed job posting as mentioned above, extensive outreach, and ensuring the posting reached a wide and diverse audience—the next important step was the interview phase. Here we got to know potential new recruits as people, and they got to know us and our collective. When Pangea reviewed Esperanza's application for a position as a front desk receptionist and operations manager, for example, her background in bank customer service immediately demonstrated her strengths in client interaction and organizational skills. We were

---

[*] See appendix I, "Job Posting," and appendix J, "Detailed Job Description (Internal)."

eager to understand how her leadership style and lived experiences might align with Pangea's shared leadership culture. During her interview, Esperanza shared her personal story as an immigrant who had been undocumented for years. Her experiences navigating the immigration system while helping her family apply for U visas highlighted her sharpness, proactivity, and care—qualities she had already developed and were essential for the role.*

From the beginning, Esperanza brought empathy, dedication, and leadership to her role as a front desk receptionist. Beyond her specified duties, she organized community members she met through her work and actively contributed to public campaigns alongside Pangea's attorneys. Her curiosity, care, and advocacy instincts shaped her approach to the role, driving impactful change from within. Pangea embraced and celebrated her leadership, offering opportunities and resources to amplify her talents, emphasizing autonomy, flexibility, and personal development as essential values in her journey and the broader workplace culture.

Esperanza's story shows how shared leadership structures can create an environment for growth when individuals' unique strengths and experiences are recognized and valued. She continuously took on leadership roles, collaborating with colleagues and the community in ways that elevated collective efforts. After a few years, she transitioned into a role as a Pangea organizer for immigrants in detention, applying her leadership skills to mobilize and support detained immigrants. Her leadership and determination culminated in a successful campaign to close the last ICE detention center in Northern California in Yuba (the facility that had held Jesus).

Esperanza's journey underscores the importance of recognizing potential beyond traditional metrics like resumes, especially for candidates with lived experiences. When people's unique strengths are valued and nurtured, they can develop their leadership and drive meaningful change. Shared leadership environments don't just benefit individuals—they create space for everyone to thrive and contribute to something bigger.

While interviewing Esperanza, Pangea was still figuring out its approach to hiring. At that time, we didn't yet have the structured, transparent practices we later adopted, but we relied on our instincts and our commitment to equity.

---

* Although we didn't do a competency assessment for Esperanza's role that year, we did do them for other roles by simulating real tasks to evaluate technical abilities and problem-solving approaches. Clear instructions and feedback were provided in some cases, helping candidates understand where they excelled and what could be improved. Though we didn't apply this process consistently, it remains a best practice for creating transparency and support during recruitment.

Looking back, we recognize how those changes could have made the process even more supportive for candidates like Esperanza. Her story highlights how leading with trust and intention can open the door for incredible possibilities.

Transparency and Interviews

Like many "professional" spaces, interview settings in social justice can unintentionally favor certain communication styles, such as confidence in self-advocacy or on-the-spot responses. In addition to having a structured process, hiring committees should examine our assumptions around professionalism and what makes a good hire. This means reflecting on how traits like eye contact, quick responses, or polished communication may not be equally accessible to all candidates. In addition to recognizing our biases, it's important to account for cultural, linguistic, or neurodivergent differences, which may impact how candidates express themselves during the hiring process. There are many resources on this topic, and this chapter offers just a brief glimpse into a much larger and evolving body of work.

There are many ways to mitigate bias in an interview setting. One helpful strategy is to give candidates their interview questions ahead of time. As Pangea's consultant kiran once suggested, unless we are hiring for the skill of charisma and thinking on one's feet, we don't actually need to surprise candidates with questions during an interview. By offering questions in advance, we allow all candidates to prepare and present their best selves. This especially supports people of color, women, gender-nonconforming folks, and others who may not have had as many chances to self-promote or showcase their skills under pressure. It helps us focus on each candidate's true potential and readiness rather than how well they handle unexpected scenarios.

With this context in mind, here are some interviewing practices that Pangea used:

- **Share interview questions with all candidates in advance** to remove the element of surprise, allowing for more thoughtful, genuine responses. This builds trust, reduces anxiety, and demonstrates the organization's commitment to equitable and transparent practices. Ask each candidate the same set of questions to maintain consistency, and avoid informal side conversations with certain candidates.
- **Always include the salary or salary range in job postings,** and commit to staying within that range. This promotes equity by ensuring that candidates

have clear expectations about compensation, helping to eliminate pay disparities, and building trust in the hiring process.

- **Use the same interview committee for all candidates** for a given position, where possible. This allows for more accurate comparisons and minimizes bias.

- **Immediately after each interview, have each committee member evaluate candidates individually and in silence** before sharing thoughts with the group. This helps maintain objective assessments.

- **Base evaluations strictly on the job description,** not in comparison to other candidates.

- **Consider using a scoring matrix or metrics** when assessing a large number of candidates. If you don't use a matrix during interviews, it can still be helpful for reference checks.

- **Conduct reference checks** for valuable insights on a candidate's past performance, working style, and reliability.[*]

Adopting these practices cultivates an equitable hiring process that actively seeks out diverse experiences and perspectives. By embracing structured, transparent methods, we invite candidates to step forward authentically, showcasing their unique strengths and stories. This enhances our ability to identify individuals who resonate with our organizational values while strengthening our commitment to collective leadership. As we open our doors wider to participation, we empower people from all backgrounds to contribute meaningfully to our mission right from the recruitment stage, enriching the tapestry of our social justice work and our collective impact.

Thorough Reference Checks

At Pangea, we learned that thoroughness during recruitment was essential for our worker collective. Before onboarding anyone, we conducted reference checks for all potential candidates, from interns to staff. The depth of the review varied depending on the role, but the purpose was always the same: to understand both how the candidate would fit into our collaborative environment and how well they could perform the specific job we were hiring them

---

* See appendix L, "Reference Checks."

to do. For interns, we kept it simple by emailing references with a rubric to fill out; for staff positions, we had in-depth conversations with references. The questions we asked during these reference checks gave us a clearer picture of a candidate's working style, adaptability, and potential for growth.* For example, asking "How does X handle constructive criticism?" or "Does X ever get defensive?" helped us understand how open they were to feedback—something critical in a collective where mutual accountability is key. Questions like "How self-aware is X?" or "What is an area where X can improve?" highlighted areas for growth and gave us insight into whether the candidate was reflective and committed to personal development.

This process helped us carefully evaluate candidates who might not have been a strong fit for our collective leadership model, and it allowed us to confirm and strengthen our confidence in candidates who shared our values and could thrive within the team. It ensured that we brought on individuals who aligned with both the culture and the specific demands of the role. Additionally, it allowed us to be realistic about areas of challenge when we did hire someone. For example, if a candidate showed great potential but struggled with speaking confidently in meetings or during client interactions, we knew ahead of time where we needed to provide additional support. In this way, our recruitment process wasn't just about finding someone who fit perfectly; it was about identifying those who aligned with our mission and had the willingness to grow within the structure.

When speaking to references, one particularly important question we asked was "Is there anything I should know before making a hiring decision?" This question sometimes surfaced valuable insights that might not have been shared in a traditional reference process. By asking this, we uncovered additional context about the candidate's interpersonal skills, leadership potential, or areas where they might need more support, which was critical for understanding their fit in a shared leadership structure.

In a worker collective, where decisions are often made collaboratively, it's essential to understand both how someone performs in isolation and how they engage with others, take accountability, and contribute to the collective process. These insights allowed us to assess not only whether the candidate could do the job but also how they would contribute to the overall joy and effectiveness of the collective.

---

* See appendix L, "Reference Checks."

Taking the Time

One of the most effective policies Pangea implemented based on kiran's recommendation was its nine-month candidacy period for new hires. This policy came into effect after the recruitment process and allowed us to take a more proactive approach to onboarding. Stretching the hiring arc beyond the initial recruitment stage created space for deeper relationship-building and mutual learning between the organization and the candidate. It also helped create a supportive environment that reduced the potential harm associated with a termination.

A candidacy period allows an organization to take its time before fully committing to hiring a new team member. This thoughtful process aligns with the insights of Maurice Mitchell, who says, "Hire slowly, always. . . . Unintentional scale is an enemy to solid structure. A healthy organizational culture should be prioritized over sheer scale. Take time in establishing and re-establishing culture as you hire."[1] While Mitchell is addressing the broader need to scale organizations thoughtfully, his advice also applies to individual hiring decisions. An intentional candidacy period policy embodies this perspective by fostering a careful, deliberate approach to onboarding. It creates a dedicated space for nurturing and reinforcing the organizational culture. However, even with the best intentions and well-structured processes, organizations sometimes face a difficult reality: having to let go of a staff member.

Many worker cooperatives, such as AORTA and the Cheese Board Collective, implement candidacy periods to integrate new members into their collective structures. These periods provide mentorship, shared learning, and opportunities for mutual feedback, fostering individual growth and collective accountability. By creating space for newcomers to build relationships, participate in decision-making meetings, and engage in community, candidacy periods strengthen connections and deepen shared responsibility, laying a foundation for meaningful engagement and belonging.

At Pangea, a candidacy period allowed a potential new staff member to explore the pathway to becoming a co-director, since all recruits were applicants on the path to co-directorship. This period also ensured accountability both for the candidate and for the entire organization, while fostering thorough integration and safeguarding against moving too quickly.

The milestones on the path to co-directorship include demonstrating an ability to fulfill the job description, aligning with Pangea's Points of Unity, and showing a readiness for sharing ownership at Pangea. Importantly, the policy states: "Pangea acknowledges that people of color and members of other historically disenfranchised groups have been most negatively impacted by policies that create barriers to access and power. . . . The policy aims to empower candidates by making clear that they will be evaluated by the co-directors with whom they have worked most closely; the timeline in which those evaluations occur; and the criteria by which they will be evaluated."*

The candidacy period serves to mitigate barriers, providing a structured, transparent, and clear way for diverse candidates to thrive and assume leadership roles. By allowing candidates to fully understand and integrate into the organization, Pangea makes sure new leaders are well-prepared to contribute effectively and sustainably to the organization in the long term.

Designing Onboarding

Onboarding policies and candidacy periods are not uncommon, but organizations have different ways of structuring them. At the Cheese Board Collective, a hiring committee similar to Pangea's HR Hub is empowered to post vacancies, collect and review applications, make a short list of interviewees, do all the interviews, and schedule what they call "tryouts." Tryouts allow applicants to meet and work with everyone so the whole group can weigh in on the decision about who will become a candidate, and applicants get a sense of whether this workplace could be a good fit for them. Candidacies take place over a six-month period, during which time staff members evaluate candidates regularly and vote on whether to continue or terminate the candidacy. Candidates who successfully complete this candidacy period are voted on as worker-owners and members of the collective. When an applicant becomes a candidate, the Cheese Board also uses "sponsors" (i.e., advocates) during this process. Sponsors help shepherd candidates through their candidacy period, and they act as liaisons, offer guidance and support, and coordinate feedback throughout the organization.

Pangea's nine-month candidacy period allowed the team to evaluate new candidates every few months based on three key criteria: their ability to fulfill their job description, their alignment with and commitment to Pangea's Points of Unity, and their readiness to share ownership at Pangea. The main purpose of a candidacy was to support a new staff member's growth at Pangea. It was an opportunity for the staff member to develop their job-related skills, receive

---

* See appendix K, "Candidacy Period Policy," which was developed by Pangea staff members Jessica Yamane Moraga and Ambri Pukhraj.

timely feedback, and learn about Pangea's worker-led governance structures and processes. It also served as an important way for both the candidate and the organization to assess their compatibility while emphasizing a shared commitment to growth. Unlike traditional probationary periods that often involve monitoring or testing the individual, which can create anxiety and competition rooted in carceral and punitive systems, the candidacy period focused on nurturing the candidate's development. This built collaboration and mutual support, and it helped new staff feel fully supported in their transition into the collective.

Collectively led organizations often design a thorough and intentional onboarding process that prioritizes welcoming new members and ensuring they are fully integrated into the organizational culture. Significant resources—such as time, training, and feedback—are dedicated to this phase to help new team members feel welcomed, build leadership skills, and understand the organization's values and operations. This resourcing goes beyond skill-building; it fosters a sense of belonging and shared ownership from the beginning.

At the same time, the onboarding process is also an opportunity for both the organization and the individual to ensure alignment in values and in meeting work expectations. As new members grow into their roles, there is a collaborative effort to ensure that their contributions align with the collective's goals and operational needs. Rather than being a one-sided test, this is a collaborative and liberatory process designed to empower individuals and the collective. Once staff members are onboarded, they enjoy a level of autonomy and decision-making power that surpasses what is found in conventional organizations.

A candidacy period is not merely a strategy; it lays the groundwork for a vibrant and leaderful work environment. Frequent and timely feedback mechanisms during the process cultivate a culture where team members can practice giving and receiving constructive input, building an atmosphere of continuous growth and mutual support. As we'll explore in chapter 10, this proactive form of conflict resolution prevents small issues from snowballing into larger ones. It also equips staff members to handle more significant challenges when they arise, because staffers are already accustomed to interacting openly and collaboratively.

Performance Evaluations as Part of the Candidacy Period

Performance evaluations were a key part of the candidacy period at Pangea. They created a structured way to communicate feedback and facilitate goal-setting for growth. They also provided an opportunity to check in on job fit, assess candidate performance over a specific period of time, and help support development and growth. Evaluations were regularly scheduled and unfolded in the following series of steps:

1. Candidates receive performance evaluations at three, six, and nine months. After the first evaluation, the criteria include areas of growth related to the job description and identified from prior evaluations. At the nine-month evaluation, additional criteria will be added related to candidates' hub duties, which begin after the first six months.

2. Candidates are evaluated by their supervisor and the four Pangea co-directors who have worked most closely with them during candidacy. This team acts as a liaison between the full Pangea team and the candidate, supporting communication and feedback in both directions.

3. The same team of four or five people conducts three, six, and nine-month evaluations. If there is a need to replace an evaluator in between evaluation rounds (if an evaluator goes on leave, for example, or if there is a major shift in personnel), the co-director who has worked with the candidate the most becomes the new evaluator.

4. After both the three-month and six-month evaluations, the evaluating team decides whether to continue candidacy. Every member of the evaluating team must vote "yes" in order for the candidate to continue their candidacy. If one or more members vote "no" during any one of the evaluations, the candidate is offboarded at that time.

5. Membership vote: After the nine-month evaluation and reaching the final stage of the hiring arc, as our consultant kiran called it, the evaluating team will vote on whether the candidate will become a co-director of Pangea. Every member of the group must vote "yes" in order for the new staff member to become a co-director. If one or more members vote "no," the candidate is offboarded at this time.

A vote of "yes" means:

a. The candidate has demonstrated an ability to fulfill their job description.

b. The candidate has demonstrated alignment with and commitment to Pangea's Points of Unity.

c. The candidate has demonstrated readiness to share ownership at Pangea.

Additional benefits of the candidacy period include

- Focusing on candidates' growth and support from the beginning, which promotes high-quality work while also strengthening team dynamics, making it less likely that difficult decisions will be needed in the future.

- Ensuring our accountability and our ability to do high-quality work and to function well as a collectively led organization.

- Protecting the team from having to make even more difficult decisions later, such as involuntary termination.

- Allowing us to hire candidates whose potential we are excited about with confidence, knowing we will learn more by working with them than we will from their resume, interview, and references.

- Facilitating the delivery of guidance to candidates and giving candidates information they need to make changes the group wants to see.

- Providing candidates with full pay and benefits during their onboarding, helping them feel welcomed while equipping them with the skills needed for effective participation in the collective structure before taking on significant responsibilities.

Actionable Takeaways

Ensure equity in interviews. Approach interviews as opportunities to find candidates who align with the mission and have the capacity to grow within a collective structure. Prioritize lived experience in addition to professional experiences. Consider sharing interview questions in advance to promote transparency, allowing candidates to engage more fully and thoughtfully.

Be transparent in hiring. Start with clear, transparent job descriptions that align with organizational values. Include details about the salary amount and structure, collective governance principles, and

participation expectations. Clearly distinguish between essential qualifications and desirable "bonus" skills to encourage a wider pool of candidates, especially those who may self-select out due to not meeting
every criterion.

Clarify job expectations. Maintain both a summary and a detailed
job description that includes estimated hours, task prioritization, and
clear expectations. A detailed job description helps manage expectations, create clarity, and establish accountability from the start, aligning candidates and the collective team to have a full understanding
of their role.

Maintain clear onboarding and offboarding policies. Maintain clear
and comprehensive onboarding and offboarding policies to set accurate expectations and provide a solid framework for evaluating fit. This
clarity helps both the organization and the candidate understand their
roles and responsibilities.

Establish a candidacy period. Implement a structured candidacy period
for new hires that promotes mentorship, shared learning, and integration
into the organization's culture. This period should emphasize relationship-
building, regular feedback, and understanding of roles to create a supportive onboarding experience.

Document lessons learned. After each candidacy period, engage in
reflection and conduct a reflective review of the process and outcomes. Documenting lessons learned can help refine the candidacy
policy and improve future onboarding practices, contributing to the
organization's overall growth and resilience.

Offboarding

Letting an employee go is one of the toughest challenges a collective organization can encounter. Because relationships are central to collectives, letting someone go can feel particularly personal and difficult. In close-knit, collaborative environments, the ripple effects of such a decision touch the entire group, making the process even more complex and heartfelt. And yet, in social justice workplaces, sometimes letting someone go is the boundary we need to set to stay true to our values.

Take the case of Bo[‡] at Insight Collaborative,[‡*] an organization committed to supporting individual growth and organizational alignment. The organization's candidacy policy required new candidates to demonstrate their ability to fulfill their job descriptions, align with the organization's core values, and show readiness for shared ownership over the course of one year. From day one, Bo and his supervisors took the process seriously, recognizing that his success was a collective responsibility. Weekly check-ins with his supervisor and additional colleagues at Insight Collaborative often stretched for several hours (a red flag),

---

* This story is a composite based on cases I have encountered in my work as a nonprofit leader and consultant. It illustrates the dynamics that can arise in such situations and the opportunities that emerge from intentionality and transparency during the candidacy and offboarding processes.

focusing on managing his calendar, ensuring enough time for tasks, and providing feedback on his work.

Despite their efforts, there was a clear discrepancy between Bo's understanding of his role and Insight Collaborative's expectations. Bo and the co-directors met every two weeks to discuss his progress and keep assignments in check, and his co-directors provided Bo with time-bound goals and specific benchmarks to help him balance deadlines and responsibilities. When Bo requested a two-month leave for a reasonable accommodation, the organization supported him, wanting to ensure they approached the situation with integrity and care. Insight Collaborative prioritized both short- and long-term impacts, even though it became clear within the first six months that Bo was struggling to meet his job requirements. The leadership team was mindful of the long-term risks, considering the potential for future conflict or morale issues if Bo later claimed he had received inadequate support. They also recognized the possibility that the reasonable accommodation might allow Bo to reset and fulfill the potential he had demonstrated in his interview. The organization's approach reflected a commitment to thoroughness, balancing immediate costs with the patience to cultivate long-term well-being, trust, and positive energy within the team. However, even after his return, Bo struggled to meet the expectations that were set out for him.

As Bo's candidacy period came to a close, the team faced a difficult decision. They realized that they had done all they could for and with Bo, on all levels—emotionally, professionally, medically, and relationally—and the care had been provided with structure and intentionality. Bo and the team had been aligned on one another's needs and expectations through clear communication and transparency. Nevertheless, it was clear that Bo was not meeting expectations. The team of co-directors designated to onboard Bo and who worked most closely with him in his first year voted unanimously to let him go. Still, voting "no" on his candidacy brought up many difficult feelings. Bo's supervisor talked with him about the collective decision and named how challenging it was, because she and others really liked him and cared for him. However, the decision also emphasized their collective accountability in upholding the organization's values and maintaining the standards everyone agreed to.

The process highlighted the clarity in boundaries that the organization's policy had created. It also modeled a way of upholding collective responsibilities to the organization's mission as well as great care for an individual. It showed Insight Collaborative's collective effectiveness in creating a supportive yet accountable environment, even when the outcome was difficult. So how can we all do what Insight Collaborative did: know when termination is warranted, and manage harm and repair in a way that aligns with our values and safeguards the well-being of the workers involved?

Implementing termination policies is difficult because it requires a great deal of emotional labor, skill, and resources from everyone involved. Leaders and workers alike often have some amount of fear around termination or separation. Concerns range from hurting someone's feelings and upending their life to leaving them stranded in a system with no financial safety net or support. In collectives, where staff don't view themselves as anyone's boss, the challenge can be even greater. Many people come to these groups with a deep commitment to solidarity, and they may lack the experience or inclination to take on the management responsibilities required for enforcing boundaries and making difficult decisions. There are fears of rejection, abandonment, and financial instability for our colleagues, and how these decisions might affect relationships or our standing within the movement spaces where we work. At Pangea, learning to balance this fear and grow into deeper management responsibilities was a significant growing edge for us. With the guidance of our organizational coach Sheena Wadhawan, we began to develop our understanding. She reminded us, "Fear teaches us things—it is a teacher—but you should never let it drive your decisions. Fear is your drunk friend who you don't give the car keys to."

When guided by compassion and a culture of care, we open the door to creative possibilities, clarity, and a sense of wholeness. Having a thoughtful offboarding policy and structure in place early on is essential for sustaining organizations in today's world. By dedicating time and resources to it up front, transitions become smoother. A candidacy period provides the perfect opportunity to address potential challenges, laying the foundation for a more respectful and supportive separation process if needed.

Coaching Out

In conventional hierarchical organizations, termination feels like the word itself: an ending, sometimes unexpected, painful, or loaded with other emotions. At Pangea, this was out of alignment with the culture of care and our fourth and fifth Points of Unity:

4. We believe in the oneness of all people, and we embrace the common humanity of every person; our interactions are guided by love.

5. We treat every person we meet as an individual with a unique story.

One way to ease into the offboarding process in alignment with those values is the practice of "coaching out." If the staff member is not able to perform their job well after the organization has offered feedback and other structural support, we assist them in transitioning out of the organization.

Authors Alison Green and Jerry Hauser describe coaching out as "an honest conversation about the employee's fundamental fitness for the role."[1] The idea is to communicate to the employee that continued tenure in the role doesn't make sense and to agree on a smooth transition plan. "The key is to talk honestly and collaboratively and recognize that the employee may simply be miscast in the role," they say.[2] It can also mean meaningfully considering what a good role for the employee might be as an alternative.

During my time at Pangea I found myself in the difficult position of having to let someone go. It was a challenging decision to make and carry out. I liked and cared for my colleague, and because we were a small team, we became close quickly, which added to the difficulty. However, they were stressed by the extreme pressures and high stakes involved in deportation defense work, and they had missed a court deadline, which was a serious and unacceptable lapse. It was clear that there was a mismatch in our hire, yet I was still torn about it. At the time Pangea had no policy and no structure for addressing accountability issues like these, although meeting court deadlines was an implied standard. I consulted with experts, colleagues outside of Pangea, and others who could offer expertise relevant to my situation. One Pangea advisor—Vivek Maru, founder of Namati, an organization that seeks to advance justice through legal empowerment— recommended the book *Managing to Change the World*. When I came across the book's section on *coaching out,* I knew that's what I had to do.

I spoke honestly with my colleague, suggesting that they might be better suited for a lower-pressure role, such as affirmative casework that is not so intensely deadline- and court-driven. I asked if they also felt this shift might be a better fit for them, and I offered to support their transition by reaching out to my contacts. The underlying principle was not to judge their performance as good or bad, but rather to consider what they could offer in a role that aligned with their strengths. This can be a big weight for an employer, but the goal here was to stretch, see the whole person, and act with care. Thankfully, they agreed. I then contacted several nonprofits and shared the situation while highlighting my colleague's strengths. One of the organizations was enthusiastic about bringing them on board,[*] and they transitioned smoothly into a new job that was a better fit for them.

---

[*] This employee's role was funded through a transferable grant, so their hiring process followed a less traditional approach.

Coaching out doesn't always involve a happy ending like that, with a carpet rolled out to a new job at a new organization. But it *is* a way of easing a staff member out of their role in a personal, responsible, and compassionate way. Done well, coaching out is a form of relational tending and can be a positive experience that is important for the well-being of the organization as a whole. "You might wonder whether a firing will lower morale among the rest of the staff," write Green and Hauser. "In fact, you will find that just the opposite occurs! . . . It's likely that your staff has spotted the problems and will be relieved when they are resolved." Staff who are unable to perform their job duties and effectively contribute to organizational goals can be a morale drain for those who do fulfill their responsibilities or who go above and beyond. The relief that comes with a shift in personnel has a wide-ranging impact for employees. As Green and Hauser state, "Their quality of life goes up when they work in environments where standards are high, accountability is clear, and they can count on their co-workers."[3] Coaching out can thus help create a respectful, values-aligned work environment where both the team and its individuals are supported in alignment with the organization's mission.

Termination can sometimes be viewed as inherently harmful, leading to a reluctance among staff to support it—even when it's clear that an employee is not fulfilling their obligations. There is sometimes a desire to accommodate staff indefinitely, even at the expense of organizational health. However, as my colleague Esperanza reminded us in our conversations about letting people go, we need to remain focused on our core purpose: to serve the community and advance the organization's mission. The purpose of our work is not to guarantee indefinite employment for every staff member but to ensure we have a team equipped to meet the needs of those we serve. While compassion and support are essential, maintaining a clear focus on the organization's well-being allows us to make these difficult decisions in a way that ultimately supports both the team and the community.

To minimize the impact of termination on an employee, and to act in alignment with organizational values, many collectives and facilitators recommend that offboarding policies include a generous severance package, where possible. Green and Hauser agree, emphasizing that it's both a supportive gesture and a strategic move. They argue that knowing the staff member will have financial support can make leadership feel more comfortable moving forward with a transition. Additionally, a well-thought-out severance package can help organizations avoid drawn-out PIPs, allowing them to manage transitions more efficiently and balance integrity with compassion.[4] Exit interviews, conducted as part of this process, can also provide invaluable insights, allowing organizations to learn from the past and improve their practices for the future.

Unlike a coaching-out process, which prioritizes mutual understanding, I was once fired from a toxic workplace. At the time, it was hard for me to see the full extent of how damaging this workplace was. I could sense the termination coming a couple of months before it happened, although the shift was dramatic: I went from being my boss's favorite, praised for my work, to suddenly becoming her least favorite, sharp criticisms replacing encouragement. The termination itself was abrupt and disorienting. I felt caught off guard and unsure of my worth. I questioned everything I had worked so hard for. Afterward, I struggled with disrupted sleep, replaying my boss's aggressions in my head, and began grinding my teeth at night from the stress. The financial pressure of being without a job weighed heavily on me, and my confidence took a serious hit. I questioned my abilities, my career choices, and whether I had made the right decisions. In hindsight, though, being let go was a turning point. It forced me to confront that workplace's toxicity, and it gave me clarity on the importance of working in a supportive, caring environment. It also strengthened my appreciation for collective leadership and a culture of care as healthier, more empowering alternatives to the hierarchical, punitive systems that so often harm individuals.

Balancing Compassion, Fairness, and Accountability

Unlike my own experience in a toxic workplace, where termination was abrupt and damaging, collective organizations have the opportunity to approach these moments with care and intention. Letting someone go is one of the hardest decisions an organization can make, especially in collectives where care and solidarity are core values. It's not just about one person—it's about balancing care for the individual being let go, fairness to other employees, and staying true to the organization's mission. These moments can stir up fears and bring up our own personal histories, like past experiences with rejection, financial insecurity, or toxic workplaces. All of that can make an already difficult process feel overwhelming.

It's a tough balance to strike. Supporting one person indefinitely when they're not fulfilling a role that meaningfully supports the organization's purpose can create inequities, harm morale, and make it harder for the team to carry out its mission. At the same time, moving too quickly or without care can break trust and leave everyone feeling unsettled. These decisions require us to hold both accountability and compassion, which isn't easy—but it's essential.

Having clear policies and practices in place can make a big difference. They help guide us through tough decisions and ensure we're handling them with care and fairness, for both the individual and the organization.

Actionable Takeaways

Clarify responsibilities from the start. Set clear job descriptions and expectations from day one. Make sure new staff understand their role, goals, and how success will be measured.

Prevent avoidable terminations by providing ongoing support.

Regular feedback: Build a culture of continuous, constructive feedback. Schedule regular check-ins to identify challenges and opportunities for growth early on.

Conflict resolution: Offer training and tools for conflict resolution so team members can address issues before they escalate to termination.

Professional development: Invest in ongoing skill-building opportunities to empower colleagues and reduce the need for termination.

Mentorship and peer support: Incorporate mentorship into PIPs, allowing co-workers to assist the individual in reaching their goals.

Two-way feedback: Create a dialogue where individuals can express concerns and challenges, fostering mutual understanding.

Use candidacy periods. Implement a candidacy period to assess fit through mentorship and collective feedback. Offer regular support and structured feedback throughout this period to gauge whether the candidate aligns with your organization's values and expectations, emphasizing transparency in the evaluation process.

Clear path for exit: Encourage mutual assessment during candidacy, making sure there is clarity in decision-making roles, responsibilities, and timelines. This process should prioritize respectful communication, with all parties in clear agreement on the decision and its execution.

Use due process and collective decision-making.

Due process: Develop a comprehensive offboarding policy that includes collective input from staff at various levels. Ensure the protocol is transparent, with clear guidelines outlining decision-making roles, responsibilities, and timelines.

Vote: Ensure a clear voting mechanism for termination decisions, to mitigate bias and ensure collective agreement. At Pangea, we followed a voting policy where a majority (51 percent) of decision-makers, typically four to five people, had to agree to let someone go after they had passed their candidacy period.

Collective decision-making in offboarding: Engage a small group of team members in the onboarding and offboarding decision-making process. This supports transparency and values alignment in making difficult decisions, like termination.

Conduct offboarding in a respectful, thoughtful manner.

No surprises: Ensure ongoing conversations and feedback to prevent surprises about termination decisions.

Gracious exit: Approach termination as a collaborative conversation aimed at preserving organizational health and individual dignity. While we can't control how someone reacts to being let go, our responsibility is to handle the process with care and respect, knowing we've done our best to support them throughout.

Consider a "coaching out" approach. If letting a staff member go is the best option, consider coaching the individual out. Have honest conversations about their fit within the organization, and explore alternative roles or opportunities outside the organization.

Provide severance and support. If possible, offer a generous severance package and transition support to ease the offboarding process.

Conduct exit interview. Use exit interviews as a tool to gather insights and learn from the offboarding experience. These conversations can provide valuable feedback on organizational culture and processes while also helping to defuse charged emotions by giving the departing employee a chance to be heard and share their perspective in a structured, respectful way.

9

Cycling Out of Executive Titles

Having organizational integrity in place—thanks to the hub model—had a major impact on Pangea, and it helped us develop best practices for onboarding and offboarding. But the journey didn't stop there; I would soon learn that letting go of titles and the authority they carried was equally important in our evolution.

In fact, before we embraced the hub structure, I had proposed an idea: removing my executive director title.[1] I had hoped, at least in theory, to make Pangea a truly collective, shared-leadership organization. But there was pushback against that idea at the time. My colleagues believed that having an executive director title was important to funders and would appease their conventional thinking about building relationships with leaders. Their perspective resonated with me; the world of funding often operates on conventional hierarchies. So we decided that I'd keep the executive director title, and in some ways I was actually relieved.

Around the same time, in 2018, our HR Hub began addressing a pressing issue: a one-time founders' compensation. My co-founder, Marie, and I had carried a heavy workload and salary imbalances from our early days in 2013–2014, and it was time to address that. Following a suggestion from our consultant, the HR Hub worked with our full team to create a special compensation committee to find a solution. The committee created a proposal, checked it against our available funds, sought approval by the full team, and coordinated with Pangea's Board Finance Committee. After confirming the resources were there and holding several discussions, the full team voted to approve it. The final step was presenting the proposal to the full board of directors, who gave their approval as well. This collaborative effort resulted in a one-time payment of $25,000 each for Marie and me. Even with this additional compensation, our annual salaries remained below market rates for senior attorneys and executive directors in the Bay Area. But it felt like a meaningful step toward addressing the imbalances and recognizing the work we had put in.

Over the next few years, Pangea experienced a profound transformation. We shifted from having one executive director to sharing the role between Bianca and me. As the hub system took root in our organization, we embraced rotational leadership and collective decision-making, but it didn't come without its challenges. Navigating the shift from traditional hierarchical structures to a more collaborative approach required us to confront our ingrained habits and expectations. We had to learn to trust each other's expertise and perspectives, which sometimes sparked tension as we adjusted to this new way of working. Yet, through open dialogue and a commitment to shared values, we gradually found our rhythm.

It became clear that although Bianca and I held the titles of co-executive directors, those titles no longer reflected the realities of our practice and hub system. We realized we didn't hold final decision-making authority on most matters, and that was perfectly fine; it was a sign of how far we'd come in fostering a collaborative environment.

By 2019, Pangea had grown into a thriving, self-sustaining ecosystem. The governance hub decided it was time to reevaluate whether we still needed the executive director titles. The organization was ready for this transition; I, however, was still sorting through my feelings about it. Letting go of a title that had been such a part of my identity and leadership journey wasn't easy. It required a lot of reflection and vulnerability as I navigated my mixed emotions around this shift. But by 2020, after some introspection, I found a new clarity.

The transition felt much like an offboarding process, but we were simply shedding titles that no longer aligned with our evolved structure. By this stage, it was clear that our organization had already shifted toward a more collaborative model, and we were just catching up our titles to reflect that reality. We decided it was time for Bianca and me to offboard our co-executive director titles, and we would all onboard the title of co-director.

This shift in titles mirrored a larger journey toward shared governance, one that I documented in an article for *Nonprofit Quarterly* titled "Why My Nonprofit Has No Executive Director." Below is an excerpt of that article, detailing the challenges and rewards of transitioning away from conventional leadership titles:

We voted to remove the executive titles altogether. Leading up to the vote, we had multiple conversations that underscored our readiness to rightsize our ED titles with our actual authorities and processes. When I returned from parental leave in 2019, our governance hub, comprised of two white male colleagues and myself, welcomed me with an invitation to remove my ED title. My first reaction was, "WTF?!" Hello, feminist-POC-mother pride coupled with insecurities of losing organizational worth and value after being on 4.5 months of leave! Despite my push for this very transition, I felt the sting of being devalued.

I had poured all my heart and energy into building up the organization. For years, I researched, read, strategized, and talked about our organization with everyone I knew. I gained valuable skills and tools in a short amount of time. I had built power and authority. But I reminded myself that I had started this conversation and was driven by values of shared or rotational leadership. By this point, Bianca and I no longer had any executive power or final say over matters unless such say was delegated to us by the hubs. Our ED titles had become symbolic. My role and work would continue as before.

It took me working with a trusted therapist to understand my feelings and not feel ashamed of them. With help, I confronted my relationships with success, achievement, performance, authority, motherhood, and self-worth within the context of US culture and the counterculture I was cultivating in my organization. As I moved through my ego, what remained was a strong feeling of pride and accomplishment in my organization, my co-workers, and myself for pushing ourselves to the next level of democratic governance.

Even at this next level, however, we needed someone to keep a bird's eye view of the organization. A significant amount of unnamed labor that Bianca and I did was not delegated to any of our hubs. This included proactively addressing staff needs, identifying gaps, acting on them, researching and presenting proposals to better the organization, fundraising (advocating in white spaces), and a great deal of other relational work. Ours was a clear example of the invisibilized yet crucial labor that is disproportionately carried out by women and gender non-conforming people of color to help organizations run well. Bianca and I continued to do some of this labor outside of the hubs before a full-time employee was hired to take on this work in May 2022. That invisible labor was essential in helping Pangea transition to a decentralized structure, and it will be key to maintaining it.

Pangea formally became a nonprofit with no ED in March 2020, and all staff (14 of us) took on the title of co-director. Although our roles, duties, and distributed leadership structure remained the same, staff ownership and accountability to the organization was elevated. For example, one employee who had never been involved in fundraising was empowered to secure a sizable grant for Pangea, at the time equivalent of one year's salary. Distributing authority and living by our values has gone hand in hand with reaping economic benefits. Pangea's financial standing and reserves are well over the industry standard for nonprofits.

Organizations don't have to get rid of their ED titles to be inclusive and leaderful. But we *should* question and push back against traditional power structures and valuations of human time, labor, professional experience, and education if we are to live in a freer, more inclusive, mutually respectful, and equitable world. As adrienne maree brown says, "How we are at the small scale is how we are at the large scale." At the small scale, nonprofits can invest in creating a culture of respect, equity, and inclusion, modeling the kind of world we want to see in our larger communities and governments.[2]

Transitioning from executive titles to sharing director titles across all staff involved more than changing labels; it also implied doing the internal work as leaders to reconcile our relationships with authority, power, and ego. As a leader, I had to reflect on and release long-held habits of control while embracing vulnerability and trust. At times, the critiques of executive titles, even when not personally directed at me, felt like a reflection on my leadership. I found myself taking these critiques to heart, wishing I could have received some of that feedback in one-on-one conversations, where it might have felt more constructive and less personal. It would have also helped to hear acknowledgment of my contributions in the larger group, recognizing the significance of holding such a title, especially as a femme of color, where those titles carry meaning and weight in our world. Acknowledging that complexity—while still striving for a more collective structure—would have softened the experience.

Despite these challenges, this transition was an important step in aligning our values with our structure, and it brought us a sense of pride in the progress we were making together. While we hadn't yet reached complete stability, we were more prepared to navigate the natural conflicts and growing pains of an evolving organization, knowing that we were building something more sustainable and equitable. At our annual retreats, my co-workers would often reflect, "What I love about Pangea is that we don't sweep problems under the rug like other places. We face them head-on, and every time we do, we come out stronger and more connected." Each difficult moment became an opportunity to grow, and the progress we made felt like an accomplishment we could all share.

Letting go of executive titles at Pangea was more than a symbolic shift; it was a step toward aligning our structure with our values and reinforcing trust in our collective governance. The title change also served as a form of accountability, ensuring that our leadership reflected the shared authority and decision-making practices we had worked so hard to build. This process of offboarding mirrored the broader work of creating clear frameworks for navigating transitions, whether in roles or relationships. By creating clear structures and cultivating a culture rooted in accountability, we established the foundation needed to address challenges with transparency, confidence, and care. This intentional shift also prepared us to engage with conflict not as a threat but as an opportunity for growth. In the next chapter, we'll explore how addressing conflict with intention can deepen trust, repair harm, and strengthen the collective fabric of an organization.

Actionable Takeaways

Here are eight tips for any ED or leadership team curious about pursuing a similar executive director title transition, adapted from my article in *Nonprofit Quarterly*:

1. **Honor your personal feelings and internal conflicts.** Follow kiran nigam's advice to "examine your personal relationships to structures of authority." My feelings stemmed from my ego. Taking time to process this helped.

2. **Begin by transferring a few major organizational responsibilities to other staff.** Give them final decision-making authority (over your own vote), and let the rest of the staff know about it. Also, give them structures and resources to support their leadership.

3. **Do research on some of the different ways shared leadership and horizontal governance can work in practice.** Talk with staff at organizations like Pangea Legal Services, Community Resource

Initiative, Sustainable Economies Law Center, Anti-Oppression Resource and Training Alliance: AORTA, RVC Seattle, and Fortify Community Health.

4. **Talk with other leaders.** Read the *Nonprofit Quarterly* article "Five Insights from Directors Sharing Power,"[3] and consider talking with the leaders referenced in it about how they share their leadership and titles.

5. **Talk about power.** Facilitate a conversation about power in your organization. Involve everyone who is directly impacted by your governance structure, including staff (at all levels) and the board. If your organization is larger than twelve people, consider having conversations in smaller breakout groups.

6. **Develop a plan.** Include collective governance and shared leadership as goals for your organization's strategic plan.

7. **Don't try to do it all overnight.**
   a. Give everyone involved time to process and talk among each other and with others outside the organization.
   b. Try a step-by-step approach. For example, try removing the word *chief* if you have C-suite titles, and try out the executive director title instead. Or try out a shift from one executive director to a team of two or more EDs.
   c. Consider a six-month pilot project rather than a permanent change.

8. **Recruit experienced collective leaders.**
   a. Bring two or more people with democratic governance experience onto your board.
   b. Hire an experienced coach or facilitator to guide your journey. There are many excellent coaches within the Nonprofit Democracy Network.

Conflict

Transforming Tensions: Generative Conflict in Action

Thirteenth-century poet Rumi suggested that our wounds can become the very channels that lead to learning and growth.[1] This wisdom is especially resonant when considering our natural inclination toward conflict. Conflict, like a wound, can be a source of pain and discomfort, yet it also presents an opportunity for healing and regeneration. From the intimate connections we have in family dynamics, to the world at large in its many iterations—societal, organizational, political—conflict is inevitable. And, if approached intentionally, conflict can become a generative, illuminating force.

In any setting with two or more people, conflicts are a natural part of our relationships. And since we all come with unique experiences, expectations, and needs, it's inevitable that there will be workplace tensions from time to time. While every person's approach to conflict is different, many people fear it, are uncomfortable with it, and avoid it. And this makes sense; along with a desire to "get along," some can't afford for the conflict to impact their employment, or they are concerned with the threat of subtle or overt retaliation. "I'll tell you a secret," writes Kai Cheng Thom, a conflict resolution practitioner and somatic coach. "For most of my life, I've been terrified—*terrified*—of conflict." She describes the emotional violence of her childhood and patterns that were played out repeatedly not just in the personal realm, but also "in the 'healing' worlds of non-profit work, social services, and mental health. . . . I don't exaggerate when I say that I've seen lives, relationships, organizations, and communities completely destroyed by conflict."[2] Most of what is modeled for us aligns with Thom's experience. Conflict often feels destructive and terrifying, leaving a trail of harm and tension. Many of us have seen relationships and organizations break under its weight. Yet, ancient wisdom tells us another story: conflict, when approached with care, can be the greatest source of healing and renewal.

"Disagreements are an inevitable, normal, and healthy part of relating to other people," says Amy Gallo in a *Harvard Business Review* article titled "Why We Should Be Disagreeing More at Work."[3] As Gallo notes, while we may be aspiring to a perfectly peaceful workplace, that kind of environment wouldn't actually benefit our organizations, our work, or our people. In reality, when disagreements are handled well, they can lead to many positive outcomes. This idea aligns with N'Tanya Lee's concept of "principled struggle," which emphasizes that we make space to engage in conflict to deepen our collective understanding and achieve greater unity. The key principles of this approach are

- Be honest and direct—while holding compassion.
- Take responsibility for your own feelings and actions.
- Seek deeper understanding; ask and read first.
- Consider that this may/may not be the container to hold what you need to bring.
- Side conversations should help us get to better understanding, not check out (test: could I bring the essence back to the group?).[4]

Lee emphasizes the need for more intentional spaces for disagreement and conflict, which is especially important in collectively led organizations. These spaces provide opportunities for small, everyday tensions to be addressed before they quietly accumulate into larger issues. They also offer chances to build deeper connections, to transform tension into understanding, and to grow.

Understanding Types of Conflict

Let's consider a few different types of conflict that manifest in organizations as harmful workplace dynamics. In the workplace, conflicts can be magnified by power imbalances and financial pressures that are part of living in our current system. Conflicts can also arise not only because of gaps or gray areas in workplace agreements and structures but also from personal dynamics between workers. While conflict takes many forms and has been the focus of extensive research, I want to focus on three types that I've seen most often in practice. First, external pressures—such as deadlines, the political state of the world, and funding challenges—can push teams to move at a pace that undermines trust and collaboration. Second, unresolved wounds or emotional patterns from past experiences can surface, leading to blurred boundaries, which can strain relationships within the team. Finally, there are the small, everyday interpersonal tensions—those tiny cuts of misunderstanding or miscommunication—that, when left unaddressed, can quietly fester and build resentment over time.

External Pressures: Moving Faster Than the Speed of Trust

The first type of conflict occurs when things move too fast, rather than "at the speed of trust," as adrienne maree brown puts it.[5] This rush often creates operational stresses and strains. In late 2016, as the immigrant community was overcome with fear after the election of President Donald Trump, Pangea and I found ourselves stepping up to organize a resistance. The immigrant community was scared of mass ICE raids, increased imprisonment and deportations, young children left without parents, and broken communities all around. We came together with partner organizations, youth activists, and community organizers, believing in our collective strength and resilience. I secured grants and facilitated dozens of workshops to prepare our communities for the challenges ahead in a matter of months.

However, despite our shared commitment to the work, some of the external chaos started to seep into our collaborative space. I felt the urgency of the moment and pushed for reports on numbers and statistics that added pressure to our already overwhelmed partners. We operated in emergency mode, racing against time. In the process, some communication channels were broken, and so was trust. People felt overworked and unheard, and tensions rose.

Looking back, I realize how important it is to slow down in moments like these. It often feels impossible at the time, but taking that pause is what allows real growth and development to happen. I also learned the importance of building proactive conflict-resolution practices into our work from the very beginning, rather than waiting until tensions arise. While we did great work and kept our relationships strong, I learned that moving at the speed of trust is vital, especially for collectively led organizations and our coalitions.

Unresolved Wounds and Enmeshment

A second way conflict frequently emerges is when vicarious or direct trauma, left unattended, impacts how we show up with each other. At Pangea, as at many justice-focused nonprofits, many of us had our own stories of harm and injustice, closely mirroring if not directly connected to the struggles faced by the community we served. This personal connection can sometimes lead to enmeshment, a concept Dr. Gabor Maté describes as a sign of unresolved trauma.

Dr. Maté explains the difference between engagement and enmeshment in this way: engagement is about being fully present and actively supporting our causes while maintaining clear boundaries between our personal experiences and our professional responsibilities. It means working with purpose and compassion without letting personal issues cloud our judgment or overwhelm our capacity to act effectively.

In contrast, enmeshment happens when our unresolved personal trauma bleeds into our work, creating a tangled web of emotional involvement. Dr. Maté describes enmeshment as a state where personal pain dominates our thoughts and actions, causing us to react from unresolved anger or distress rather than from a place of balance and awareness.

At Pangea I experienced enmeshment myself. My strong sense of urgency, especially when working with detained clients or those separated from their children, was driven by my own unresolved childhood wounds related to separation from my primary caregivers and the loss of relatives in prison. This urgency sometimes led me to perceive colleagues as being less committed if they didn't match my level of intensity. As a result, my emotional enmeshment created an unnecessary pressure for my peers and our organization, despite all of our genuine dedication to the work.

Dr. Maté's key insight is that to truly engage in our work without getting enmeshed, we need to acknowledge and tend to our personal issues. Self-awareness is vital, especially when our work hits close to home. By working through our past wounds, we can avoid unnecessary conflicts and handle any conflicts that do come up with greater clarity and empathy. This self-awareness helps us approach both our work and our relationships with a clearer, more balanced perspective, making it easier to work effectively and address issues as they arise. As Dr. Maté wisely puts it, "As long as you are driven by unconscious dynamics, you're not free."[6] If we're working to liberate others, we have to first liberate ourselves. This personal liberation is connected to taking accountability—for our actions, our impact on others, and how we show up in our relationships.

Accountability has to begin within ourselves, and it must be rooted in our own internal reflections and values. As adrienne maree brown writes, "A first step toward ending cycles of harm . . . is honing our internal sense of accountability" so we can act in alignment with our values rather than fearing external callouts.[7] Without this internal clarity, she warns, we become fragile and susceptible to cycles of harm by "outsourcing our accountability" to others.

When we leave our inner work undone, the unresolved wounds from our personal histories can resurface in the workplace, showing up as re-creations of family roles and childhood dynamics among colleagues. This connection is difficult to untangle and shows up in subtle ways. Take Sara[‡] and Tom[‡] as an example. Sara, a longtime middle manager at a nonprofit in New York, found herself in a difficult conflict with Tom, who struggled to meet the expectations of his role. This resulted in a significant additional workload for Sara and other team members. In addition to his work performance issues, Tom was often self-aggrandizing and defensive, which opened up unresolved wounds from Sara's past. Yet Sara's colleagues saw things differently; they defended Tom, dismissing Sara's concerns as personal bias.

While Sara's reaction to Tom was reasonable, it was also deeply tied to her childhood and the dynamics she experienced at home. She had grown up with a father who suffered from undiagnosed mental illness—something no one in her family acknowledged. Sara's father was a constant source of fear and frustration; his controlling nature and harsh behavior made everyday life unbearable. When Sara tried to speak up or share her feelings, she was met with scorn and denial.

Yet, to the outside world, her father was the perfect picture of charm and selflessness. He was the kind of person who would help a neighbor in need, always quick with a smile and a kind word in public. In front of others, he acted like a proud and loving parent, even while he belittled and controlled Sara behind closed doors. This disconnect left Sara feeling isolated, as the people around her only saw her father's public face. Over time, Sara learned to bury her truth and adopt the public's as her own, disconnecting from reality.

Years later, when Sara encountered Tom at work, those old wounds began to reopen. Tom's behavior in the workplace reminded her of her father in ways she couldn't initially articulate. Like her father, Tom was charming and polite in group settings but condescending and dismissive when it came to people he deemed less important. He took credit for others' work—especially women's work—and always seemed to find a way to put himself in the spotlight, despite his underwhelming performance. Sara felt concerned and frustrated, and she knew something needed to be addressed, but his performance shortcomings were ignored.

For Sara, this wasn't just about a difficult co-worker who didn't meet his work expectations; it was also about the resurfacing of emotional wounds from her family of origin—in the workplace. When Tom eventually moved on to another job four years later, she felt some relief, but the impact lingered. The dynamics from her family life were playing out with her colleagues. It took her years to recognize how Tom's traits had mirrored her father's, influencing how she reacted in that situation. At the time, she struggled to separate her past wounds from the present need for accountability from Tom. But through sustained inner work, the help of her therapist, and the care of her community, she gradually learned to confront those older wounds and break the cycle. Sara also began to wonder if Tom had his own personal struggles that complicated their work relationship, and if what she believed to be a simple performance issue was something more complex for him as well.

A workplace may not be able to address every individual's personal issues or family wounds, but it can play a crucial role in recognizing and validating harmful experiences that repeat at work. It's challenging when someone like Sara can't fully articulate or understand their own struggles, but acknowledging their feelings and offering support can make a big difference. In a collectively governed organization, there's a focus on creating a caring culture and supportive conflict structures. This means actively setting aside time and space to address issues involving anyone who feels harmed, no matter how small or personal the conflict might seem to others. It's about finding a balance between recognition and the practical limits of what the workplace can manage. Transformative approaches to conflict (discussed more below) can help in this regard, providing a framework for validating personal experiences while tending to the dignity of all parties involved and exploring possibilities for repair, however big or small.

Even though a workplace isn't responsible for resolving personal wounds, dismissing conflicts like those between Sara and Tom as "personal issues" or "interpersonal dynamics" ignores the deeper dynamics at play. Beyond Sara's enmeshment, her story also underscores the complexity of conflict, as it highlights the structural gaps and the need for safeguards to protect organizational values and principles of equity—and to guard against individuals who might exploit a collective structure.

In Sara's case, the absence of a clear evaluation process for Tom's performance and alignment with the organization's values was a structural gap. This could have been addressed with a formal evaluation process, a candidacy period, and clear steps for Sara to address performance concerns, as outlined in chapters 4 and 7. Additionally, feedback and conflict communication skills, discussed further in the section on feedback below, could have helped Sara and Tom navigate these challenges more effectively.

Recognizing how our own internal struggles—influenced by our pasts and subtle daily dynamics—influence our interactions at work is just as important as addressing structural issues. Acknowledging and validating each person's experiences of subtle, harmful dynamics, regardless of their title or position, is a vital first step in addressing conflict effectively and building our accountability muscles. If these experiences are dismissed or downplayed, they can spiral into larger, longer, more complex workplace conflicts. But when approached with care, they can nurture a culture of growth and respect, honoring the values of collective care and fostering stronger, more supportive relationships. The next step involves addressing these dynamics—both personal and collective—so they don't interfere with our work.

Small Cuts, Big Impacts: Addressing Everyday Interpersonal Conflicts

Minor interpersonal issues, or "small cuts," are a third type of conflict that can manifest within an organization. While these minor conflicts may seem insignificant at first, they are the most common. If left unresolved, they can fester, repeat, and accumulate, ultimately affecting team morale and the organization's overall health. In Sara and Tom's case, what initially seemed like minor misunderstandings and performance issues grew into signs of larger structural gaps within the organization. Without adequate feedback or evaluation processes in place, their managers and team ignored these tensions, hoping to move past them. However, the lack of space for addressing these issues allowed the small cuts to grow into larger frustrations that impacted everyone.

In collective workplaces, trust and relationships are at the core of everything we do, so we are uniquely poised to transform conflict. It is crucial to address conflict early, before it becomes a full-blown crisis. As transformative justice educator Mia Mingus points out, "A lot of times really great work falls apart . . . because of the internal dynamics." She emphasizes the importance of tending to conflicts when they are "at a very low scale." These are the small cuts that add up until they become the proverbial death by a thousand cuts. "There may not even be harm yet," says Mingus, but left unattended, they quickly become the source of greater conflict.[8] Skills, tools, and practices to address conflict in a timely, effective, liberatory way can be built into the work routine. By tending to the small cuts of conflict, we can prevent individuals and organizations from being harmed and move toward growth, resilience, and deepening of relationships.

Effective feedback systems that address issues before they escalate, transformative justice practices and training, and periodic coaching for all staff—even if just a few times per year—are valuable routines. They function much like maintaining dental health: brushing your teeth daily, scheduling regular cleanings, and addressing small cavities early to prevent bigger issues later. In the words of Sonya Shah, co-executive director of the Ahimsa Collective, "We need to get to making 'Hey, do you think you need to be accountable or responsible for that?' as common as saying 'Hey, did you put your seatbelt on?'"[9] Shah's analogy underscores the importance of normalizing accountability conversations, making them as routine and nonjudgmental as everyday safety checks. By addressing conflicts early, as we would go to a dental cleaning appointment, we build a culture of care and prevention that reduces the need for larger, more disruptive measures down the road.

Even when larger conflicts arise, tending to smaller conflicts is still invaluable. Practicing how to address minor tensions builds the skills and confidence needed to move through more significant challenges. By starting small, we are better equipped to handle major conflicts with clarity and care.

The worker collective Movement Generation is one great example of how groups can intentionally and proactively address conflict. Founded in 2006, Movement Generation operates through consensus-based decision-making, using the fist-to-five gradient voting method (explained in chapter 5) to gauge group alignment. Salaries are equal across the board: $105,000 per year for full-time employees as of 2023, with generous benefits packages. Staff collaboratively set their own working hours every six months, all while holding themselves to high standards of accountability and maintaining clear expectations for work and engagement. By making room for disagreements and principled struggle, Movement Generation has been able to identify structural gaps in social and political education among their staff, which they have proactively addressed. Movement Generation has taken time to explore internal issues or dynamics, often through multiyear processes that were focused and intentional. These processes allowed staff to bring up concerns, analyze structural problems, offer solutions, and engage in collective reflection.

Over the years, as part of their work to create intentional spaces, Movement Generation created various processes on topics like gender, race, and disability justice. Co-founder Mateo Nube explained to me that these processes are "part of building self-awareness and being deliberate about our work." They are not one-off meetings; they are continuous and can range from multiyear study processes to real-time conflict resolution, allowing the team to address issues, learn from one another, and enrich their understanding of the subject over time. These gatherings are facilitated by external experts as well as team members, creating a collaborative environment for growth and reflection. Recently, Movement Generation's disability justice team facilitated a ninety-minute discussion on neurodiversity, exploring how neurodiversity impacts the personal lives of all staff members and how these issues intersect with their work together. This conversation helped bring visibility to different needs within the team and deepened the collective understanding of how to better support one another in a work environment.

In collectively led organizations like Movement Generation, disagreement, development, and growth are intentionally woven into the fabric of their structure. These teams understand that dialogue and disagreement are critical to building resilient, values-driven movements. Struggle, reflection, and growth are a core part of their collective approach.

Frameworks for Addressing Harm: What Is Transformative Justice?

Acknowledging and addressing harm are essential to fostering a culture of trust, accountability, and healing. Harm can have a great impact on individuals and our organizational communities. While conflict or disagreement may revolve around differences in opinion or perspective, harm involves actions or dynamics that violate trust, cause emotional or physical injury, or perpetuate injustice.

Transformative justice offers vibrant, heart-centered alternatives to punitive systems, focusing on healing, accountability, and community-driven responses to harm. It's a vast field, with many experts, rich frameworks, and books exploring its depths. While this section is just a brief introduction to this powerful practice, it provides a glimpse into how we can address harm in our workplaces.

Mingus and Shah both work in the field of transformative justice. Their work goes beyond punishment as a response to harm or unmet expectations, focusing instead on repair, healing, and accountability. The idea of punishment as "justice" finds its most extreme expression in the military-industrial complex and the criminal legal system, and it ripples across other areas of life, such as school, family, and the workplace. In the workplace, imagine an employee who keeps missing deadlines, resulting in members of his team doing extra labor to tend to the needs of the organization impacted by the delays. With a punitive approach, the response might be to give him a formal warning, cut back his responsibilities, or even let him go. This method focuses on penalizing the employee without really digging into why the deadlines were missed and what can be done to repair the situation for the colleagues, the clients, and even the employee himself.

In contrast, transformative justice seeks to actually address harm at its root and restore wholeness. For example, imagine the situation discussed above with Sara and Tom; only this time, instead of focusing solely on missed deadlines and their consequences, all the people involved—Tom, Sara, and any other affected parties—come together to understand the underlying issues. The group might explore whether Tom needs more support or clearer instructions, or is dealing with personal challenges. However, the process doesn't stop at identifying those needs; the group also works to understand the impact of Tom's actions on Sara, the team, and clients. They collaboratively create practical solutions like offering additional training, adjusting deadlines, or improving communication channels. Importantly, in this process, there's clarity around roles and responsibilities. Tom's work cannot be quietly shifted back to Sara or anyone else unless the team collectively agrees that such changes serve the organization's broader goals.

Transformative justice frameworks are valuable in addressing harm and promoting healing, but they can face challenges when a person who has caused harm resists genuine accountability or pretends to engage without making meaningful change. The voluntary nature of this model requires authentic participation, and if the impacted parties are not fully committed, the process may fail to bring about true transformation. This is where a possible limitation of transformative justice surfaces, because it depends on the willingness of the person who caused harm to engage in self-reflection and commit to change. In some cases, this can lead to outcomes that feel more performative than transformative. However, when supported by strong community structures, ongoing follow-up, shared accountability, and transparent evaluation processes, transformative justice can still be an effective governance tool for collectively led organizations.

Importantly, transformative justice acknowledges the broader social and historical systems of domination that contribute to harm, seeking not only to address individual conflicts but also to transform the underlying conditions that gave rise to them. It centers community involvement and healing, focusing on creating systemic change from within the community where harm occurred. "How do we restore ourselves back to that relationship that existed before the harm happened?" adrienne maree brown asks. "So someone stole your purse, you get an apology. They do some community service. . . . But for me, I always say that doesn't go far enough. Because if the original conditions were unjust, then returning to those original conditions is not actually justice. Right? You're just going to have someone who's like, 'Great, now I returned everything to you. I still don't have anything and I'm still hungry and I still need something.' So, we need to go further." How much further? According to brown, we need to go "all the way down to the root system of the harm."[10]

This means turning toward one another with intention, holding space for collective accountability, and addressing both the harm and the underlying conditions that allowed it to happen. In Sara and Tom's case, it meant addressing harm and performance issues as well as confronting the inequities and patterns that allowed them to persist. While their conflict included performance issues, it also exposed a broader, more subtle pattern of inequity where women's contributions were devalued and charm and self-promotion were rewarded. Without clear evaluation processes and accountability structures, these dynamics remained invisible and unchallenged. Transformative justice invites us to create intentional structures—like liberatory feedback systems and transparent evaluations—that disrupt these patterns and repair harm at its root. This is the work of building equity, trust, and collective accountability, transforming not just individual conflicts but the systems that perpetuate them.

Incorporating Transformative Justice Principles into Daily Practice with Feedback

Healthy communication and feedback mechanisms are the foundation for transformative conversations that help us prevent misunderstandings and unnecessary conflict. They also allow us to prepare for larger conflicts. This skill set is essential for every staff member, from entry-level staff to senior management and executives. As a founder of Pangea, I rarely received feedback from my colleagues, even though Pangea is a horizontal organization. When we created space during meetings to welcome feedback, I could feel my colleagues' reluctance to share it, especially with me. Except for myself and a couple of other senior attorneys, few colleagues offered feedback to each other regularly.

The term *feedback* has a negative connotation for many of us. We might have been given ineffective feedback in the past or have had it delivered in ways that felt hurtful. This can lead to us often thinking of feedback as critique, but when it's given in the context of relationship and authenticity, feedback is an act of care. In teams and collectives, the key to harnessing lessons from mistakes is feedback that emphasizes connection and growth.

Staff are often understandably reluctant to share feedback with managers or founders, who may respond with dismissiveness or even subtle forms of retaliation. In most workplaces, it is management who provides feedback, not the other way around. But in collectivist organizations, and for those committed to equity, effective feedback channels running both ways are crucial to our growth and healthy relationships. As part of embracing our growing edges, Pangea sought out training on how to give feedback. Organizational coach Sheena Wadhawan offered Pangea a training that asked team members to think of an unforgettable lesson we'd learned through conflict and to share the story behind it. We had all learned lessons, gained insights, and grown through conflict. "Perfection is a fiction," Sheena told us. The most valuable lessons come from mistakes and challenges.

Sheena helped us reframe feedback as an act of care and vulnerability based on our belief in someone, and as a way to set them up for success. "Feedback is a gift," she said. According to Sheena, a healthy feedback mechanism has three major elements: reflection, consent, and regularity.

Reflection, Consent, and Regularity

Incorporating reflection, consent, and regularity into feedback practices is key to building a thoughtful, collectively governed workplace. These three elements are profoundly intertwined, forming the foundation of effective communication, especially when navigating conflict.

A strong communication and feedback practice starts with self-reflection and a commitment to openness and growth. According to Priya Rai, executive director of API Chaya, a nonprofit for and by survivors, reflection includes questions such as "How do I give a good apology? How do I have hard conversations with people in my life? How do I try to be intentional about the way I interact with people in my life in the tiniest ways every day?"[11] Focusing on small moments is foundational.

Consent is also key. Asking colleagues if they are open to feedback and how they prefer to receive it supports a culture of mutual respect and consideration.

It's essential to ensure feedback is delivered and received when everyone is grounded and well-resourced. Understanding whether a person prefers to receive feedback immediately or at a later time, and respecting their preferred method of delivery, enhances its effectiveness and respectfulness.

Many consultants agree that making feedback a regular routine in social justice work is important. Rai, at API Chaya, further explains that routine feedback protocols are the "everyday building blocks of transformative justice."[12] By weaving these reflection and consent practices into daily routines, like in supervision check-ins, we can create a more thoughtful, supportive environment. This helps nurture continuous growth while addressing power dynamics and promoting equity. Incorporating specialized training makes these habits even stronger, building a workplace where learning, respect, and collaboration thrive.

Trying It On

At Pangea, Sheena's coaching and training helped us create a thoughtful and supportive approach to giving feedback. Here is a key part of the framework that shaped our practice:

PREPARE YOURSELF:

- Am I physically, mentally, and emotionally ready to give feedback?
- Have I eaten, had water, or rested enough to ensure I can show up well?
- What is my intention behind giving this feedback? What need am I addressing?

REFLECT ON THE CONTEXT AND RELATIONSHIP:

- Do I know my colleague's preferences for receiving feedback, and is this the right time and place?*
- Is my colleague resourced and ready to receive feedback?
- What is the power dynamic between us, and how might that inform my preparation for this interaction?

---

* See appendix N, "Feedback Preference Chart."

DISCERNMENT AND READINESS:

- Is it my role to give this feedback, and is it aligned with our organizational values?
- Have I checked to see if the recipient has the capacity to engage in this conversation right now?

DELIVERING FEEDBACK:

- Be specific—focus on the actions or behaviors that need attention, rather than making judgments about the person.
- Avoid passive-aggressive tendencies. Instead, be direct and clear.
- Keep the conversation constructive, focusing on mutual growth and understanding.

This framework helped us ensure that feedback was clear, delivered with care, and nurtured a culture of mutual respect and continuous improvement.

Finally, we strove to make feedback a natural, everyday part of how we worked together. "Let feedback be so routine that it becomes boring," Sheena said during Pangea's coaching. By making feedback a regular part of our check-ins and supervision, we took the pressure off, which makes it feel less intimidating or stressful. This helped us diffuse the powers of cultural norms around perfectionism and made giving and receiving feedback feel easier and more comfortable for everyone. When feedback is routine, it builds trust and lets us address small issues before they become bigger problems. Collectively led spaces especially tend to have a culture where feedback is normal, expected, and a way for us all to grow together.

To weave feedback into the culture of our organizations, it's important to do the following:

- Set an intention and start from a place of care.
- Hold processes with integrity; take the necessary time to honor them.
- Introduce accountability early on, starting with the onboarding process.
- Bring in neutral third-party coaches and trainers to mediate issues and assist in the practice of healthy feedback protocols.
- Make sure there are frequent and timely feedback mechanisms that allow staff to practice giving and receiving constructive criticisms.
- Establish a practice of regular training for new staff and for those of us who might forget its components.

At Pangea, staff who missed Sheena's live feedback training were given access to a recording of it so everyone would have a baseline understanding. In hindsight, it's apparent that an annual refresher on feedback practices would have been a valuable addition to reinforce these skills over time.

Receiving Feedback

Defensiveness is a natural and common reaction to feedback, but it often gets in the way of growth and connection. The key to receiving feedback effectively is to recognize this instinct, set it aside, and stay open. By centering the other person's experience, we demonstrate accountability and turn feedback into a tool for learning and building trust.

With this in mind, the following practices are essential when receiving feedback:

- **Assess** our readiness to receive feedback; ask for additional time or support if needed.
- **Affirm and validate** the feelings and impact experienced by the person offering feedback.
- **Avoid** sharing your intentions at this stage, as it can invalidate the impact and experience being shared by the other person. Focus on their perspective first.
- **Reflect** back what you heard, to ensure clarity and understanding.
- **Center** the experience of the person giving feedback throughout the process.
- **Acknowledge** the *impact* of our actions.
- **Take responsibility** for your actions, and avoid defensiveness.
- **Clarify** any misunderstandings. (Notice the order of these elements: clarification comes after affirmation, validation, reflecting back, and taking responsibility.)
- **Commit** to addressing the feedback and making improvements.
- **Seek** additional clarification or support, if needed to respond effectively.

At Pangea, we initially struggled with our communication. Reluctance and unspoken tensions often made it difficult to address problems in a timely way. However, after getting trained in effective feedback practices, we were able to address tensions before they grew into larger issues, creating a more connected and collaborative environment. Personally, I began receiving feedback in a way I hadn't experienced before, and it became something I valued greatly. I saw it as a gift and a true investment in my growth—one that showed my colleagues believed in me. It was a sign of trust and commitment, which made me feel supported in my role and ultimately strengthened our relationships.

Proactive Structures and Culture for Conducting Transitions Justly

For collectively led organizations committed to social justice, feedback plays a crucial role in addressing tensions before they escalate. However, when feedback isn't received or acted upon, a new boundary sometimes has to be drawn—such as letting an employee go. As discussed in chapter 8, having clear, well-crafted policies for offboarding is essential for navigating these difficult decisions in a way that aligns with organizational values. These policies should be transparent, widely communicated, and firmly rooted in the organization's commitment to both staff well-being and accountability.

Equally important is fostering a culture that aligns with these structures. Proactive communication about the organization's policies should happen when the organization is stable and not in crisis. This helps build trust, address fears early, and prevent misunderstandings. While letting someone go is never easy, combining thoughtful feedback practices with clear, values-driven policies ensures that transitions are handled with care and compassion, protecting both the individual and the organization.

Securing External Support

Sometimes, conflicts within an organization need an external perspective to be resolved effectively. While finding someone completely impartial is challenging, bringing in an outside viewpoint can provide valuable insight and help transform conflicts. External support doesn't always mean hiring a costly mediator; there are creative, collaboration-based methods that can also be effective.

The Cheese Board Collective's approach to conflict transformation is an inspiring example of this. Members of their Conflict Resolution Committee participated in intensive training with the SEEDS Community Resolution Center, focusing on nonviolent communication and building a shared language for feedback. Through this training, they realized how challenging it would be to mediate conflicts among co-workers and then transition back to their regular work responsibilities—a dynamic that could be emotionally draining.

Acknowledging these challenges, the Cheese Board, in collaboration with the Arizmendi Association and other worker-owned cooperatives such as Rainbow Grocery Cooperative and Other Avenues Grocery Collective, came up with a resourceful solution: mediating each other's conflicts. This arrangement involved holding space for difficult conversations, developing actionable steps, following up with the involved parties, and maintaining confidentiality. This collaboration shows how organizations can creatively share resources and leadership to transform conflicts.

The Cheese Board example underscores the importance of bringing in external support. When resources are available, expert consulting cooperatives like AORTA and Harmonize, and coaches like Sheena, specialize in facilitating healing circles and guiding organizations through collective conflict transformation processes that are more comprehensive. In the case of Sara and Tom described above, they might have taken the following steps:

- **Consulting all parties:** Engaging everyone involved through listening circles, anonymous surveys, or one-on-ones to collect detailed information about the conflict and understand different perspectives at play. Encouraging transparency and regular check-ins where staff can voice concerns early to prevent escalation.

- **Naming major harms:** Identifying and articulating the major harms and actions that led to these harms. Mediators invite staff to reflect on and contribute to this understanding, ensuring all perspectives are considered.

- **Normalizing conflict resolution skills:** Offering regular training in conflict resolution and transformative justice to equip staff with tools to address issues proactively.

- **Engaging in collective dialogue:** Facilitating a group discussion where all parties can openly share their perspectives, discuss the impact of the conflict, and work towards mutual understanding.

- **Providing tools and language:** Offering tools and language to help staff express and understand the harms and their impacts. This can include frameworks for discussing difficult topics and techniques for effective communication.

- **Prioritizing accountability and self-reflection:** Encouraging self-accountability, where staff reflect on their actions and impact, to help create a shared understanding of responsibility.

- **Creating space for individual expression:** Allowing each individual to share their experiences and the harm they've endured, providing a supportive space where their experiences are recognized and validated by others.

- **Inviting genuine apologies:** Encouraging those who have caused harm to offer sincere apologies, following best practices for accountability, such as those outlined by Mia Mingus, which emphasize the art of making a genuine apology.[13]

- **Creating clear, accessible processes:** Developing and documenting transparent, equitable processes for addressing future conflict, and ensuring staff understand how and when to use these processes.

Securing external support helps transform conflicts while reducing the strain on staff who already carry significant responsibilities in mission-driven work. By addressing issues proactively, as the Cheese Board Collective did through collaboration with other cooperatives, even resource-constrained organizations can reduce the burden on their teams. This ultimately saves time, money, and resources. It also strengthens relationships and creates a more supportive environment for everyone involved.

Actionable Takeaways

Start by embracing the gifts of conflict. Conflict is a natural part of any workplace. By acknowledging this and implementing effective structures to address issues, organizations can turn conflicts into valuable opportunities for growth and improvement.

Establish clear conflict transformation guidelines. Develop clear structures and policies for handling both minor and major conflicts. Ensure there is a straightforward process for support and resolution, with mechanisms for accountability. Investing in fair practices now can prevent bigger problems later. See chapter 6 for more details on creating effective policies.

Address conflict early. Early intervention is crucial for maintaining trust and positive relationships, particularly in environments where personal and professional lives overlap. Use tools like structured feedback, transformative justice practices, and regular coaching to address small issues before they escalate.

Consider holding caucuses or hosting focused learning sessions over an extended period. This approach is inspired by organizations like Movement Generation. Use these spaces to deepen understanding of systemic issues and develop shared language around topics that impact your team, such as neurodiversity, disability, race, gender, and other intersecting identities.

Skill up on communication. Invest in training to enhance conflict communication skills. Improving these skills helps everyone in the organization manage conflicts more effectively and fosters a supportive work environment.

Create healthy feedback mechanisms. Establish safe spaces for staff to discuss conflicts and provide feedback. Effective feedback practices help prevent misunderstandings and reframe feedback as a caring, collective commitment. Regularly reflect on how feedback is given and received and ensure everyone's comfort and boundaries are respected.

Make feedback routine and part of the structure. Use structured feedback mechanisms, like regular check-ins and goal-setting meetings, to support staff and their commitments. Address discrepancies through frequent, clear, and time-bound feedback as a routine part of work.

Use a third-party mediator or designate a role within the organization to address conflict. It is crucial to have a designated person who is responsible, trained, and well-resourced to navigate conflicts in a constructive, timely, and proactive manner. If your organization has the means and resources, consider engaging an external coach or third-party mediator for conflict management.

Explore collaborative solutions. If hiring a mediator or coach isn't feasible, partner with another organization. Train staff from both groups in conflict transformation skills, and support each other when issues arise. Even if impartiality isn't perfect, an outside perspective can be valuable.

11

Funding Abundance

Funding the Future

When some funders first learned that Pangea operated with a collective governance model, they raised concerns that we wouldn't be able to retain good attorneys with that kind of structure. It wasn't just funders, either. In 2015, an executive director from a well-established, well-funded nonprofit echoed this sentiment: "You can't get foundation support with a flat structure. Funders need to see who is in charge." The skepticism around nontraditional leadership models was hard to ignore.

Rather than dismiss these concerns, I recognized an opportunity for education. It became important to proactively communicate the strengths and values inherent in Pangea's democratic governance model. I understood that to build credibility and secure funding, we had to share our story—one that illustrated how our collective structure built the leadership of every team member and strengthened our ability to fulfill the organization's mission.

Fundraising had long been one of my primary responsibilities as both executive director and co-director. Over the years, we strengthened our fundraising hub (the Income Hub) by onboarding new members, sharing institutional knowledge, introducing them to funders, including them in funder meetings, and distributing responsibilities like writing applications and reports. The dedication of the team members on the hub, combined with ongoing integration and collaboration, was instrumental in Pangea's continued achievements. After I left Pangea, the organization successfully applied for and secured a $2 million

Yield Giving grant. This achievement underscores how the hub's collective governance model and the groundwork we laid enabled others to confidently take on leadership and carry the work forward. Our hub made sure that no one person was ever solely responsible, allowing the organization to grow beyond any one individual's contributions.

Conventional Funding and Nonconventional Models

Upon reflection, the questions about Pangea's flat salary structure should have come as no surprise. The conventional philanthropy model has the same institutional roadblocks and bureaucratic shortcomings as conventional top-down business models. Most funders are set up as hierarchies, with boards that approve of funding and are often removed from their grantees and the communities they serve.

Nonprofits often have to navigate the challenge of treating each funder differently, each with its own distinct processes and reporting requirements, which adds a burdensome layer to an already complex system. There is little, if any, transparency in this process. There is also an inherent interest in keeping power centralized and in the hands of a few, because funder boards and a select group of decision-makers hold most of the control over where funds go and how they are distributed.

Meeting immediate community needs often goes hand in hand with the work of advocating for more just practices in philanthropy. With an organizational strategy of abundance, rather than one of scarcity, we often find ourselves needing to educate funders about our values and inviting them to become more equitable partners in our mission to serve communities and the world. We are not just deconstructing systems we oppose but also actively building the ones we want to see. Philanthropic organizations committed to social justice could greatly benefit from learning about the alternative governance approaches with which nonprofits are experimenting. This understanding would further enable funders to better support nonprofits as they interact with traditional funding systems that are often shaped by deep-rooted structural and historical inequities.

The Cost of Repair

Philanthropic funding, like corporate funding, often comes with strings attached that can reshape or even harm collectives and community-focused systems. Just as global financial institutions impose tough conditions on countries in economic crisis, philanthropic funders can set strict terms that may impact the way organizations operate and serve their communities. For example, funders might demand quick results and detailed reports, which can force nonprofits to prioritize short-term goals over long-term community needs.

A common example of philanthropy being directive with nonprofit organizations is when a funder offers a significant grant but with strict conditions attached, steering the nonprofit's work in a specific direction. For instance, a funder might offer a grant to a nonprofit working on housing justice but only on the condition that the funds be used solely for a specific part of a housing project in a particular city, rather than allowing the nonprofit to decide where the need is greatest. Another common example is when a funder offers a significant grant but underestimates the actual cost of labor and time required to fulfill the work. For instance, a funder might provide funding for a nonprofit's new environmental justice initiative but allocate resources only for basic project execution, leaving essential overhead costs like staff training, data analysis, and community outreach severely underfunded. These restrictions can force an organization to either stretch its resources thin or divert other funds to cover the unfunded work.

The implications of this are significant. While the funding may fill an immediate financial gap, the nonprofit may end up compromising its broader mission or neglecting other areas that align more closely with the needs of the communities they serve. Over time, this can create a situation where the nonprofit is more focused on meeting funder expectations than on serving its community in the most effective way, diluting its impact and shifting its priorities away from its core values.

In a collectively led organization, a directive from a funder would be handled through a participatory process involving team members and possibly community stakeholders. Instead of simply accepting the terms, the group would openly discuss whether the funding aligns with their values and mission, and how it might impact their ability to serve the community. If the conditions were deemed too restrictive, they might negotiate for more flexibility or even reject the funding to preserve their principles. This transparent approach would ensure that decisions reflect the organization's values and prevent overreliance on funders who may not fully understand community needs.

Breaking the Scarcity Mindset

Power dynamics between funders and nonprofits can create harmful competition in the nonprofit sector. To keep programs and services going, nonprofits often have to accept the terms set by funders. This can lead nonprofits to compete with one another, offering more services or deliverables for the same amount of funding just to secure grants. In my experience, the pushback and gatekeeping by peers in the social justice space were often stronger than at the philanthropic level. Social justice advocates inadvertently adopted philanthropy's scarcity mindset regarding resource distribution, power, and inclusion. This pattern, sometimes called the "nonprofit starvation cycle," creates a scarcity-driven mindset that leaves organizations struggling with low wages, burnout, and limited ability to focus on long-term change.[1]

The Sylvia Rivera Law Project (SRLP) is an organization that has worked to break this cycle by building collaborative, rather than competitive, relationships with allied groups. The SRLP is a nonprofit that offers free legal services to low-income transgender, intersex, and gender-nonconforming people of color, while also striving to build a nonhierarchical collective by developing the leadership of these communities and ensuring that the SRLP's organizational practices align with the values they are fighting for. They share grant opportunities and intentionally avoid competing for funding better suited for smaller, less-recognized organizations.[2] They approach fundraising with a clear understanding of its challenges, knowing it's necessary but also aware of its flaws. By doing this, they focus on building long-term change rather than getting caught in a cycle of scarcity-driven competition and short-term fixes.

Scarcity-driven funding can sometimes have the following ripple effects on organizations:

- **Fear-based decision-making:** A nonprofit may make decisions based on fear of losing resources or funding, rather than considering what is best for the organization and its goals.

- **Short-term planning:** There is an overemphasis on short-term survival, planning, and fundraising, which can compromise the long-term vision for large-scale systems change.

- **Overreliance on volunteer labor to meet deliverables:** Although volunteers are important to nonprofit organizations, the fight to keep organizational costs low may result in overreliance on volunteer labor, leading to burnout and a lack of capacity to achieve goals. In legal nonprofits, managing pro bono lawyers with limited time can cause more work for staff.

- **Overstretching staff:** Taking on more work without hiring more people leads to overstretching staff. Staff absorption of extra labor, even in incremental amounts, adds up over time, leading to burnout and turnover.

Additionally, recruitment becomes difficult, especially for positions that effectively ballooned into the equivalent of multiple full-time roles due to these increased demands.

- **Limited investment in staff development:** A nonprofit may respond to financial pressures by limiting investment in staff development, leading to a lack of skill-building, poor job satisfaction, and low morale.

- **Tight budget constraints:** Nonprofits reliant on philanthropic funds may place tight budget constraints on aspects of their administrative work and operations, causing the organization to have insufficient resources to achieve their goals effectively.

- **Competition rather than collaboration with peer organizations with shared goals:** This duplicates labor, may lead to distrust, and can make the work harder instead of easier.

The scarcity mentality is not limited to philanthropy; it's also common with government funders, whose expectations often mirror the rigid, top-down models of financial institutions. Breaking free from this mindset requires more than collaboration; it demands intentional pushback against funders, government agencies, and even peers who have internalized and perpetuated scarcity-driven practices. As the SRLP demonstrates, this work involves educating partners, advocating for equity, and challenging systems that prioritize control over care. Nonprofits often have to expend significant effort just to reach a neutral place where their values and practices aren't undermined by the very systems meant to support them. Breaking free from the scarcity mindset often requires nonprofits to expend significant effort just to reach a neutral place—but this work also creates another pillar for transformative change and collective leadership.

An Abundance Mindset

The solution was difficult to achieve, but easy to see: We need to operate from a sense of abundance rather than scarcity, and we need to build generous organizations capable of asking for and building what our communities deserve.

This was how we moved forward with Santa Clara County legislators when advocating for legal defense attorneys for immigrants like Jesus and Rosa who were facing deportation and detention. At the time there were no publicly funded state programs in California that provided legal representation for imprisoned immigrants. In the midst of an advocacy campaign for funding to represent detained and nondetained immigrants in deportation proceedings, one legislator in Santa Clara County asked, "Where is the bang for my buck? What's the economic argument for representing so few people at such a high cost?"

The premise of the legislator's question reflects a flawed understanding of humanitarian needs and the underlying values of care and responsiveness to our communities. Framing the issue as a search for economic viability reduces the lives of detained immigrants to mere numbers. This perspective also overlooks the principle of due process, which guarantees fair treatment in courts. Our campaign for detained immigrants in Santa Clara County was a reflection of this commitment. No other area of US law allowed people to be locked up and forced them to navigate complex legal battles against trained government attorneys without access to legal representation. Studies consistently showed that the majority of immigrants in detention lacked attorneys, while those who did receive legal support were over five times more likely to succeed in their cases.[3] It was frustrating to reduce such a crucial issue—a person's freedom—to a "bang for the buck" calculation, as it dismissed the inherent dignity and rights of our communities. This is one of many examples of how nonprofits can get tied up in knots trying to work within the funder's mindset.

Pangea and our peer organizations persevered with Santa Clara officials. We called for a model of holistic legal representation that included resources for social workers, psychologists, community organizers, and community members to lead and participate in the deportation defense of their loved ones. We used photographs to help us tell powerful stories about clients like Jesus and Rosa, and we showed how holistic legal representation significantly decreased the chances of deportation and family separation. With adequate support, we were able to prevent tragic outcomes like permanent family separation or even death. Through these stories and data, the people were always at the heart of our work. In the end, it wasn't just about policies; it was about hope, resilience, and the power of community to drive meaningful change.

In spite of our best efforts to focus on humanity, we were continuously asked to justify the economics of our campaign. When Santa Clara County finally passed legislation to distribute $3.5 million in new funding, we were disappointed to see that it came with onerous reporting requirements, high deliverables, carve-outs that excluded some immigrants from services, and no wraparound support.[4] In response, we organized a campaign asking people to call in and send letters asking the county to change this inadequate and exclusionary policy. In the end, they still went ahead with their budget as it was, and the request for proposals went out. We didn't win this battle, and it was a setback.

But we came back with a multipronged strategy to try to demonstrate that the county could meet its goals and serve the community in a more holistic way. Out of the gate, we refused to apply for Santa Clara's removal defense funding in 2017, and we clearly stated why through a campaign we led in partnership with a dozen grassroots organizing groups. We organized and mobilized relentlessly. Over the previous year, I had been flying back and forth between Northern and Southern California, meeting with partners and coordinating advocacy strategies for our programs. It was a constant whirlwind of drafting proposals for philanthropy, San Francisco County, Santa Clara County, and the state of California. We worked on fact sheets, reports, talking points, op-eds, and other materials to keep the pressure on. We mobilized our clients to testify at public hearings in Sacramento, who shared their stories about the impact of these policies. We coordinated letters signed by over one hundred organizations, rallied hundreds of community members in front of San Francisco City Hall, and garnered support from key figures who wrote op-eds on our behalf. The energy was undeniable; the community was alive and engaged, and so was I. But before we reached this point, I had already faced significant resistance. Many questioned our ambitious goals, raising concerns about limited resources and pushing back against our broader vision. It was challenging, but in the end, this resistance revealed a valuable truth to me: Some of the strongest pushback can come within our own ranks, even among trusted partners.

Coalitions and Compromise

Recognizing and navigating this internal resistance became one of the most difficult yet transformative parts of our work. Many of our peers and leaders operated from a scarcity and overwork mindset, which was sometimes a bigger challenge than negotiating with funders. When working in coalitions, I spent countless hours in emotional labor, negotiating with peers at other organizations over our funding asks. While some wanted to push for high-volume, low-cost representation, Pangea's focus was on lower-volume representation with higher funding for holistic work. We wanted to stop deportations and family separation, a goal that requires more than legal representation—it takes community, collective organizing, and sometimes a full campaign. We pushed for wraparound services and more resources for this deeper work, driven by a vision of possibility. At one point, our original funding proposal boldly included housing alternatives to ICE detention, inspired by successful models shared by our partner organization, Freedom for Immigrants.[5] We imagined a future where immigrants and refugees would be supported in homes, not cages, with social workers and alternative housing replacing incarceration. However, resistance from our peers forced us to scale back, reducing the ask to just attorneys and some funding for ancillary services, sacrificing parts of our dream to move the effort forward.

Although we made compromises with both our peers and local and state government, we won something much bigger—something that hadn't existed before: publicly funded removal defense programs and representation for detained immigrants in Santa Clara County and San Francisco, and across California.

Soon, together with leaders and coalitions across the state, we were able to secure approximately $50 million in funding statewide and across Northern California counties.[6] Philanthropy played a crucial role in this effort. Tessa Trouverol-Callejo, then at the San Francisco Foundation, mobilized counties and matched funds to expand the model. We openly shared the frameworks and proposals that had been effective in San Francisco and Santa Clara, recognizing the importance of collaboration over competition. Our programs became a national model. Soon, organizers and immigrant rights activists from Chicago, Pennsylvania, and beyond began requesting our advocacy materials to help establish public immigration defense programs in their own regions. Sharing these resources felt natural; spreading the abundance mindset and partnership was always at the heart of our efforts.

Over the next six years, people like Rosa, Irani, and Jesus benefited from the newly created, publicly funded legal representation programs. They no longer had to use their below-living wages to pay for attorney fees. They qualified for public representation to get out of jail and stop their deportations. In the face of a relentless deportation machine, publicly funded legal representation was a welcomed resource for organizations that had been doing the work in its absence. But the whole effort took extraordinary patience and a steadfast commitment to our values, which meant we had to model those values and show up in the world for funders the way we wanted others to show up for us.

Sharing the Vision

High-quality work is essential, as we demonstrated with our model of publicly funded legal representation for immigrants. At Pangea, we built a reputation for excellence by advocating for every case, working in community, pursuing appeals in the highest courts when necessary, and earning respect from peers, judges, and even ICE. This dedication made all the difference to our clients.

When we're engaged in resource-intensive work like organizing or systemic change, educating funders about what quality work entails and its true costs becomes essential. Funders will not envision our ideal future for us. We have to articulate it clearly and show what it takes to make it a reality. Justice is as expensive as injustice.

From the beginning, Pangea did more low-volume work than other organizations that were primarily doing nonremoval defense immigration work. This is in part because removal defense takes a lot more work. When funders asked for larger deliverables, I learned to push back. Once, a Nicaraguan Muslim mother was cited for fraud after she tried to cash the bad check her employer gave her. She was detained by the police and then transferred to an ICE prison facility. We mobilized our community to request her release, and just as we launched a national public campaign, ICE released her. Another time, a Korean father with a college-age drug conviction from several decades prior was detained. After we successfully advocated for his release, President Biden featured his story in a national policy proposal. "Our cases are low volume, but they have a ripple effect and high impact," I told funders.

Hundreds of thousands of people found out about our cases when we did public campaigns, and this is how many learned that resisting and organizing for social change were both possible and worthwhile. When funders said "I want to see high-volume work," I would reply, "We will give you a high impact." Sure, in the time we spent representing the detained Nicaraguan mother and reuniting her with her three children, we could have helped fifteen people prepare green card applications. But who can say one is more important than the other? We need both kinds of work, not just one or the other. The Nicaraguan mother's case set a precedent in the media and the public at large, with over three hundred thousand TV viewers who watched her story on the news. It activated congressional representatives and their constituents. While some funders began to recognize the value of our high-impact (and sometimes high-profile) cases, others remained focused on stories with larger numbers.

At Pangea, we faced pushback from funders and others around us, whether in our nontraditional methods of advocacy and litigation or in our distinct approach to internal governance. Those less impacted or further removed from the issues we tackled were often slower to catch on. Still, we persisted, staying true to our vision.

Fundraising for collectively managed organizations means going beyond describing the true cost of our external work; it requires us to share the vision behind our internal structure as well. This involves bringing our collective approach to life for funders. We can do this through various channels such as grant applications, reports, in-person meetings, newsletters, and social media. One example I shared with funders was Pangea's high staff retention rate over the course of ten years, far exceeding those of similar organizations. I connected this achievement to our collective governance approach and the supportive culture of care we cultivated. Sharing these kinds of compelling stories helped funders understand and connect with our collective structure. It took time, but with consistent and thoughtful communication, we gradually built the support we needed.

To strengthen our relationships with funders and external partners who doubted the effectiveness of collective governance, we used these strategies to communicate its value:

- **Present the benefits of shared leadership.** We emphasized how distributed decision-making increases accountability, reduces burnout, and cultivates creativity. We highlighted how our model led to more sustainability and resilience as an organization because responsibilities were shared, reducing the pressure on any single individual.

- **Demonstrate stronger team retention.** We highlighted how shared leadership improved team retention by creating a more empowering and engaging environment. Staff felt more valued by and invested in the organization, reducing turnover and creating stability.

- **Align with funder values.** We drew connections between shared leadership and the values funders prioritized, like equity, inclusion, and community-driven change. We showed them how collective governance allowed for these values to come to life internally—cultivating care for our staff and reflecting the participatory, collaborative approach we took in our community work.

- **Highlight stronger decision-making.** We explained how collective decision-making processes brought in a broader range of perspectives, leading to more thoughtful, innovative, and well-rounded decisions.

- **Showcase transparency and accountability.** We reassured funders that shared leadership models are built on transparency and accountability, with clear roles and structures in place. This meant that decision-making processes were open, and everyone involved held themselves and each other accountable, resulting in more trustworthy and credible outcomes—values funders hold in high regard.

A Trust-Based and Participatory Approach to Funding

Pangea's holistic immigrant justice approach often led to positive litigation precedents that impacted tens of thousands of people across the United States, precisely because we pushed the envelope on the constraints of conventional funding models, leaning into what's now called trust-based and participatory philanthropy.

Trust-based philanthropy aligns closely with the principles of collective governance by emphasizing shared decision-making and mutual respect. Just as collective governance involves diverse voices collaborating to make decisions and shape the direction of an organization, trust-based philanthropy values the input and expertise of nonprofits in shaping how funds are used. According to the *Nonprofit Quarterly* article "Philanthropy Needs to Trust the Real Experts," this involves funders stepping back from micromanagement and providing flexible support that allows nonprofits to leverage their deep understanding of their communities.[7]

Trust-based and participatory models of philanthropy offer a much-needed shift toward transparency and a redistribution of power, allowing the communities being served to have a real say in decisions that impact them. In her article "The Historical Case for Participatory Grantmaking," philanthropy consultant Cynthia Gibson argues that these models are gaining momentum as organizations, including philanthropic ones, adapt to a rapidly changing world. Gibson emphasizes that these approaches are not only ethical but also practical, given the growing demand for greater transparency, inclusiveness, and collaboration in addressing societal challenges. She observes that participatory models acknowledge that the people closest to the problem are also closest to the solution. Acknowledging that solutions to today's complex challenges can't come from the top down, she says they require "partnership with people who can bring their lived experience to bear in making important decisions about their lives, communities, and futures."[8]

Gibson traces the roots of participatory philanthropy back to the 1970s, noting that although these models are not entirely new, their resurgence reflects a growing recognition of their potential to democratize philanthropy and challenge entrenched power dynamics. However, shifting power and decision-making to communities isn't easy. It takes time and persistence, especially in a sector like philanthropy, which often moves slowly and remains anchored in conventional, pyramidal models. Funders also understandably want evidence that new approaches will work. As Gibson points out, initiatives like the thirty-four-member panel created by Community Foundations Leading Change offer promising examples. This interdisciplinary group—which included voices from philanthropy, government, academia, and community organizations—called on foundations to engage directly with residents as equal partners in change. Their work directly evidenced that participatory grant making leads to more innovative and locally tailored solutions, with communities both benefiting from the outcomes and actively shaping them.

Forging New Paths in Philanthropy

The push to see these new models flourish in the philanthropy world has only just begun.

Trust-based philanthropy represents a shift in how we approach giving and supporting communities. At its heart, this model is about putting confidence in the people who truly understand the issues—those who live them every day. For Pangea and our partner organizations like Faith in Action Bay Area, this meant fostering the leadership of undocumented immigrants and community leaders to take the lead in advocacy campaigns. Instead of imposing top-down solutions, we trusted those with direct experience to guide our efforts and drive real, impactful change. With funders, we nonprofit leaders aimed to drive the change, and for the most part, our funding partners listened.

Justice Funders, a nonprofit that partners with and guides philanthropy, exemplified these principles by becoming a worker self-directed nonprofit organization with a shared leadership structure in 2021. The term *worker self-directed nonprofit* has its roots in cooperative and democratic governance traditions, and refers to an organization where decision-making power is shared among workers rather than centralized in a traditional hierarchy. In an article titled "If We Are Not Prepared to Govern, We Are Not Prepared to Win," Justice Funders executive director Dana Kawaoka-Chen puts this development into perspective: "What is even more meaningful about these organizational shifts is that they are expressions of the kinds of shifts we are working toward in philanthropy and in our world: the democratization of power, the care of the collective and the self-determination of all."[9] This underscores the organization's commitment to more just and participatory frameworks.

Collective practices can and should be embraced at all levels. Organizations can listen to and follow the lead of the communities we serve; funders can empower organizations and communities to decide and lead the way; and philanthropy itself can take these principles further by adopting collective structures internally. These shifts are not only possible—they are already happening.

By adopting such models, we're doing more than supporting change; we're making sure it's driven by those who know best. For example, the community-driven effort to free Jesus, as highlighted in chapter 1, was fueled by the unwavering commitment of undocumented youth and advocates. When we collaborate with organizers and activists and we deeply engage with the community, we also bring the same level of dedication and authenticity to our relationships with funders, whether they are government agencies, foundations, individual donors, or other supporters.

We should be in the driver's seat with foundations, just as our clients should steer their own journeys and our communities should lead in policy advocacy and actions. Funders may offer us road maps or inquire about our destination, but it's important to understand that sometimes the most direct route is littered with obstacles that could impede our mission. Sometimes, funders want the fastest way: just focus on the legal part. But legal work on its own often leads to deportations because the legal system is full of roadblocks. As Mananzala and Spade point out in "The Nonprofit Industrial Complex and Trans Resistance," nonprofits can provide essential services and build leadership, but we still have to recognize the limits of the nonprofit structure: It can sometimes maintain the status quo rather than push for real change.[10] That's why advocacy and organizing are just as crucial, even though they are resource-intensive and indirect. These efforts are what truly lead to wins and liberation. Just as we, as advocates, trust the wisdom and leadership of communities closest to the issues, funders too can lean into this—both internally and externally—to help guide transformative change.

Some funders are starting to understand this. The California Dignity for Families Fund (CDFF) is one example. Through a $25 million partnership with the state, CDFF put immigrant justice leaders at the forefront, ensuring a clearer understanding of migrants' needs and the nonprofits supporting them. They committed to multiyear legal funding, recognizing that immigration cases can take years to resolve, and organizations need consistent support to provide uninterrupted services. By investing in holistic solutions like language access, mental health services, and support for BIPOC-led nonprofits, CDFF showed that when funders prioritize sustainability and follow communities' lead, the impact is deeper and more lasting.

For instance, during Pangea's advocacy campaign for representation for detained immigrants, we received invaluable support from two key philanthropic organizations. The Silicon Valley Community Foundation and the Grove Foundation organized a meeting at the Grove office and invited the California governor's immigration staff. This meeting bridged the gap for our community to directly share our needs and speak to them. Their willingness to listen and amplify our collective concerns resulted in the creation of statewide programs that had never existed before, unlocking millions of dollars in public funding for our communities.

By respecting our expertise and our journey, funders can help us achieve what might seem impossible. Social justice ecosystems need more of these supportive partnerships where funders recognize and empower our leadership, helping us turn bold (but also basic) dreams into reality.

Money Smarts for Meaningful Change

Social justice nonprofit organizations typically rely on a variety of funding sources to support their work, and navigating the diverse world of nonprofit funding is a bit like steering a ship through changing waters. This is especially true for organizations committed to collective leadership. Each funding source brings its own set of benefits and challenges, whether it's the flexibility of individual donations, the more substantial but often restrictive grants, or the vibrant energy of fundraising events. For instance, individual donations can rally community support and provide adaptable funding, but they also come with the unpredictability of varying income streams. Similarly, foundation and government grants offer stability for targeted initiatives but can sometimes restrict the freedom needed for meaningful societal change. Fundraising events and corporate sponsorships heighten visibility and bring in resources, yet they require careful balancing to ensure they don't compromise the organization's core values and collaborative spirit. Earned income and membership revenue offer dependable support and foster deeper community ties but can sometimes unintentionally limit access due to costs or require intense ongoing effort.

Here's a broad look at some of the benefits and challenges of different funding sources in the context of collective leadership.

Individual Donations

These contributions from individuals offer flexible funding for various needs. Individual donations come in different forms, such as one-time gifts that address immediate needs or specific initiatives, and recurring donations that provide a steady and predictable flow of support.

BENEFITS:

- Provides adaptable funding, allowing the organization to quickly respond to community-driven priorities.
- Engages the community directly, creating a shared sense of ownership and support.

CHALLENGES:

- Income can be unpredictable, requiring ongoing effort to build and sustain donor relationships.
- Heavy reliance on donations might make long-term planning a bit challenging.

Grants from Foundations

This financial support is aimed at specific programs or projects to take on particular issues. It can also come in the form of general operating support that is flexible. Grants from foundations can be targeted in various ways, such as program grants for specific initiatives, operating grants that cover general costs, or capacity-building grants designed to strengthen the organization's infrastructure.

BENEFITS:

- Can offer substantial funds for various initiatives, helping to make a meaningful impact on specific areas.
- Supports detailed planning and aligns with collective goals of taking on key issues.

CHALLENGES:

- Application and reporting processes can be demanding and may take focus away from collaborative decision-making.
- Restrictions on grant usage might limit the ability to adapt to changing needs or pursue bold new directions.

Government Funding

These are grants or contracts from county, state, or federal government agencies supporting direct services. Government funding may come in several forms, including competitive grants awarded through an application process, formal grants distributed based on predetermined criteria, and contracts for delivering specific services.

BENEFITS:

- Provides stable and often significant funding for essential services, helping to keep the organization running smoothly.
- Supports key services that align with the community's needs and the organization's mission.

CHALLENGES:

- Comes with strict regulations and oversight that might limit flexibility and the ability to advocate for broader changes.
- Focuses mainly on direct services and high-volume work, which might not support advocacy or systemic change initiatives.
- Contracts are not paid in advance and typically pay less than equivalent government employee wages, leading to cash-flow problems and financial strain.

Fundraising Events and Campaigns

This refers to revenue generated through organized events and campaigns, which also raise awareness and engage supporters. Fundraising efforts can include high-profile galas and auctions, local community events that build engagement, and online campaigns that leverage digital platforms to reach a wider audience.

BENEFITS:

- Boosts visibility and community involvement, helping to build strong networks and partnerships.
- Energizes the community and highlights the organization's mission in a fun and engaging way.

CHALLENGES:

- Planning and running events can be resource-intensive, which might stretch the organization's capacity.
- Revenue from events can be unpredictable, requiring constant effort to keep the momentum going.

Corporate Sponsorships and Partnerships

This is financial and in-kind support from businesses that contribute financial resources and/or expertise. Corporate support can come in the form of event sponsorships, where businesses fund specific events; in-kind donations of goods or services; or strategic partnerships that align with both the organization's and the business's goals.

BENEFITS:

- Brings additional resources and opens up valuable networking opportunities.
- Strengthens partnerships that align with the organization's goals and mission.

CHALLENGES:

- There can be concerns about aligning corporate interests with the organization's values.
- Sponsorships might come with expectations that could influence decision-making or priorities.

Earned Income

This is revenue generated from fees for services or products provided by the organization. Earned income can include fee-for-service models where charges are applied for specific services, product sales related to the organization's mission, or licensing and royalties from intellectual property.

BENEFITS:

- Offers a reliable income stream, supporting long-term sustainability and operational independence.

- Aligns closely with the organization's mission by providing valuable services or products to the community.

CHALLENGES:

- Fees could limit access for those with fewer resources, potentially conflicting with the organization's commitment to inclusivity.

- May strain the organization's ability to sustain its comprehensive social justice work, as charging low-income communities the full cost of services is often not feasible.

- Requires significant business knowledge to generate an effective earned income revenue model and can divert focus from the core mission.

Membership Revenue

These are dues paid by members to support the organization while fostering engagement and active participation. Membership revenue can come from individual memberships, where people pay regular dues, or organizational memberships, where businesses or other groups contribute to support the nonprofit.

BENEFITS:

- Encourages active involvement and strengthens the organization's community ties and resilience.

- Builds a sense of shared ownership and commitment among members, supporting values of collaborative governance.

CHALLENGES:

- Keeping members engaged and satisfied can be demanding, requiring ongoing effort and resources.

- If membership levels decline, it could impact the organization's revenue and engagement.

Planned Giving

Planned giving includes bequests specified in wills, charitable remainder trusts that provide income during the donor's lifetime with the remainder going to the organization, and gifts of life insurance or retirement assets.

BENEFITS:

- Provides significant future funding, helping to ensure long-term sustainability and support for the organization's mission.
- Engages supporters in a meaningful way, often leading to larger gifts than immediate contributions.

CHALLENGES:

- Planned gifts are realized in the future, making them less useful for addressing immediate financial needs.
- Requires effective communication and stewardship to encourage and manage planned giving commitments.

Social Media Fundraising

Social media platforms can be used to engage supporters and raise funds for the organization through campaigns, events, and direct appeals. Social media fundraising can involve crowdfunding campaigns, donation drives, or leveraging viral content to encourage small donations from a broad audience.

BENEFITS:

- Expands the organization's reach, allowing access to a larger and more diverse audience beyond traditional donor bases.
- Encourages engagement and community-building.
- Provides real-time feedback and data, helping organizations tailor their messaging and fundraising strategies based on audience response.

CHALLENGES:

- Requires a significant investment of time and resources to create engaging content and maintain an active online presence.
- May lead to donor fatigue if campaigns are not varied or engaging enough, potentially causing supporters to disengage.
- The unpredictable nature of social media algorithms can limit the visibility of fundraising efforts, making it difficult to reach potential donors.

Budgeting with Our Values

A key fundraising challenge is coordinating funder requirements with colleagues in a collaborative, participatory way. For example, in conventional nonprofit setups, an executive director might secure a grant for a project, like helping immigrants with citizenship applications. While they might seek input from management, the staff doing the actual work often don't have a say in deciding how the funds are used or what the project's priorities should be. This can lead to a disconnect between the goals set by funders and the real needs and challenges faced by those on the ground.

In contrast, collectively governed organizations take a more expansive approach. At Pangea, for example, when we were awarded the Levi Strauss Pioneers in Justice Fellowship, we were promised $150,000 over the course of two and a half years. The fellowship aimed to support BIPOC women, femme, and non-binary leaders, including myself and peers like Zahra Billoo, executive director of the Council on American Islamic Relations, San Francisco Bay Area chapter, and Cat Brooks, executive director of Justice Teams Network/Anti Police-Terror Project. Each of the twelve fellows led an organization, and each of these organizations had the freedom to use its fellowship funds as needed while collaborating to shape activities like healing justice, communications training, and resource mobilization. We were excited about the opportunity to build community. However, at the beginning of the program, after the initial $50,000 of the grant had been issued to our organizations, the Levi Strauss Foundation made the surprising decision to terminate the fellowship granted to Zahra Billoo. Zahra, a bold and inspiring Muslim leader known for her outspoken advocacy on Palestinian issues, was removed after expressing her views during the fellowship.

In response, Cat and I organized a discussion within our cohort of twelve leaders. We wanted to understand the implications of Zahra's removal and how it aligned with our collective values. I first reached out to the Income Hub at Pangea, seeking input on whether to take a stand in support of Zahra and risk losing $100,000 in funding. My colleagues reminded me that a decision like this required a full team vote. Given the time-sensitive nature of the situation, one of our Income Hub members who was aligned with taking a stand took the lead in coordinating with the full team. She sent out an email sharing detailed information about the foundation and Zahra's situation, explaining that this wasn't a vote but a temperature check. Everyone was asked to respond by noon, giving us time to weigh in before my meeting with the cohort and the foundation later that day, where we planned to discuss taking a stand in support of Zahra.

The process was democratic. Despite the time limitation, every team member had the chance to voice concerns and share perspectives. Everyone responded: The Pangea team was unanimous in supporting the decision to back Zahra, despite the potential financial risk. Some raised concerns about filling a budgetary gap if we lost the funding. Finance Hub members quickly provided numbers from our bookkeeper, confirming that we had strong reserves and outlining how many months of operations were covered. After reviewing this information, the team unanimously supported the decision, both in terms of values and financial well-being. Several colleagues even offered to mobilize external networks, including labor councils and Jewish allies for Palestine, in case we needed to launch a public campaign. This collective alignment allowed me to enter the fellowship meeting with confidence. If our team hadn't been aligned, I would have adjusted my approach in that meeting.

Our collective decision to support Zahra and demand her reinstatement— even if this meant risking our remaining $100,000 in funding—was aligned with the entire fellowship cohort. Accordingly, we gave the foundation three days to reconsider their decision. In the meantime, Cat began mobilizing and planning a fundraising campaign to ensure that if all twelve organizations lost the foundation's funding, they could fill their respective budgetary gaps. Ultimately, the foundation reinstated Zahra, which was a significant relief and a testament to our collective strength. However, two months later, the foundation decided to end the entire program. Although we all received our funding, the experience highlighted the importance of collective decision-making and alignment with our values.

Ultimately, though, our values should not have to be up for sale.

Similarly, when Santa Clara County introduced a funding policy that excluded immigrants with certain convictions from accessing legal services, it directly conflicted with our values at Pangea. We believed that everyone has a story and has the right to move, relocate, and rebuild their lives without enduring a system stacked against them. Immigrants face double punishment—first through the criminal legal system, often for poverty-related offenses, and then through the immigration system, where even minor infractions can lead to detention or deportation. This unjust system enforces hyper-incarceration and denies immigrants the resources to defend themselves in court. Our values were grounded in a commitment to love and compassion, extending to both our community members and even policymakers we may disagree with. In response to the exclusionary policy, we didn't just make an internal decision; we took it to the public. We led a community advocacy campaign, mobilizing our members to call county supervisors and voice our concerns. Our voices were loud and clear, and while we made the tough call to decline the Santa Clara County funding, our relentless advocacy made waves. And it paid off soon after!

Not long after these exclusions were introduced, the county moved to weaken its sanctuary policy, which had been established around 2011. This policy was meant to protect immigrant residents by preventing local authorities from cooperating with ICE, but now the county sought to exclude certain groups from its protections. Building upon the energy generated by our recent campaign to oppose new restrictions on immigrant access to legal services, we launched a full-scale community advocacy campaign, pushing for a stronger sanctuary policy and calling on the county supervisors to defend immigrant residents against these harmful changes.

We packed public hearings, invited clients to speak, and demanded that the supervisors listen to the community. The memories of our previous mobilization to resist the exclusions in the legal representation program were still fresh in their minds. Our clients and community members gave powerful testimony, making it clear that any attempt to roll back protections would directly harm the people they were elected to serve. With sustained advocacy, we flipped one of the supervisors who had initially opposed us, and through ongoing negotiations, we gradually garnered the support of additional supervisors. Our collective efforts ultimately led to the drafting of the strongest sanctuary policy language we had seen anywhere in the country. It was a powerful example of how organized, community-driven action can create real, lasting change. By embracing collective decision-making and building leadership both internally and within our community, we were able to not only resist unjust policies but also to create long-term, values-based policy change that reflected our commitment to justice and belonging.

Even with tough financial decisions and less-than-ideal funding, a collective process that incorporates feedback helps an organization stay aligned with its values while considering the impact on its reputation and relationships. When a state-level funding opportunity came up that was similar to the exclusionary Santa Clara County funding, Pangea faced another tough decision. This state funding offered us the chance to secure more substantial, long-term support, allowing us to provide free services to clients who were otherwise paying thousands of dollars in small installments over several years. For many on our team, the prospect of removing that financial burden from our clients was incredibly compelling. The funding was also substantial, and it could fill a critical gap in our budget that we needed to address. However, it came with a significant compromise: an exclusionary policy that prohibited immigrants with certain convictions from accessing legal services—something that clashed directly with our values.*

Our structure and process made this a collective decision, and we knew the importance of handling this decision with care. We held thoughtful, transparent discussions across the team, ensuring everyone's concerns were heard and fully understood. We recognized the value of sustainable, long-term funding, but we also knew the weight of what we were compromising. The process of deciding wasn't easy; there were time constraints, financial pressures, and the looming knowledge that this funding could make a real difference for our clients. Unlike some nonprofit staff, who hadn't been informed of critical conditions attached to similar funding opportunities, our collective structure ensured that everyone involved had access to the full picture.

After thoughtful and democratic discussions, we knowingly compromised by deciding to accept the funding—though not enthusiastically. We learned that not every decision we make as a collective will fully align with our ideals, and that's okay. It's part of navigating the reality of nonprofit work. Although we weren't proud of accepting funding that clashed with our values, it helped us understand why other organizations and leaders sometimes make similar compromises. The difference was that we reached our decision transparently and with participation from everyone on the team.

We recognized that balancing immediate needs with long-term goals some-times requires trade-offs. In the end, we also accepted that sometimes decisions come with unenthusiastic consent, and that's part of navigating complex challenges in a democratic, collectively led organization. While we strive for full alignment with our values, we also understand the need to compromise at times to sustain our mission. That's the power of collective leadership: making informed choices, and learning from each milestone along the way.

One additional thing that set our process apart was that even as we com-promised, we reinforced our values in practice. We made sure that accepting this funding wouldn't mean abandoning those who were excluded by the state

---

* See Pangea's Points of Unity in appendix B, "Statement of Values and Principles": "1. We believe that all people are equal in rights and should be free to move. We dream of a world with-out borders. . . . 5. We treat every person we meet as an individual with a unique story."

policy. As a team, we committed to using other funding sources to continue serving every client, regardless of their exclusion under the state's rules. This way we ensured that no one would be left behind. Additionally, we pledged to launch advocacy campaigns to push for change, building a case around the injustices of the exclusionary policy. It was our collective process that pushed us to think creatively and find ways to refine our compromises. It empowered us to make better-quality decisions across the board—more thoughtful, well rounded, and values aligned—even as we faced difficult financial challenges.

Navigating complex funding decisions within a collectively governed organization requires intentionality, clarity on long-term goals, and organizational integrity. Here are some potential questions to consider together when accepting funding:

- Does accepting this funding compromise our mission or long-term goals?

- How does this funding source align with our collective values and strategic priorities?

- Are those directly impacted by the funded project involved in the decision-making process?

- What consent-based decision-making tools do we have in place to ensure timely and inclusive input?

- How can we ensure that the perspectives of marginalized voices are central to this decision?

- How will our shared leadership structure handle and document the decision-making process for this funding?

- What are the potential positive and negative impacts of the deliverables, and how can we mitigate any downsides collectively?

- How do we navigate any political or ethical misalignment with the funder while maintaining our integrity?

Balancing the Organization's Needs

Balancing organizational needs requires ongoing intentionality, especially in collectively led organizations. During my yearlong executive certificate program with One Justice, which is like business school for nonprofit leaders, I learned the importance of focusing on a few key income sources rather than spreading resources too thin. Managing each funding type demands significant capacity, so it's smarter to diversify within a category instead of across too many categories. For instance, if we rely on foundation and government grants, we should seek funds from various different foundations and various local, state, or federal programs. This would help us build stronger connections and expertise without overextending our capacity. Additionally, by focusing on a few funding categories, we can streamline our advocacy for collective governance structures because we can tailor our messaging to similar funding sources.

When Pangea launched, we relied 100 percent on earned income by charging low fees for our legal services.[11] Our fee structure at the time wasn't just a financial tool; it was a key part of how we steered our organization toward meaningful impact. We received no income for the other work we did, such as community empowerment, organizing, public campaigns, and local, state, and national policy advocacy work. If we think of sources of funding as a vehicle to help us drive toward social justice, then the fees we charged and income we earned allowed us to be the drivers of the vehicle. Instead of being constrained by the fixed routes dictated by external funders or another driver, our fee-based revenue gave us the control to choose our path based on what best served our clients and our mission. But we needed more to sustain us over the long term, and fees placed a burden on clients who were already struggling financially. There was a crucial intersection between financial sustainability and accountability in our work.

While Pangea's fee-based revenue model prioritized client-driven accountability, the Sylvia Rivera Law Project (SRLP) emphasizes community-driven support to maintain independence and integrity. They highlight the importance of grassroots fundraising for building strong movements, and they believe that "a large donor base of community members and allies is a more sustainable approach to movement building than receiving support primarily or exclusively from a few foundations and wealthy individuals. Raising money from the organization's constituency and its allies makes the work more accountable to that constituency and helps ensure that the mission and program will not shift in response to wealthy philanthropists' visions."[12] Their funding model underscores the importance of building financial structures that reinforce the accountability and integrity of an organization's mission, rather than becoming dependent on the influence of a few wealthy funders.

Although SRLP's vision of grassroots fundraising is easier said than done, their analysis resonates with my journey at Pangea. Even as our reliance on fees for services freed us from external funder-driven agendas, it also placed a disproportionate financial burden on our clients. Similar to SRLP's grassroots model, shifting toward diversified and community-centered funding sources later helped us distribute that financial weight more equitably while maintaining our organizational independence and alignment with our core values.

When I left Pangea in 2023, the budget mostly consisted of diversified grants from foundations and local governments, with client fees for services contributing a smaller part. However, even though fees were a minor piece of the budget, they played an important role in allowing us to continue to be the drivers in the values-aligned way we did our work. For example, when a client's case required us to launch a public campaign or make challenging demands of legislators, our previous fee structure gave us the confidence and freedom to act decisively. We knew that even if our actions risked jeopardizing external funding, we could rely on our earned income to support our work. We could fully support our clients' needs and remain true to our values, which allowed us to become known as the organization that took on the toughest cases with relentless determination.

Budgeting Transparently and Collectively

Transparent budgeting practices and participatory discussions about cost management help maintain trust and ensure that resources are allocated in a way that aligns with the organization's mission. At Pangea, we approached fundraising as long-term relational work with funders that we housed within the Income Hub. However, to maintain checks and balances and distribute authority effectively, we separated the responsibilities for managing income from the responsibilities for managing expenses. While the Income Hub was responsible for bringing in funds, it had no control over budgeting or spending decisions. These tasks were assigned to a separate hub, ensuring that financial decisions were made collectively and transparently. This division of responsibilities wasn't just about financial management; it was also about distributing power. By assigning different teams to handle income and expenses, we decentralized decision-making and gave more people a say in how resources were managed. This distribution of financial authority is one way we sought to prevent the concentration of power in a few hands, ensuring that control over money—and, by extension, over organizational priorities—was shared across the collective. This also allowed for a more equitable distribution of the financial burden during times of constraint, because the entire team was involved in finding solutions.

For example, in Pangea's early years we faced a serious challenge with making payroll. With only two months of reserves and expenses climbing, the situation felt overwhelming. I had never managed such a large budget before, so I felt the pressure intensely. Rather than taking on this challenge alone, I brought the issue to our team, and together we created a thoughtful and participatory plan together.

We decided that no one would be laid off if we hit a financial rough patch. Instead, we agreed that, if necessary, everyone's pay would be temporarily reduced, with a commitment to repay any reductions once our financial situation improved. Although we didn't need to implement these measures thanks to new funding that came through, the brainstorming process surfaced valuable fundraising ideas, which we parked for future use. Our collaborative approach proved invaluable. By sharing the burden and working together, we navigated the challenge with resilience, creativity, and a strengthened sense of collective accountability.

The stress was considerable, however, and it was clear that although collective decision-making is invaluable, it has its limits. For large organizations, involving everyone in every stressful decision, particularly in crisis situations, would not be practical or efficient. Even for our small organization it took an emotional toll on staff. Just as it wouldn't be wise to involve an entire staff in HR decisions, most decisions are best handled by smaller, more focused groups. However, maintaining a participatory spirit by inviting feedback and meaningfully incorporating it, wherever feasible, will continue to embody the principles of collective governance.

To fund abundance, we have to break through the prison bars, the police, and ICE, like Rosa and Jesus did. We have to go beyond existing funding practices and break free from scarcity-driven approaches and entrenched systems that prioritize control over care. The work of building abundance starts with us—by trusting the expertise of our teams, leaning into collaboration, and daring to ask for what our communities deserve. It's not about incremental change; it's about boldly reshaping systems to meet the scale of the challenges we face. This is where we begin.

Actionable Takeaways

Rethink "investment." Funders often expect to see a quick turnaround (one to two years) and a return on investment, which has caused many nonprofits to cut back on things like wages and health benefits in order to produce high-volume, low-cost results in a short amount of time. These short-term goals are harmful and perpetuate structural issues. Focus on the true cost of justice and long-term goals.

Plan for visionary growth. Consider building time for retreats where you can do twenty- to one-hundred-year visioning. Some organizations also reflect back one hundred years in those same retreats and ground their plans in the paths of Indigenous ancestors. In the words of Judith LeBlanc of the Native Organizers Alliance, "We need to see our plans for the next five years as part of a 100 year path. We need to know that how we walk in the present is what will sustain us in the future because it is guided by the past experiences."[13]

Funding experimentation and capacity-building is key. The traditional philanthropy model is hierarchical, with little connection between funders and grantees or the communities being served. This needs to change through a concerted effort by nonprofit leaders and values-aligned funders. As leaders, we can continuously educate funders about the benefits and effectiveness of a collective structure. Similarly, funders need to be proactive and commit to funding at scale. This includes supporting the building of infrastructure needed to run collectively governed organizations.

Fund all labor, including invisible work. Request funding that covers both visible and behind-the-scenes efforts that are essential for operations, including administrative, emotional, and community engagement labor. While volunteer labor can be a stopgap solution and temporary benefit, funding abundance means funding all labor. (The Cheese Board even pays for job applicants' time when they come in for a tryout after an interview.)

Use proactive staffing to stay below full workload. As much as feasible, aim to keep workloads manageable and ensure staff aren't stretched thin by hiring in advance for emerging roles and scaling labor according to demand. Protecting staff members' workloads will allow for creativity, new projects, and an ability to respond to emergencies. Importantly, it will also reduce staff burnout and turnover.

Collaborate instead of competing. Collaborate rather than compete with peer organizations that share similar values and goals to yield more abundance. Consider the example of organizations like the SRLP that take this a step further by intentionally deferring grant opportunities to smaller organizations.

Highlight victories as well as challenges. In grant applications and grant reports, give examples of the successes of collective governance at your organization. Shine a light on growing edges, and make a case for how philanthropic partners can provide support at scale.

Move with abundance in mind. Advocate for what you need and for what the communities you work with deserve. Rejecting shortsighted demands and sticking to your values will actively produce steps toward long-term structural change, even if it doesn't always meet short-term goals. Work with funders to help them understand the importance of adaptive funding. Advocate for grant flexibility so the organization can respond to evolving needs and dedicate resources toward both immediate and visionary goals without restriction.

High-impact work is as important as high-volume work. Visionary work, or work that hasn't been done before, requires changing funders' frame of mind. You can tell funders who are pushing for short-term, high-volume results that you strive for high impact instead of high volume. For example, short-term work like processing green cards is vital, but so are the long-term impacts of things like reuniting families and setting legal precedents for decades to come.

Fundraising is long-term relational work. The relationships and trust you build within your organization should be reflected outwardly in the way you deal with donors. Treating values-aligned donors as thought partners helps build trust and opens opportunities in terms of new relationships and opportunities.

CONCLUSION

As we look to the future, the path forward is clearer than ever. The world of work is shifting, and with it the way we govern ourselves, care for each other, and build organizations. In this new era, our future is collective. The rise of worker-led organizations—those where shared leadership and shared responsibility are the backbone of decision-making—is not a mere trend; it's a transformation in how we understand power and community. The change has already begun, and the seeds planted in collective governance are sprouting in real time.

But for these models to thrive, they need commitment from all sides. It requires those at the top and those coming down from the top to be vocal in their support, to model the behaviors of shared power, and to make space for others to lead. Workers, too, need to lean in, both to do their jobs and to take responsibility for the whole. It's uncomfortable at times—asking people to take ownership of something that isn't just theirs but all of ours, and allowing leaders to step back and let others lead. But in this discomfort, growth happens. The challenges are real, but so are the possibilities. When we create spaces where everyone is invited to participate, to have a say, and to lead in their own way, it opens up a whole new world of possibility. It's not just about fairness or equality; it's about creating a better, more supportive way of working together. And we're seeing this already in places like the nonprofit sector, where workers are pushing back against the "do more with less" mentality that has so often dominated our culture, even in social justice spaces.

Workers are reorganizing their workplaces, yes—and they're also building something more. They're pushing for deeper, systemic changes that go beyond just wages and benefits. They're pushing for a culture of fairness, transparency, and collective power. The rise in worker-led governance models in the non-profit sector (along with a renewed surge in public-sector union organizing)[*,1] is showing us that people are ready to reclaim power, not only in how much they're paid or what benefits they receive, but in how decisions are made and how they're treated. Nonprofits especially are looking at their internal structures and realizing that they need to change. It's a slow, steady process, but it's happening. Workers are taking control, demanding fair treatment, and saying, "We deserve better—and we can create it." But as the great thought leader Audre Lorde reminds us, achieving real liberation takes more than a fight against oppression; it requires a thorough deconstruction and rebuilding of the systems that perpetuate it.[2] The challenge here is not only to fix the problems we see but also to dismantle the structures of power that created them in the first place. This is why shifting from a strictly hierarchical, top-down system to one of participatory, collective governance isn't just about equity and inclusion—it's about the profound and necessary act of rebuilding how we work, how we lead, and how we treat one another. It's about justice. We are not simply asking for better conditions within the old systems. We are evolving into something new.

But let's be real: it's not going to happen overnight. It takes time—at least three to five years of sustained effort—for real transformation to occur within an organization.[3] And we can't expect perfection from the start. Transforming how we work, how we lead, and how we make decisions is a long-term investment. It takes time, patience, and a willingness to be uncomfortable. It takes experimenting, making mistakes, learning from them, and trying again. The kind of collective governance we dream of doesn't happen in one big leap; it happens through incremental progress. We start with small changes, perhaps by creating a new decision-making process in a team, or introducing a regular meeting for everyone to voice their concerns. It's in the small, intentional shifts that we begin to build something bigger.

I've seen this up close. When I was part of Pangea Legal Services, we took a step toward formalized co-governance, and it was far from easy. At first, I found myself reluctant to relinquish control and let others take the lead, especially when I thought I knew better. I had to learn to trust others, reconcile my ego, lean back, and allow mistakes to happen. But over time we saw how much

---

* The surge in union organizing and activism that we've seen over the past decade shows a clear hunger for change. Over sixteen million workers in the United States were represented by unions in 2022, and union membership has been growing rapidly in the public sector where one in three workers is unionized.

stronger we became. When leadership was shared and decisions were made collectively, we found new ways of doing things—sometimes better ways than I could have imagined. And the results were there: The year after I left, my colleagues continued to thrive and raised millions of dollars in new, unrestricted funding—an extraordinary achievement for a twenty-person nonprofit, especially after a founder transition. We continually proved to ourselves that this model works, and it was because we made the decision to embrace collective leadership, even when it was hard.

When we look to history for guidance, we can see how seemingly small and thoughtful actions have led to enormous change. In the 1960s, the Black Panther Party launched its Free Breakfast for Children program, not as a temporary fix but as a way to meet basic needs and challenge systemic inequalities. What began as free school breakfasts in local communities eventually inspired statewide programs and national policies. Meaningful change often starts small—one organization, one community, one movement at a time. If we want to transform the future, we have to start where we are and build from there. We have to live the change we want to see now. We have the power to create the future we envision; the key is to begin practicing it every day in our workplaces, our homes, and our communities.

This is our generation's work: to create organizations that are efficient and serve an immediate need while also being holistic and human-centered—organizations where everyone has a voice and every person feels empowered and accountable. We will create spaces where workers can lead and decision-making is shared, and we will build systems that reflect our deepest values of care, respect, and justice. This vision is not a distant dream. It's happening now, and each of us has a role to play.

So where do we begin? There are as many starting points as there are individuals and organizations, but one thing is clear: We begin with values and points of unity. We ground ourselves in shared values, we build relationships, and we create what we can with what we have. We don't wait for the perfect conditions. And in this practice, in this steady, deliberate work of transforming our workplaces from the inside out, we create a future that reflects our highest aspirations.

Change starts with the choices we make and the values we commit to embodying. Each time we prioritize collaboration over competition, equity over expediency, and care over control, we lay the groundwork for something transformative. As these principles take root in our actions and relationships, the change deepens and expands, offering not just a new way of working but a new way of being together. We may not have all the answers yet, but we have the capacity to shape the future. And that future is collective.

APPENDICES

APPENDIX A

Board Resolution for Worker Self-Direction and Distributed Authority

Board Resolution Approving Staff Self-Governance

The Board hereby resolves that, in accordance with Pangea's Point of Unity #12 ("We are committed to equity regarding compensation, responsibilities, and shared ownership"), the successful track record of Pangea's staff and activities, the staff's robust set of internal policies and procedures for self-governance, and emerging principles and best practices for the management of nonprofit organizations, it is in the best interest of Pangea and most effectively and efficiently advances Pangea's mission if Pangea staff primarily direct the strategy, policies, and tactics of the organization.

The Board affirms that Pangea staff may make day-to-day decisions and set longer-term policies and strategy for the organization until [enter DATE, one year from the present], at which time the Board shall review and may reaffirm or revoke this resolution, in view of the best interests of the organization.

As a member of an organization with a shared leadership structure, each Pangea staff member serves as a steward of Pangea's mission and day-to-day activities. Each staff member is a point of direct accountability for the organization, listening to and responding to the needs of communities we serve and work with. As such, staff have heightened responsibility and should have heightened influence to make decisions and shape their own programs and realms of work. In order to carry out their heightened responsibilities, staff require agency and autonomy to respond appropriately in the best interests of the public and the organization. As such, staff shall continue to implement a governance structure that distributes power among the staff and engages each staff member in decision-making processes.

Regardless of the above, the role of the Board shall always be to fulfill its duty of care by closely monitoring the activities of the organization, regularly reviewing financials and budgets, monitoring compliance with the law, reviewing internal policies adopted by staff, and intervening in decisions it believes to be harmful, overly risky, illegal, threatening to the organization's tax-exempt status, or contrary to the mission of the organization. The Board shall also review and approve any decision that could result in personal financial benefit of $1,000 or more for any staff member, including staff compensation and benefits.

APPENDIX B

Statement of Values and Principles

Pangea's Points of Unity

January 2015

1. We believe that all people are equal in rights and should be free to move. We dream of a world without borders.

2. We were created to fill a gap in free and low-fee deportation defense services.

3. We recognize that education, legal empowerment, and policy advocacy are essential to changing perspectives around migration and migrants' rights.

4. We believe in the oneness of all people, and we embrace the common humanity of every person; our interactions are guided by love.

5. We treat every person we meet as an individual with a unique story.

6. We are committed to excellence and providing high-quality services.

7. The law is a living document. Its flaws do not constrict us. We use it strategically to ask boldly for the best for our community.

8. We are positive and solution oriented. We value fresh attitudes, innovation, and creativity. We challenge conventional thinking in order to redefine what is possible.

9. We practice humility. We listen, learn, reflect, evaluate, and grow.

10. We value our team's individual and collective well-being. We create mechanisms to support well-roundedness and our team's mental, physical, and spiritual health.

11. We recognize a tension between serving as many people in need as possible, taking challenging, legally complex cases, and valuing our own health and well-being. We strive to maintain a balance between these three goals.

12. We are committed to equity regarding compensation, responsibilities, and shared ownership.

13. We strive to create an organization that is both financially sustainable and autonomous.

APPENDIX C

Task Redistribution Chart

	ADMIN HUB (SAMPLE)			PROGRAM HUBS	OTHER	
HUB NAME AND POINT PERSON >>	E.g. Governance Hub (name of point person)	E.g. Finance Hub (name of point person)	E.g. Legal Services Hub (name of point person)	E.g. Supervision (see tab 2)	E.g. Coalitions/Liaisons	E.g. Other Activities
HUB MEMBERS >>	Name 1	Name 1	Name 1			
	Name 2	Name 2	Name 2			
	Name 3		Name 3			
Name	Board liaison/relations	Hub member	Hub member	Names of people supervising	Names of coalitions and groups	10-year anniversary party planning committee
	Legal compliance point person	Spending lead	LexisNexis Incubator Program point person			Coordinator for the creation of Party Hub
	All-team meetings	Accounting	Impact litigation point person			10-year anniversary party planning committee with board
	Hub goals/midyear review	Pay bills/reimbursements	Mentorship scheduling			
	Meta Hub chart review	Budget lead	Workload subcommittee			
	Health of org structure point person	IRA disbursements				
	Task redistribution lead	Budget co-lead				
		Audit property tax filings				

APPENDIX D

Decision-Making Flowchart and Table

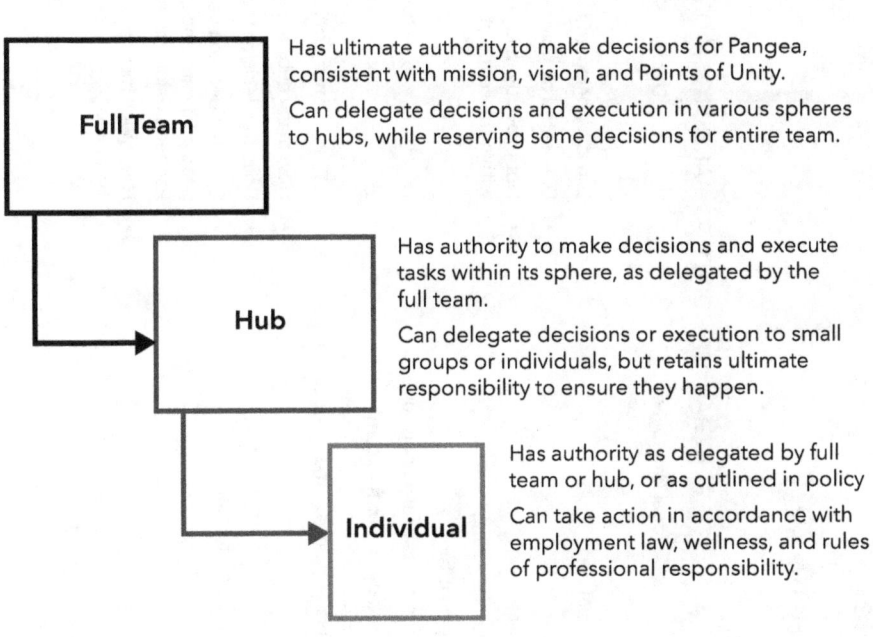

Full Team

Has ultimate authority to make decisions for Pangea, consistent with mission, vision, and Points of Unity.

Can delegate decisions and execution in various spheres to hubs, while reserving some decisions for entire team.

Hub

Has authority to make decisions and execute tasks within its sphere, as delegated by the full team.

Can delegate decisions or execution to small groups or individuals, but retains ultimate responsibility to ensure they happen.

Individual

Has authority as delegated by full team or hub, or as outlined in policy

Can take action in accordance with employment law, wellness, and rules of professional responsibility.

Pangea Authority Table

Officially Adopted August 10, 2018

	WHO HAS AUTHORITY TO MAKE DECISIONS?		
	Individual Employees	Decision-Making Hubs	Full Team
Where does the decision authority come from?	• Internal policies • Points of Unity • Job descriptions • Personal well-being • Employment laws • Rules of professional responsibility • Delegated by hub or full team	• Explicitly delegated by the full team • Delineated by policy • Not explicitly delegated by the full team but within the scope of the work area	• Mission and vision • Points of Unity • Board
What factors should be considered?	• Does this only impact me, or does it impact the group? • Legality • If no policy, go to hub	**If not explicitly delegated:** • How many hubs are involved? • Does the decision involve a change in policy? • Does the decision potentially conflict with Pangea's political stance, or is it intertwined with Pangea's vision and mission? • How much money is involved? Refer to Spending Policy.	

WHO HAS AUTHORITY TO MAKE DECISIONS?

Examples	What decisions can each individual employee make on their own, without consultation?	What decisions can hubs (or those delegated authority by hubs) make on their own?	What decisions must be made by the full team?
	Per Policy • Purchase USPS labels • Spend money on business-related travel, within established policy • Schedule vacation days following established policy **Per Job Description** • Make strategic decisions about client representation **Per Personal Well-Being** • Remove oneself from a hub • Organize one's workspace • Organize one's schedule within established policy • Hang art **Per Employment Laws** • Report misconduct **Per Rules of Professional Responsibility** • Withdraw from case	**Per Explicit Delegation** • Eliminate candidates during recruiting process • Hire non–full-time staff/interns • Set average caseloads **Per Policy** • Terminate an employee in accordance with termination policy • Approve spending in accordance with spending policy **Per Scope of Work Area** • Make decision on health coverage affecting single individual	• Delegate authority to hubs • Appoint hub members • Create management structure • Approve salaries • Approve budget • Approve health coverage plan • Approve full-time staff hires • Accept funding with strings attached

List of Hubs

ADMINISTRATIVE HUBS

Communications: Responsible for ensuring positive messaging in line with our Points of Unity, mission, and vision; displaying our achievements and disseminating information about Pangea's work and values.

Finance: Manages and oversees Pangea's expenses, budget, accounting, and taxes.

Function Junction: Oversees general and daily business operations in our San Francisco and South Bay offices. Ensures that the organization functions as smoothly as possible, to support high-quality services.

Governance: Manages organizational rules that govern how Pangea operates. Ensures that Pangea processes and policies meet organizational goals, governs the structures, and creates and manages the connections between hubs.

HR: Responsible for benefits, team wellness, and team life cycle recruitment and retention.

Income: Responsible for overseeing and maintaining diversified cash flows rooted in organizational values, our budget, Pangea's needs, and team needs.

PROGRAM HUBS

Legal Services

Community Empowerment and Policy Advocacy

APPENDIX E

Decision-Making Policy and Gradient Voting Tool

VALUES

Everyone should be heard.

Getting everyone to yes: We want to work toward everyone being on board, with full team buy-in.

DECISION-MAKING PROCESS

Pangea Legal Services makes decisions by a modified form of consensus. The group uses the "gradients of agreement" to help guide discussion. Consensus is defined as 51% of team members voting 4 (abstain/no opinion) or above to pass a proposal. Individuals do not hold the right to block. However, even if the 51% threshold is reached, if 25% or more of individuals present and voting are an 8 on the gradient, that is not sufficient support for the group to move forward with the proposal. Team members are encouraged to vote 8 if they truly cannot support a proposal.

"Consensus on a decision means that each team member says they buy-in to the decision and actively support its implementation, even if they do not think it was the very best decision." (From *Team Decision-Making: The Gradients of Agreement*, by Steve Joyce, TeamSTAR Project)

QUORUM

A quorum of 75% of staff members is required to make decisions. Staff members on long-term leaves approved by the group (health leave, parental leave) and new staff who do not yet hold decision-making power do not count when calculating the quorum. For example: if Pangea has 15 staff

members, 1 is on leave and 1 is a new staff member who does not yet hold
decision-making power, the quorum is 75% of 13, which would be 10 staff
members.

NEW STAFF MEMBERS

New staff members who have been with the organization for less than six
months may bring forth ideas and are encouraged to participate in discussions but do not hold decision-making power.

GRADIENTS OF AGREEMENT

(From *Team Decision-Making: The Gradients of Agreement*, by Steve Joyce,
TeamSTAR Project)

	Enthusiastic Support	
1	Fully support	"I like it!"
2	Endorsement with minor concerns	"Basically I like it."
	Lukewarm Support	
3	Agree with reservations	"I can live with it."
4	Abstain	"I have no opinion."
5	Stand aside	"I don't like this, but I don't want to hold the group up."
	Meager Support	
6	Disagreement, but willing to go with majority	"I want my disagreement noted, but I'll support the decision."
7	Disagreement, with request not to be involved in implementation	"I don't want to stop anyone else, but I don't want to be involved in implementing it."
	Strong Objection	
8	Can't support the proposal	

FROM IDEA TO DECISION

If a staff member has an idea, they begin by bringing that idea to the hub
under whose scope of work the idea falls. They may do research or gather
quotes to develop their proposal, especially if there is a question of major

financial impact or long-term decision-making. The hub may take on the idea or proposal as part of their work and research or refine it, implementing it via their own decision-making process, or bringing it to the whole group if needed.

CONSENSUS

1. Facilitator checks for shared understanding of the issue and restates for clarity.

2. If there is a proposal, the proposal's authors share it with the group.

3. We start by asking questions about the proposal.

4. We can then get a sense of how the group is feeling by asking people to show how they feel on the gradient of agreement.

5. We then move into discussion of the proposal. We can amend it to strengthen it during our discussion. During our discussion, we center our values of everyone being able to be heard and moving toward the highest amount of buy-in possible.

6. Facilitator summarizes where the discussion is and tests for consensus, again using the gradients of agreement. If there is not sufficient support for the group to move forward, the group can continue discussion, can task a person or small group with bringing a new, refined proposal later, or can table the conversation. If there is adequate support, the group moves on to #7.

7. Facilitator restates the decision. We clarify how the decision will be implemented, including specific commitments and responsibilities.

8. If the decision resulted in a new policy, the staff member who brought the proposal to the team should follow the steps in "Addendum II: You just passed a policy. Now what?" [See appendix G.]

OFFERING FEEDBACK/VOTING BY EMAIL

Staff proposing an item to be voted on should try to give notice by email ahead of time to the team, if practicable, in the form suggested in "Addendum I: Email Proposal Template." [See appendix F.] If a staff member will not be present at the meeting, they can provide feedback about proposals or meeting topics in advance of the meeting. This feedback may include a request that the proposal not be decided upon without them, with a date indicated by which they will be available to participate in decision-making.

If a team member would like to propose an amendment or a change to the proposal, they should send feedback approximately 24 hours before the discussion of the proposal. A staff member who will not be present may also enter a vote over email in advance of the meeting. This email vote will count for quorum only if the proposal is not changed during the meeting. If the proposal is changed and the email vote is needed for a quorum, the proposal has not passed until the team has informed the absent staff member about the change and that person has agreed to the proposal as amended.

We recognize that circumstances sometimes prevent members from providing timely feedback on proposals that they have a vested interest in discussing, and we will determine on a case-by-case basis whether it is appropriate to leave a 7-day window during which the absent member(s) may provide feedback before the decision goes into effect.

DECISION-MAKING BY EMAIL

For smaller decisions, or decisions that have already involved a strong level of staff participation, we may choose to make the decision by email without a meeting. We avoid lengthy conversations or debates by email; if it becomes clear more discussion is needed, the proposal will move to a meeting.

For proposals by email that **have not been** the subject of recent, full-team discussion:

- All staff (with the exception of those who do not count for quorum) need to vote 4 (abstain) or above for the proposal to pass by email. Otherwise, it will be brought to a meeting.

- In cases where an urgent (time-sensitive) decision is needed on such a proposal, the proposal may pass with a quorum of staff members voting by email, and 51% or more voting 4 or above.

- For proposals by email that **have already been** the subject of recent full-team discussion:

  - Pangea's normal consensus voting system applies (see "Decision-Making Process," above.)

  - However:

    - All staff (with the exception of those who do not count for quorum) need to vote for the proposal to pass by email.

- **If a staff member was not present** at the full-team discussion, they should read the notes/watch the recording before voting. They may provide feedback on the proposal via email before the voting deadline.

  - Reminder: If a staff member knows beforehand that they will not be present at a full-team discussion of a proposal, they are encouraged to provide feedback in advance of the meeting. This may include a request that the proposal not be decided upon without them, with a date indicated by which they will be available to participate in decision-making.

- **If a staff member *chooses*** not to vote on an email proposal, they will not be counted for quorum.

  - Reminder: One of the duties of a Pangea staff member is to participate in the collective decision-making process. Refusal to do so is a refusal to fulfill the expectations of collective membership.

- Once email voting is done, the staff member who brought the proposal should

  - Send an all-team email with the results (e.g., passes with strong support, requires discussion, etc.).

  - If the vote resulted in a new policy, follow the steps in "Addendum II: You just passed a policy. Now what?" [See appendix G.]

LARGER-SCALE DECISIONS

Some decisions that we make are inevitably larger in scope and scale, where the impacts of cost are more far reaching—time, money, emotional labor. We seek to be thoughtful and ask hub point people or individuals bringing forth larger-scale decisions to the group to do a deeper level of research. Some types of information we may want to consider bringing forward to the group include

- **Alignment** with organizational priorities, values, Points of Unity, strategic plan, and personal interests

- **Project budget**

- **Market research:** Who else is doing similar stuff? What are they charging? Who are they serving?

- **Effective date or implementation deadline:** If this is a new protocol or amendment, when does it start/change? If it is a special project or other proposal, what are the time constraints?

- **Pros:** Why is your proposal an improvement over the present situation or a good use of our resources?

- **Objections:** Issues of consideration, or trade-offs

- **Social impacts:** What impact will this proposal have on the social fabric of our organization?

- **Other resources and impacts:** If other resources are necessary, how will their use affect the rest of our operations?

- **Responsible party:** If approved, who will implement this proposal?

(Last adopted and updated December 9, 2021.)

APPENDIX F

Email Proposal Template

ADDENDUM I: Email Proposal Template

Adopted April 19, 2019

Goal: This Email Proposal Template aims to assist the team in streamlining the decision-making process, and ensuring that team members come prepared to RDVs[*] ready for thoughtful discussion and voting on any proposal.

Team members are asked to send out proposals that will be voted on at RDV at least a week before, if practicable, to give ample time for questions, feedback, and counterproposals to be circulated before RDV. *Counterproposals raised at RDV for the first time are highly discouraged.*

THE EMAIL SHOULD INCLUDE THE FOLLOWING SECTIONS/ITEMS:

- **Proposal:** State your proposal. Include any information you believe would fortify your proposal or background you think is necessary for the team to understand.
- **What authority do you have?** Explain the authority you and the team have to make/vote on/implement the proposal (with reference to the Authority Chart and Hub charts).
- **Feedback deadline:** Unless this is an emergency, this deadline should be at least five days away.
- **RDV voting date:** When you would like your proposal to be voted on. Please ensure that you have also added the proposal to the RDV agenda using [Proposal and Vote].

---

[*] RDV: Short for *rendez-vous*. This term was used for Pangea's regular staff meetings, to add some fun, inspired by our French co-founder.

EXAMPLE:

To: Pangea Team

From: Paul Robeson

Re: [Proposal] Margarita Machine

Dear team,

On behalf of the Football Hub, I am making the following proposal, which will be voted on at RDV next week:

Proposal: That Pangea buy a margarita machine. See the specific model we are suggesting in the attached Word document.

Authority: The Football Hub has been delegated authority by the team to propose purchases that would make our football-watching more fun; the entire team has to approve any purchases.

Feedback deadline: Please send me initial thoughts and counterproposals by next Tuesday.

RDV voting date: Friday 5/14.

Please let me know if you have questions.

In solidarity,
Paul

APPENDIX G

Handling Newly Passed Policies

ADDENDUM II: You just passed a policy. Now what?

Adopted 12/08/21

1. **Title it this way:** [NAME OF POLICY], effective [DATE]
2. **Save the policy in its own folder in box.**

    a. The folder should only have one document in it—the most recent effective policy.

    - The policy drafter can decide where this folder should live in box.
    - All drafts and prior versions of the policy should be saved elsewhere (for example, in the hub meeting notes).

3. **Update the Index of Policies and Key Documents** (found at 0 INTERNAL MANUALS)

    a. Direct the user to the folder with the effective policy in it.

    Include date of the effective policy, so the next person updating the handbook will know what they have to update.

APPENDIX H

"Life Happens" Policy

Human Resources Hub ("HR") envisions an organization where individual needs are met, confidentiality and privacy are honored, and the sustainability of our organization is maintained.

Because of Pangea's organizational structure, HR does not have the authority to make individualized exceptions to our policies.* Only the full team can grant such an exception. However, HR encourages requests for exceptions because they help us identify ways in which our existing policies can be improved to benefit the entire team.

A Pangea employee can request an exception to an HR policy by contacting Pangea's Life Happens point person. This person's name will be listed on Pangea's internal task redistribution chart. Upon receiving such a request, the Life Happens point person will share the request with HR.

HR will take the following steps:

1. **Determine whether the request is a request for a reasonable accommodation under applicable law.**

   a. If it is, HR will follow the Reasonable Accommodations Policy.

   b. If it is not, HR will proceed to step 2.

2. **Consider creating or amending a generally applicable policy that addresses the request.**

   a. HR will follow Pangea's policy-making protocols, including getting full-team approval when required. See HR Authority Chart.

---

* See Pangea's Points of Unity in appendix B, "Statement of Values and Principles": "1. We believe that all people are equal in rights and should be free to move. We dream of a world without borders. . . . 5. We treat every person we meet as an individual with a unique story."

- If full-team approval is required, HR will make efforts not to disclose the identity of the requestor to the full team, absent the requestor's approval.

   b. If a policy is created or amended to address the request, the "Life Happens" process is complete.

3. **If creating or amending a policy is impracticable for reasons of time or for any other reason, HR will ask the requestor if they would like proceed to step 4.**

   a. If the requestor says yes, proceed to step 4.

   b. If the requestor says no, the "Life Happens" process is complete. Pangea will not make the requested exception.

4. **Ask the full team to vote on a one-time exception to an existing HR policy.**

   a. If the vote passes, Pangea will make the requested exception.

   b. If the vote fails, Pangea will not make the requested exception.

APPENDIX I

Job Posting

Position Announcement: Experienced Removal Defense Attorney (San Francisco, CA)

[Editor's note: This position was posted in 2022.]

A little about us!

Our vision is to live in a world where people have the right to move and resettle across borders with dignity and respect. We work toward this vision through our mission: defending immigrants against deportation, promoting community education and empowerment, and engaging in policy advocacy. We also work toward this vision internally by building a horizontal, consensus-based organization.

Our team: We started in 2013 with a team of 1.5 and now are 21 (4 based in San Jose and 17 in San Francisco). Our majority POC staff and board of directors are diverse in their migration backgrounds and are extremely supportive of each other. What brings us together is our dedication to our work, each other, and the larger movement for immigrants' rights.

Our work: We operate on three levels: direct legal representation, policy advocacy, and community empowerment and education. Attorneys at Pangea participate in traditional lawyering—zealously representing immigrants in their removal proceedings and appeals. Attorneys also act as movement lawyers—working with clients, their families, grassroots organizers, legislators, and media to create systemic change. Our goal for representation is not only to achieve positive legal outcomes for each client but also to provide our clients with opportunities for politicization and social transformation, thus advancing the larger movement for immigrant justice.

Our offices: Pangea's main office is located in downtown San Francisco near key immigration offices, including the detained and nondetained immigration courts, ICE, USCIS, and the asylum office. Our San Francisco office is also within a few blocks of Muni and BART. Pangea's Santa Clara County office is located in the San José Unified School District office, allowing us to partner with and serve parents, teachers, and students. We work in our physical offices 2 days per week.

Our internal work: Pangea is more than a job; it's an opportunity to become a director and share ownership in an organization that reflects the values we want to see in the world. Over the last 9 years, we have built an organization where everyone receives equal pay, authority is delegated by consensus, and everyone's responsibilities are equally important regardless of organizational role. All employees serve on 1-2 organizational "hubs" that help run, build, and strengthen our organization. After 9 months of employment, new employees are voted on to become co-directors of the organization and voting members of at least one hub. We are committed to continuing to develop our organizational model guided by our social justice ideals, and we invest significant time in its upkeep and growth.

We are hiring an immigration attorney to primarily represent asylum seekers in removal proceedings.

JOB TITLE: IMMIGRATION ATTORNEY
PRIMARY RESPONSIBILITIES

- Represent immigrants in nondetained removal proceedings (primarily asylum seekers)
- Represent clients in I-765, I-730, I-485, and other asylum-adjacent filings
- Create opportunities for clients to share their stories, participate in community empowerment activities, collaborate with organizers and public campaigns, and join the larger movement for immigrant rights
- Help to maintain and grow Pangea as a democratically run organization, and actively participate in 1-2 organizational "hubs"
- Review colleagues' written materials on an ongoing and as-needed basis

REQUIRED SKILLS AND EXPERIENCE

- License to practice law in the United States
- Spanish language proficiency
- Excellent written communication skills

- Attention to detail, while still able to see the big picture
- 8+ years of removal defense experience, 10+ years preferred

BONUS SKILLS AND EXPERIENCE

- Spanish language fluency, proficiency in other languages
- Experience in movement-building/community organizing
- Experience working with survivors of trauma
- Excellent verbal communication skills
- Ability to wear multiple hats and juggle various responsibilities/roles

ALIGNMENT WITH PANGEA'S POINTS OF UNITY

We are looking for someone who can relate to and embody our Points of Unity. These are the internal organizational principles that our team created together in 2015, and we frequently turn to them when creating new policies or making difficult decisions.

- We believe that all people are equal in rights and should be free to move. We dream of a world without borders.
- We were created to fill a gap in free and low-fee deportation defense services.
- We recognize that education, legal empowerment, and policy advocacy are essential to changing perspectives around migration and migrants' rights.
- We believe in the oneness of all people, and we embrace the common humanity of every person; our interactions are guided by love.
- We treat every person we meet as an individual with a unique story.
- We are committed to excellence and providing high-quality services.
- The law is a living document. Its flaws do not constrict us. We use it strategically to ask boldly for the best for our community.
- We are positive and solution oriented. We value fresh attitudes, innovation, and creativity. We challenge conventional thinking in order to redefine what is possible.
- We practice humility. We listen, learn, reflect, evaluate, and grow.
- We value our team's individual and collective well-being. We create mechanisms to support well-roundedness and our team's mental, physical, and spiritual health.

- We recognize a tension between serving as many people in need as possible, taking challenging, legally complex cases, and valuing our own health and well-being. We strive to maintain a balance between these three goals.
- We are committed to equity regarding compensation, responsibilities, and shared ownership.
- We strive to create an organization that is both financially sustainable and autonomous.

All about benefits and compensation.

First 9 months: The first 9 months at Pangea are considered a candidacy period. During this time, an employee receives and absorbs significant training and orientation around our horizontal model. During the candidacy period, an employee is a nonvoting member of the team and receives the same salary as all other teammates (currently $74,000/year).

After 9 months: After successfully completing the sponge period, an employee is voted on as a full member of the team. Their title is updated to that of co-director, and they get voting rights.

IN TERMS OF BENEFITS:

- Staff have a 4-day work week (Mon.–Thurs.), and our physical office is closed Fridays.
- We offer health insurance through Kaiser (Silver Plan) at no cost to staff, and we cover 50% of dependent premiums.
- We offer up to $2,400 in health reimbursements for things like glasses, therapy, or co-pays.
- We offer up to $3,500 in childcare reimbursements.
- We have a Simple IRA plan with an automatic 2% employer contribution.
- We pay for professional membership fees, trainings, coaching, and staff development.
- Our vacation benefits start at 15 days in the first year and increase with tenure up to 25 days per year.
- We close our office for 16 holidays a year, which are aligned with school closures.

Application Instructions.

The start date of this position is flexible. Applications will be accepted on a rolling basis. We will start evaluating applications on November 7, 2022, on a rolling basis. Please submit a cover letter, resume, and three references to jobs@pangealegal.org. In your cover letter, please answer the following two questions:

1. How has your personal background or experiences, professional or otherwise, prepared you for the kind of immigration work Pangea does?

2. What experiences do you have with collectively run organizations, or what draws you to a nonhierarchical organization?

Please indicate "Immigration Attorney Application" in the subject line of your email.

We encourage immigrants and those directly impacted by Pangea's work to apply. Pangea is an equal opportunity employer. We celebrate diversity and are committed to creating an inclusive environment for all employees.

APPENDIX J

Detailed Job Description (Internal)

Job Description of Pangea Bird's-Eye View and Project Coordinator

General overview:

This position is created to 1) support staff wellness and development; 2) enhance and support the work of hubs; and 3) set Pangea up to grow healthily and sustainably. This role will not replace the baseline hub duties and admin work all staff are required to do. This person will be a permanent member of HR and Governance Hubs and will act as a primary delegee for hub tasks and to-dos.

Staff Well-Being and Development - 20%

- Coordinate and execute annual reviews for all 18 staff members
- Revamp and implement our supervision system
- Coordinate resources and trainings for staff professional development, including trainings on community organizing
- Regularly meet with staff to check in on well-being, struggles, needs, desires, projects; research and follow up where needed

Governance Work - 20%

- Coordinate task redistribution
- Coordinate and implement annual budget process
- Identify gaps in our current hub and meeting structures, and help fill them, including internal communication and document sharing

- Plan and carry out all-team meetings (e.g., retreats, compensation discussions, org structure check-ins), including bringing in outside facilitators when necessary
- Act as board liaison or co-lead
- Coprepare and review our taxes with our CPA
- Keep us on track toward 5-year goals
- Create an open source platform online for our policies and internal structure documents with Governance Hub

Organizationwide Coordination - 60%

- Shadow all hubs, membership in HR and Gov Hub; take on 40% of hub tasks and spearhead policy drafts
- Update the handbook annually
- Be the point person for our 10-year anniversary celebration and planning
- Strategize, develop, plan, and implement an individual donor database system with Income Hub
- Spearhead or edit our quarterly newsletter with Comms Hub
- Create structure for all staff to engage clients in ComPA work on a regular basis
- Revamp our website annually by updating pictures, stories, and other content with Comms Hub
- Support conflict resolution and PIP leads in times of need by coordinating with outside contractors and staff, offering research, and securing related resources

APPENDIX K

Candidacy Period Policy

Becoming a Co-Director of Pangea

(Last voted on 6/30/2022; edited 12/29/2022)

To further Point of Unity #6 ("We are committed to excellence and providing high-quality services") and Point of Unity #12 ("We are committed to equity regarding compensation, responsibilities, and shared ownership"), Pangea is creating a policy for when and how a new staff member becomes a full member ("co-director") of Pangea after 9 months of candidacy. "Candidates" are applicants who are invited to work with Pangea on the path to co-directorship.

The primary purpose of candidacy is to support a new staff member's growth toward co-directorship of Pangea. Candidacy is an opportunity for the staff member to develop their job-related skills, receive timely feedback to support their growth, and learn about Pangea's worker-led governance structures and processes.

A secondary purpose of candidacy is to allow both Pangea and the candidate time and opportunity to assess whether we are a good fit for one another before the candidate becomes a co-director, a role that carries significant responsibility and power over the future of Pangea.[*]

Pangea acknowledges that people of color and members of other historically disenfranchised groups have been most negatively impacted by policies that create barriers to access and power. The reason for creating the present policy is to ensure accountability not just for the candidate but for the entire organization. The policy aims to empower candidates by making clear that they will be

---

[*] We call this "candidacy" and not a "probationary" or "trial" period for two reasons. First, as an abolitionist organization, we avoid propagating words and concepts associated with the carceral system. Second, the primary purpose of candidacy is to support the candidate's growth, not to monitor or test the individual, whom Pangea has already hired.

evaluated by the co-directors with whom they have worked most closely; the timeline in which those evaluations occur; and the criteria by which they will be evaluated.

Policy

The first 9 months of employment at Pangea are considered a "candidacy period." During this period, the performance improvement policy and involuntary termination policy do not apply to the new staff member. Instead, the following process applies:

- **Performance Evaluations**
  - Candidates will receive performance evaluations at 3, 6, and 9 months. The evaluation criteria for each candidate will be based on their job description; after the first evaluation, the criteria will include areas of growth identified from prior evaluations. At the 9-month evaluation, additional criteria will be added related to candidates' hub duties, which begin after the first six months.
  - Candidates will be evaluated by their supervisor and the three Pangea co-directors who have worked most closely with them during candidacy. This team will act as a liaison between the full Pangea team and the candidate, supporting communication and feedback in both directions.
  - The same team should conduct the 3-, 6-, and 9-month evaluations. If there is a need to replace an evaluator in between evaluation rounds (such as if an evaluator goes on leave, or if there is a major shift in who the candidate is working with), then the co-director who has worked with the candidate the next most should become the new evaluator.
  - After each of the 3- and 6-month evaluations, the evaluating team will decide whether to continue candidacy. Every member of the evaluating team must vote "yes" in order for the candidate to continue their candidacy.
  - A vote of "yes" to continuing candidacy means:
  1. Confidence in the staff member's ability to fulfill their job description;

2. The candidate has demonstrated alignment with and commitment to Pangea's Points of Unity.

- **A vote of "yes" does not mean** that the candidate does not have room for improvement. It simply means "yes" to criteria 1–2 above.

- **Membership vote**

  - After the 9-month evaluation, the evaluating team will vote on whether the candidate shall become a co-director of Pangea.

  - Every member of the group must vote "yes" in order for the new staff member to become a co-director.

  - **A vote of "yes" means:**

  1. The candidate has demonstrated an ability to fulfill their job description;

  2. The candidate has demonstrated alignment with and commitment to Pangea's Points of Unity;

  3. The candidate has demonstrated readiness toward sharing ownership at Pangea.

  - **A vote of "yes" does not mean** that the candidate does not have room for improvement. It simply means "yes" to criteria 1–3 above.

- **Notification**

  - The candidate will be notified of the result of the vote no later than 48 hours after the vote, and the team no later than one week after the vote.

Disclaimer

- This policy does not affect the fact that all Pangea staff are at-will employees whose employment can be terminated with or without cause.

Notes

- The motivation for this policy is to have the first 9 months of employment be distinct from co-directorship, for the following reasons:

  - It helps ensure our ability to do high-quality work and to function well as a worker-led organization.

- It protects the team from having to make even more difficult decisions later, such as involuntary termination.

- It allows us to hire candidates whose potential we are excited about with confidence, knowing that we will learn more by working with them than we will from their resume, interview, and references.

- Regular evaluations of candidates facilitate the delivery of guidance to candidates and give candidates information they need to make changes the group wants to see. Evaluations create a structured way to communicate feedback, both positive and negative, and facilitate goal setting for candidates. They also provide an opportunity to check in on job fit, assess candidate performance over a specific period of time, and help support change and growth. Evaluations are regularly scheduled, not responses to specific events.

- kiran's advice:

  - Yes/no voting is preferable to the consensus scale (1–8) for hiring and termination decisions.

  - Requiring a unanimous vote creates a bias in favor of *not* making someone a co-director. This is important in worker-led organizations, where each co-director has significant power and responsibility over the direction of the organization.

  - At AORTA, there was a one-year candidacy period for potential worker-owners.

Authority

- HR Hub proposes job candidates to the full team. Full team approval is needed to hire.

- Gov Hub proposes overarching structural changes to Pangea. Full team has to approve.

APPENDIX L

Reference Checks

Reference Check with Rubric for Pangea Legal Services Interns

Dear _____ ,

    X has applied for a [summer law intern] position with Pangea Legal Services. Before we [conduct the interview/make a decision], we'd like to get a quick sense of their work in the categories listed below. I would be grateful if you could indicate how you view this applicant's work and habits. If you would like to add anything, please do. But it's not essential. Thank you.

    Sincerely,

    [Sender's name]

	POOR	OKAY	GOOD	FANTASTIC
Detail Orientation				
Team Work				
Resourcefulness				
Dependability				
Written Communication				

Reference Check Questions for an Immigration Attorney Position

1. In what context did you know X?

2. How does X compare to other immigration attorneys that you've worked with? Would they fall into the top 5% category? Top 20%? 50%? Why?

3. How dependable is X? If given a task, how will they handle it until completion?

4. Can you describe X's written communication?

5. Can you describe X's spoken communication?

6. How does X handle constructive criticism?

   a. Does X ever get defensive?

7. [only if relevant] How self-aware is X?

8. How quickly does X learn new things? How much supervision do they need?

9. What is an area in which X can improve?

10. Would you hire X as a staff attorney if you had the funds? Why or why not?

11. Is there anything I should know before making a hiring decision?

12. Is there anyone else I should talk to before making a hiring decision? Anyone else you know who worked closely with X?

13. If you were going to bring X on as a new hire, what would you do in the first three months to ensure success? Particular to this candidate. Or what would you recommend we do during the first three months if we were to hire this candidate to ensure success?

APPENDIX M

Performance Evaluation
for Co-Directors

Peer assessment provides core staff an opportunity to give feedback to other members of our team. Each staff member has at least three evaluators who will give feedback that ideally acknowledges both effective behavior and areas that might be improved.

In our yearly review process, we value genuine, honest, and kind communication that is transparent, supportive, constructive, and based on clear criteria. Our goals are to foster ongoing professional growth and excellence in a supportive environment.

GUIDANCE

- Reflect on the entire evaluation period (i.e., the whole year, not the last few months).

- Consider all of the criteria separately (i.e., try not to let one issue color the entire evaluation).

- Don't be afraid to use N/A; it may be appropriate for many questions.

- Notice if you have a pattern of weighing toward 1, toward 5, or toward the center. Try to use the whole scale.

- If you mark "needs improvement," try to include specific direction for what improvement would look like (e.g., "Aim to respond to emails within 24 hours" vs. "You're terrible at email").

Goals from the Previous Evaluation Period

These goals will be sent in a separate email. Please reflect on the goals that this person sent out last year. How well is this person meeting their goals from the last evaluation period? Check all that apply.

	1	2	3	4	5
Goal 1					
Goal 2					
[Add goals as needed]					

KEY: 1—No growth or improvement, 2—Some growth/improvement; needs improvement, 3—Good growth/improvement; still room to grow, 4—Goal was met, 5—Fantastic; goal exceeded

Goals Elaboration

Please try to elaborate on the person's previously stated goals and/or give at least one specific comment about their performance and your evaluation metrics.

Legal Services

Legal Services: Attorney

Does this attorney . . .

	N/A	1	2	3	4	5
. . . write clearly, concisely, and effectively? This includes writing briefs, declarations, and memos, and conducting the corresponding fact development and legal research to make that writing effective.						

	N/A	1	2	3	4	5
. . . prepare themselves and their client(s) to speak capably in court? This includes anticipating and practicing questions and arguments from the judge and opposing counsel, and intervening adequately during hearings.						
. . . assess their cases for potential public campaigns and coordinate with internal and external partners to execute campaigns?						
. . . communicate with their clients in a clear, responsive, and empowering manner? This includes communicating effectively in Spanish or other languages, conferring with clients about strategy decisions, communicating important dates, adequately preparing clients for interviews and hearings, and responding to current client inquiries.						
. . . communicate effectively with outside entities? This includes identifying and contacting relevant agencies, courts, hospitals, friends/family members, etc. to obtain documents and information; and advocating in a persuasive and professional manner even in challenging situations.						
. . . keep track of case deadlines, prioritize work tasks accordingly, and prepare materials with enough time in advance for adequate supervisory review(s) before a filing deadline?						
. . . maintain records and enter data in a timely and organized manner? This includes updating the workflow management platform, case lists, and case notes, and keeping up with and filing mail.						
. . . express their case-related expectations, assignments, and/or instructions in a clear, concise, and timely manner to other staff?						
. . . carry a caseload and deliver a work product that are comparable with other staff who are similarly situated, and follow Pangea's relevant protocols and policies around caseloads?						
. . . review and edit their fellow attorneys' work?						
. . . attend legal trainings (including mentorship) to continue improving their legal skills?						

KEY: N/A—I don't have enough information to answer, 1—Needs major work, 2—Needs improvement, 3—Good, room to grow, 4—Great, doing well on this, 5—Fantastic, exceeded goal

Legal Services: Paralegal

Does this paralegal . . .

	N/A	1	2	3	4	5
. . . write (e.g., declarations and motions) in a clear and concise manner?						
. . . translate case-related documents and interpret verbal communications accurately and in a timely manner?						
. . . communicate effectively with outside entities? This includes identifying and contacting relevant agencies, courts, hospitals, friends/family members, etc. to obtain documents and information; and advocating in a persuasive and professional manner even in challenging situations.						
. . . maintain records and enter data in a timely and organized manner? This includes updating the workflow management platform, case lists, and case notes, and filing mail as assigned.						
. . . communicate information to clients in a clear and timely manner? This includes communicating effectively in Spanish or other languages.						
. . . keep track of internal deadlines, prioritize work tasks accordingly, and prepare materials with enough time in advance for adequate supervisory review(s) before a filing deadline?						
. . . communicate information obtained from clients or outside entities to the primary attorney in a timely manner?						
. . . carry a caseload and work product comparable with other staff who are similarly situated, and follow Pangea's relevant protocols and policies around caseloads?						

KEY: N/A—I don't have enough information to answer, 1—Needs major work, 2—Needs improvement, 3—Good, room to grow, 4—Great, doing well on this, 5—Fantastic, exceeded goal

Legal Services: Front Desk

Does this front desk staff . . .

	N/A	1	2	3	4	5
. . . ensure that callers and walk-ins are able to contact Pangea? This includes ensuring that all callers are able to leave a voicemail and are called back at least once, and that the SF office front desk is staffed Mon.-Thurs. during business hours.						
. . . screen and schedule consultations according to Pangea's case priorities and collect necessary documentation for attorney review?						
. . . communicate with clients and visitors over the phone and in person in a professional and compassionate manner?						
. . . process incoming mail, faxes, and packages promptly and accurately? This includes promptly informing clients and their primary attorney about scheduled biometrics appointments and ensuring clients have a physical copy of the appointment notice.						

KEY: N/A—I don't have enough information to answer, 1—Needs major work, 2—Needs improvement, 3—Good, room to grow, 4—Great, doing well on this, 5—Fantastic, exceeded goal

Comments on Legal Services

Please try to give at least one specific comment about their performance, and/or feel free to explain your your previous evaluation metrics.

Community Empowerment for Non-Organizers

Does this person . . .

	N/A	1	2	3	4	5
. . . maintain relationships with coalition partners?						
. . . involve clients in the community?						

KEY: N/A—I don't have enough information to answer, 1—Needs major work, 2—Needs improvement, 3—Good, room to grow, 4—Great, doing well on this, 5—Fantastic, exceeded goal

Comments on Community Empowerment Work

Please try to give at least one specific comment about their performance, and/ or feel free to explain your evaluation metrics.

Community Empowerment and Policy Advocacy

Community Empowerment and Policy Advocacy: Organizers

Does this organizer . . .

	N/A	1	2	3	4	5
. . . hold one-on-one meetings with directly impacted individuals and their families on a regular and consistent basis?						
. . . hold meetings, workshops, and trainings for directly impacted persons to develop and lead campaign strategies (e.g., to close all detention centers)?						
. . . actively recruit new directly impacted individuals (including nonclients, when relevant) to build and grow our base?						

	N/A	1	2	3	4	5
. . . create and/or seek out popular education tools and materials to engage and train individuals?						
. . . plan and coordinate "train the trainer" workshops to support directly impacted leaders to develop other leaders?						
. . . communicate with their clients in a clear, responsive, and empowering manner? This includes communicating effectively in Spanish or other languages; conferring with clients about strategy decisions and important dates; adequately preparing clients for interviews and hearings; and responding to current client inquiries.						
. . . build and maintain relationships with coalition partners?						
. . . keep the team updated about advocacy projects?						
. . . bring opportunities to the Pangea team to involve clients and directly impacted individuals in policy advocacy?						
. . . communicate Pangea's position on advocacy issues effectively in coalition meetings and sign-on proposals?						
. . . carry a caseload and work product comparable with other staff who are similarly situated, and follow Pangea's relevant protocols and policies around caseloads?						

KEY: N/A—I don't have enough information to answer, 1—Needs major work, 2—Needs improvement, 3—Good, room to grow, 4—Great, doing well on this, 5—Fantastic, exceeded goal

Comments on Community Empowerment and Policy Advocacy

Please try to give at least one specific comment about their performance, and/ or feel free to explain your previous evaluation metrics.

Bird's-Eye View Coordinator

Does the Bird's-Eye View Coordinator . . .

	N/A	1	2	3	4	5
. . . support the well-being and development of staff?						
. . . map roles and ensure organizational health and efficiency?						
. . . build up Pangea's practices around communication and transparency?						
. . . fine-tune our old structures and develop new ones to meet our needs as we grow?						
. . . hold big-picture goals like our strategic plan, and hold staff accountable to them?						
. . . connect dots, pause, redirect traffic, and ask us to slow down where needed?						
. . . coordinate and execute annual reviews for all staff members?						
. . . coordinate revamping and implementing our supervision system?						
. . . plan and carry out all-team meetings (e.g., retreats, compensation discussions, org structure check-ins), including bringing in outside facilitators when necessary?						
. . . lead work on the open source platform online for our policies and internal structure documents with Governance Hub?						
. . . shadow all hubs, with membership in HR and Gov Hub; take on 40 percent of hub tasks; and spearhead policy drafts?						
. . . serve as the point person for our ten-year anniversary celebration and planning?						

KEY: N/A—I don't have enough information to answer, 1—Needs major work, 2—Needs improvement, 3—Good, room to grow, 4—Great, doing well on this, 5—Fantastic, exceeded goal

Comments on Bird's-Eye View Coordinator

Please try to give at least one specific comment about their performance, and/or feel free to explain your previous evaluation metrics.

Core Staff Responsibilities

Governance Duties and Organizational Stewardship

Does this person . . .

	N/A	1	2	3	4	5
. . . follow Pangea's processes and protocols?						
. . . follow Pangea's decision-making process and structure?						
. . . keep the team updated on work and projects: hub, policy, advocacy, program duties, etc?						
. . . share important information with the team?						
. . . participate in meetings (hub, staff, etc.)?						
. . . share opinions openly and honestly?						
. . . work to ensure others are heard/able to share?						
. . . bring a positive and solution-based approach to problem-solving and change?						
. . . respond with openness and curiosity when people disagree?						
. . . anticipate organizational needs and demonstrate big-picture thinking about Pangea?						
. . . take initiative in researching and seeking outside expertise when we need help?						
. . . develop resources responsive to group needs, e.g., internal policies, organizational structures, handouts, curriculum, and manuals?						
. . . help others take the lead/show an ability to follow the leadership of others?						

KEY: N/A—I don't have enough information to answer, 1—Needs major work, 2—Needs improvement, 3—Good, room to grow, 4—Great, doing well on this, 5—Fantastic, exceeded goal

Elaboration on Governance Duties and Organizational Stewardship

Please try to elaborate on the performance metrics chosen above, and/or give at least one specific comment about their performance.

_____

_____

Responsibility to the Team

Does this person . . .

	N/A	1	2	3	4	5
. . . strive to create harmonious working relationships?						
. . . solicit and hear constructuve feedback with minimal reactivity or defensiveness?						
. . . integrate constructive criticism/demonstrate growth from feedback?						
. . . offer supportive yet constructive feedback to coworkers?						
. . . help others with their work?						
. . . notice, name, and appreciate the contributions of others?						
. . . practice setting healthy boundaries, not acting as a martyr or holding resentment?						
. . . trust others when they take on responsibility?						
. . . effectively communicate thoughts verbally (noncase work)?						
. . . effectively communicate thoughts in writing (noncase work)?						

KEY: N/A—I don't have enough information to answer, 1—Needs major work, 2—Needs improvement, 3—Good, room to grow, 4—Great, doing well on this, 5—Fantastic, exceeded goal

Elaboration on Responsibility to the Team

Please try to elaborate on the performance metrics chosen above, and/or give at least one specific comment about their performance.

_____

_____

Reliability

Does this person . . .

	N/A	1	2	3	4	5
. . . demonstrate timely and reliable communication?						
. . . volunteer for tasks?						
. . . follow through on tasks, commitments, and delegations?						
. . . demonstrate reliable punctuality?						
. . . show attention to detail?						
. . . meet team deadlines?						

KEY: N/A—I don't have enough information to answer, 1—Needs major work, 2—Needs improvement, 3—Good, room to grow, 4—Great, doing well on this, 5—Fantastic, exceeded goal

Elaboration on Reliability

Please try to elaborate on the performance metrics chosen above, and/or give at least one specific comment about their performance.

Embodiment of Pangea's Points of Unity

Listed below are Pangea's Points of Unity:

1. We believe that all people are equal in rights and should be free to move. We dream of a world without borders.
2. We were created to fill a gap in free and low-fee deportation defense services.
3. We recognize that education, legal empowerment, and policy advocacy are essential to changing perspectives around migration and migrants' rights.

4. We believe in the oneness of all people, and we embrace the common humanity of every person; our interactions are guided by love.

5. We treat every person we meet as an individual with a unique story.

6. We are committed to excellence and providing high-quality services.

7. The law is a living document. Its flaws do not constrict us. We use it strategically to ask boldly for the best for our community.

8. We are positive and solution oriented. We value fresh attitudes, innovation, and creativity. We challenge conventional thinking in order to redefine what is possible.

9. We practice humility. We listen, learn, reflect, evaluate, and grow.

10. We value our team's individual and collective well-being. We create mechanisms to support well-roundedness and our team's mental, physical, and spiritual health.

11. We recognize a tension between serving as many people in need as possible, taking challenging, legally complex cases, and valuing our own health and well-being. We strive to maintain a balance between these three goals.

12. We are committed to equity regarding compensation, responsibilities, and shared ownership.

13. We strive to create an organization that is both financially sustainable and autonomous.

Elaboration on Embodiment of Pangea's Points of Unity

How well does this person embody these Points of Unity? You may provide a general response and/or list any points that they embody particularly well or can improve on embodying.

_____

_____

Job Description and Workload

Please review this person's most recent job description throughly before answering the following questions.

Does this job description feel relevant, appropriate, and descriptive of what this person actually does? If not, what would you change?

_____

_____

Does this person have the tools and skills they need to achieve this job description? If not, what support or resources do you think they needed?

_____

_____

WHAT IS YOUR OPINION OF THIS PERSON'S WORKLOAD?

O Too low, needs adjustment

O Low

O Appropriate

O High

O Too high, needs adjustment

O N/A, I don't have enough information to answer this question

Are this person's time, skills, expertise, and interest/passions being used to the best benefit of the organization? If not, what shifts would you suggest?

_____

_____

Any additional comments on job description or workload?

_____

_____

Additional Questions

- What are the major strengths and contributions this person added to the organization over the last evaluation period? (Name up to three.)
- Where does this person most need to improve? What direction can you share on what improvement may look like? (Name up to three.)
- What advice would you give this coworker?
- Do you have any concerns about this person violating Pangea's policies or rules? (If yes, please explain.)
- Any additional comments?

Evaluation Suggestions

Please share any suggestions you may have for how we may improve our evaluation process.

_____

_____

APPENDIX N

Feedback Preference Chart

INSTRUCTION: EACH STAFF TO ENTER THEIR OWN PREFERENCE

- **Name:** *enter your name, e.g.*: Nilou

- **Place:** *enter where you'd like to receive feedback (by email, phone, in person, etc.), e.g.*: I prefer to receive feedback by Zoom or in person so I can both see and hear the emotions and tone of the conversation.

- **Manner:** *enter how you like to receive feedback, e.g.*: I would like feedback to be direct and simple, not sugarcoated. I prefer to get a heads up that feedback is coming by email with a few words describing the context or topic of the discussion. (For example, "Hi Nilou, I have some feedback for you regarding what you said in our staff meeting last week. I saw on your chart that you prefer a conversation by Zoom or in person. I see that we will both be in the office on Friday. Would that day work for you?")

- **Timing:** *enter how much notice you'd like, e.g.*: I would like to receive most feedback in real time or as early when relevant as possible. If it's a bigger issue, I would like to get a heads up, schedule a time to meet to receive the feedback, and then either have an opportunity to respond right away or have a day to think about it and then follow up.

ACKNOWLEDGMENTS

This book reflects the collective insights and labor of my incredible community. It exists because of many contributions, thoughtful guidance, and generous support. Each name here holds a place in this journey, and for anyone I may have missed, I ask for your understanding and hope you feel my deep gratitude.

Support on the Book

JAZMÍN DELGADO-SHAH For your exceptional editorial support, thoughtful insights, and tireless work in reshaping the first draft manuscript. Your ability to hold and honor so many perspectives has been an invaluable gift.

SHEILA QUINTANA AGUILAR For your hands-on guidance in transforming the second draft manuscript and for the profound lessons you shared along the way.

DEBRA OLLIVIER For your thoughtful writing support and exceptional skill in refining and reorganizing the third draft manuscript.

ARYN BRITTANY HONIG For your thorough research and invaluable writing support.

TAMILA GRESHAM For being a magician! And for reorganizing and editing the final draft manuscript with so much expertise and care.

RACHEL NEUMANN AND THE WAVE LITERARY TEAM   For believing in this work, connecting me to resources, and offering guidance at every step.

THE NORTH ATLANTIC BOOKS TEAM (TIM MCKEE, JASMINE RESPESS, TRISHA PECK, BRENT WINTER, JOE FINLAW, JULIA SADOWSKI)   Thank you for your trust in this work and bringing this book to life. Your values alignment, care, and enthusiasm for this work have been incredibly encouraging.

ADDITIONAL THANKS TO   Abdi Soltani, Bella Roberts, Edgar Zaragoza Guzman, Efrén Olivares, Elica Vafaei, Hossein Tajik, Kabir Bavikatte, Katie Dilks, Kristina Lorch, Matthew Parker, Meredith Bell, Nancy Wiltzek, Negar Tayyar, Nicholas Doctor, Riane Briones, Suzanne Rotondo, Sydney Rogers, Teresa Vargas, Tirien Steinbach, Ufot Umana, Jr., Zach Norris, and the team at New Degree Press.

Interviewees

Thank you to those who shared your wisdom and time: Anders Fremstad, Areca Smit, Ananda Valenzuela, Charlie Harding, Chris Tittle, Janelle Orsi, Jenna Peters-Golden, Kendal Nystedt, Liliana Plumeda, Maria de Lordes Diaz Cruz, Marc Swan, Margi Clarke, Marisela Ortega, Mateo Nube, Melody Martinez, Nadia Qurashi, Nicole Wires, Rek Kwawer, Rob Everts, Roshni Sampath, Sheena Wadhawan, Simon Mont, Targol Mesbah, Tecolocoyotl, and Vanessa Vichit-Vadakan.

Pangea Colleagues & Partners

To my former colleagues and close partners at Pangea, our collective leadership and dedication shaped this journey, and many also shared your insights as interviewees for this book. The contributions listed here barely scratch the surface of all there is to thank you for – I am deeply grateful for the many ways you brought our work and shared vision to fruition:

MARIE VINCENT   Your teachings, wisdom, and gifts are beyond words; thank you for being a thought partner and like a sister to me.

BIANCA ZAMBELLO SANTOS   Your wisdom, thoughtful editing, and meticulous fact-checking strengthened this book in countless ways. Thank you for being a cherished and enduring friend and thought partner.

KIRAN NIGAM   For your expertise, care, and guidance in collective governance from the beginning.

ESPERANZA CUAUTLE   For always grounding us in our values and collective care, especially during moments of struggle, and for your consistent organizing and ability to bring community together in meaningful ways.

CELINE DINHJANELLE   For advocating for boundaries while modeling them with care and grace.

SHELBY MALVOSO   For your teachings, generosity, and meticulous care in maintaining clean financial records, the invisible yet essential labor that supported us since the very beginning.

LUIS ANGEL REYES SAVALZA   For creating a political home for us.

SEAN LAI MCMAHON   For your calm leadership and focus through the storms.

JESUS RUIZ DIEGO   For lifting up the power of organizing, hope, and persistence - both on Pangea's board and on staff.

LORENA MELGAREJO   For your loving partnership, showing us the magic of community organizing, and turning impossible dreams into reality.

Also, heartfelt thanks to Adoubou Traore, Adriana Guzman, Alejandra Hilsaca, Ambri Pukhraj, Ana Avalos, Ana Builes, Anny Patino, Bernardo Merino, Blanca Vazquez, Caitlin Bellis, Cara Jobson, Charles Jackson, Claire Solot, Dalia Nava Jacobo, David Bennion, Dulce Guerrero, Etan Newman, Eunice Hernandez, Gerardo Gomez, Gladys Hernandez, Irma Wilson, Jeff Adachi (rest in power), Jehan Laner Romero, Jessica Yamane Moraga, Joe Sciarrillo, Joseline Gonzalez, John Pingel, Juan Camilo Mendez Guzman, Katie Lynn Anderson, Kiki Tapiero, Laila Ayub, Leslie Dorosin, Madahy Mendoza, Manuel Santamaria, Maria Palacios (*a.k.a.*, "the Goddess on Wheels"), Mariel Villarreal, Marili Iturde Guadarrama, Maya Karp, Mohammed Abdollahi, Nallely Romayor Reynoso, Pete Weiss, Railyn Aguado, Rev. Deb Lee, Roxana Moussavian, Saamia Haqiq, Sandy Valenciano, Sara Campos, Sara Hundt, Tessa Trouverol Callejo, Valerie Edwards, Vanessa Godinez, Victoria Sun, Wogai Mohmand, Ximena Valdarrago, Yadira Sanchez, and Yvette Borja.

Pangea Board of Directors & Key Advisors

To our board members and advisors, your expertise, encouragement, and belief in this work have been invaluable. Thank you:

MICHELLE GAUDET   For your encouragement, strong values, and helping us build a solid foundation.

BILL ONG HING   For your invaluable time, guidance, connections and generous support – both in our work and in the creation of this book.

LEAH CHEN PRICE   For your thought partnership, committed work, and boundless energy.

ELAINE ORR   For your wisdom, resourcefulness, and connections.

GEORGE MADRIGAL   For your financial insights, kindness, and teachings.

LEO KURTYSH   For your invaluable contributions to our systems and infrastructure.

ORLANDO MONTALVO   Your enthusiasm and kindness mean so much.

SUMAN MURTHY   For your vital role in improving our communications systems and providing hands-on support.

SARA STEPHENS   For elevating our collective governance structure at the board level.

JEN KARLIN   Thank you for your research, guidance, and support.

KRISTI TARNSTROM   For your time, insights, and hands-on support in our start up phase.

RYAN STAHL   Thank you for your behind-the-scenes advice and "worst-case scenario" warnings that helped us make informed decisions.

VIVEK MARU   For your early advising, connections, and invaluable guidance.

ANGELA CHAN, CHRISTINE STOUFFER, FRANK POCIANO, JON RODNEY, LAURA LUCAS, MARK SILVERMAN, RAHA JORJANI, ZAHRA BILLOO   Thank you for your collective insights, dedication, and support throughout Pangea's journey.

To my family and friends: Thank you for your endless love, patience, and encouragement. Your belief in me, your steady presence, and your warmth have been my foundation through this book journey and beyond. I feel lucky to get to move through life with you.

HOW TO SUPPORT
The Future Is Collective

First off, thank you. Thank you for being here, for engaging with this work, and for believing in the power of collective leadership and cultures of care. This book isn't just mine; it belongs to all of us building toward something different, something more just, more liberatory, more human.

If *The Future Is Collective* resonates with you here is an invitation to help spread the word and bring these ideas and tools to more people:

1. **Share on social media.** Post about the book on LinkedIn, Instagram, Facebook, BlueSky, or X. Share a quote that moved you, a key takeaway, or how you're applying the ideas in real time. Take a photo of the book, highlight your favorite section or tool, or share a passage that resonates. Tag me so I can join the conversation! (Example: "Just finished The Future Is Collective by @NilouKhonsari. It's giving me so much to think about when it comes to shared leadership and care in the workplace!")

2. **Write a book review.** Reviews help others find the book! If you found *The Future Is Collective* valuable, consider writing a short review on **Amazon, StoryGraph, Goodreads, Bookshop.org,** or wherever you purchase and review books online. A few sentences about what resonated with you can make a big difference. You can also add the book to your "Want to Read" list.

3. **Host a conversation.** Gather a few folks for a book club, a staff discussion, or a community dialogue on shared leadership and collective care. Let's make these ideas real and actionable together.

4. **Invite me to speak.** I love being in conversation with teams, organizations, and movements figuring out how to do this work in practice. If a talk, workshop, or fireside chat would be useful, let's make it happen.

5. **Buy the book.** For yourself, for a friend, for your leadership team, for that one person in your life who keeps talking about "a better way" but isn't sure where to start. Every purchase helps amplify this work.

6. **Ask your local bookstore or library to carry it.** This helps make the book more accessible to folks who might not otherwise find it.

7. **Recommend it to funders and philanthropic networks.** If you're connected to funders, donors, or networks invested in reimagining leadership and capacity building, I'd love for this book to be part of the conversation.

8. **Let me know how it lands for you.** I want to hear what resonates, what sparks ideas, what shifts how you approach your work. Your insights, stories, and reflections keep this conversation alive.

Every bit of support—big or small—helps create momentum around this work. If *The Future Is Collective* speaks to you, let's get it into the hands of those who need it most.

Much love,
Nilou

NOTES

Introduction

1 Diomande, Mantin. "Did Nonprofit Leadership Become More Racially Diverse After 2020?" *Candid*, May 2, 2024. *https://blog.candid.org/post/is-nonprofit-leadership-more-diverse-after-2020-demographic-data-insights.*

2 OnePoll. "Vagaro: Self-Care Habits." December 2020. *https://www.onepoll.us/portfolio/vagaro-self-care-habits/.*

3 Fuller, Joseph, and William Kerr. "The Great Resignation Didn't Start with the Pandemic." *Harvard Business Review*, March 23, 2020. *https://hbr.org/2022/03/the-great-resignation-didnt-start-with-the-pandemic.*

4 Higgins, Eoin. "As the World Burns, Organizers Are Burning Out." *The Nation*, July 28, 2022. *https://www.thenation.com/article/activism/organizer-burnout/.*

Chapter 1: From Revolution to Evolution

1 "Immigration Enforcement Actions: 2012." Accessed October 28, 2024. *https://www.dhs.gov/sites/default/files/publications/Enforcement_Actions_2012.pdf.*

2 "Detention Quotas." Detention Watch Network, March 21, 2022. *https://www.detentionwatchnetwork.org/issues/detention-quotas.*

3 Pangea Legal Services. "Breaking: Dreamer Jesus Ruiz Freed from ICE Detention After 90 Days, but Still Facing Deportation." December 19, 2012. *https://www.pangealegal.org/news-and-updates/2012/12/18/breaking-dreamer-jesus-ruiz-freed-from-ice-detention-after-90-days-but-still-facing-deportation.*

4 Gordon Nembhard, Jessica. *Collective Courage: A History of African American Cooperative Economic Thought and Practice.* University Park: Penn State University Press, 2024.

5 Wires, Nicole. "Making Economic Democracy Work: How to Practice Shared Leadership." *Nonprofit Quarterly*, November 28, 2023. *https://nonprofitquarterly.org/making-economic-democracy-work-how-to-practice-shared-leadership/.*

6 Pangea Legal Services. "Mission & Vision." Accessed October 9, 2024. *https:// www.pangealegal.org/mission-and-vision*.

7 Le, Vu. "The Default Nonprofit Board Model Is Archaic and Toxic; Let's Try Some New Models." *Nonprofit AF*, July 6, 2020. *https://nonprofitaf.com/2020/07 /the-default-nonprofit-board-model-is-archaic-and-toxic-lets-try-some-new-models/*.

8 Tittle, Chris. "Workplace Democracy in Nonprofit Organizations." Sustainable Economies Law Center, June 3, 2015. *https://www.theselc.org/workplace _democracy_in_nonprofit_organizations*.

9 Hicks, Kendra. "Resist as a Worker Self-Directed Nonprofit: Part One." Medium, January 3, 2019. *https://medium.com/@ResistFoundation/resist-as-a-worker-self -directed-nonprofit-part-one-6746a5ce51b7*.

10 Le, "Default Nonprofit Board Model."

11 California Code, CORP 5210. Accessed October 28, 2024. *https://leginfo.legislature .ca.gov/faces/codes_displaySection.xhtml?lawCode=CORP&sectionNum=5210*.

12 Le, "Default Nonprofit Board Model."

13 Le, "Default Nonprofit Board Model."

14 Robert, Henry M., Daniel H. Honemann, Thomas J. Balch, Daniel E. Seabold, and Shmuel Gerber. *Robert's Rules of Order: Newly Revised*. New York: Public Affairs, 2020.

15 Dallaire, Rachelle. "In Indigenous Nonprofit Governance, Values Matter More Than Tools." Imagine Canada. Accessed October 9, 2024. *https://imaginecanada .ca/en/360/In-Indigenous-nonprofit-governance-values-matter-more-than-tools*.

16 Dallaire, "Indigenous Nonprofit Governance."

17 Dallaire, "Indigenous Nonprofit Governance."

Chapter 2: Learning to Share Power

1 Balch, Oliver. "New Hope for Argentina in the Recovered Factory Movement." *The Guardian*, March 12, 2013. *https://www.theguardian.com/sustainable-business /argentina-recovered-factory-movement*.

2 Piellusch, Michael. "Is the 'Chain of Command' Still Meaningful?" *War Room*, February 13, 2023. *https://warroom.armywarcollege.edu/articles/chain-of-command/*.

3 Mueller, Carol. "Ella Baker and Origins of Participatory Democracy." Accessed October 9, 2024. *https://collectiveliberation.org/wp-content/uploads/2013/01 /Mueller-Ella-Baker-and-origins-of-participatory-democracy.pdf*.

4 Gordon Nembhard, Jessica. *Collective Courage: A History of African American Cooperative Economic Thought and Practice*. University Park: Penn State University Press, 2024.

5 Romeo, Nick. "How Mondragon Became the World's Largest Co-Op." *The New Yorker*, August 27, 2022. *https://www.newyorker.com/business/currency/how-mondragon -became-the-worlds-largest-co-op*.

6 Romeo, "World's Largest Co-Op."

7 Endenburg, Gerard. *Sociocracy: The Organization of Decision-Making*. Delft: Eburon, 1998.

8 Laloux, Frédéric, and Ken Wilber. *Reinventing Organizations: A Guide to Creating Organizations Inspired by the Next Stage of Human Consciousness*. Brussels: Nelson Parker, 2014.

9 Prentice, Jessica. "The Most Dangerous Notion in 'Reinventing Organizations.'" Medium, May 25, 2016. *https://medium.com/@jessicajprentice/the-most-dangerous -notion-in-reinventing-organizations-9032930295e2*.

10 Kimmerer, Robin Wall. *Braiding Sweetgrass*. Minneapolis: Milkweed Editions, 2022.

Chapter 3: Equity-Based Salaries

1 "Systemic Racism and the Gender Pay Gap: A Supplement to the Simple Truth." AAUW, n.d. Accessed January 16, 2025. *https://www.aauw.org/app/uploads /2021/07/SimpleTruth_4.0-1.pdf*.

2 Guzman, Gloria. "Median Income of Non-Hispanic White Households Increased While Asian, Black and Hispanic Median Household Income Did Not Change." United States Census Bureau, September 10, 2024. *https://www.census.gov/library /stories/2024/09/household-income-race-hispanic.html*.

3 Brown, Madeline, Mingli Zhong, Signe-Mary McKernan, Apueela Wekulom, Michael Neal, Ofronama Biu, Damir Cosic, et al. "Nine Charts About Wealth Inequality in America." Urban Institute, April 25, 2024. *https://apps.urban.org /features/wealth-inequality-charts/*.

4 Konish, Lorie. "63% of Workers Unable to Pay a $500 Emergency Expense, Survey Finds. How Employers May Help Change That." CNBC, August 31, 2023. *https://www.cnbc.com/2023/08/31/63percent-of-workers-are-unable-to -pay-a-500-emergency-expense-survey.html*.

5 Baldwin, James. *Nobody Knows My Name*. New York: Knopf Doubleday, 2013.

6 Steele, James, and Lance Williams. "Who Got Rich off the Student Debt Crisis?" *Reveal News*, June 28, 2016. *https://revealnews.org/article/who-got-rich-off-the -student-debt-crisis/*.

7 Mananzala, Rickke, and Dean Spade. "The Nonprofit Industrial Complex and Trans Resistance." *Sexuality Research & Social Policy* 5 (2008): 53–71.

8 Mananzala and Spade, "The Nonprofit Industrial Complex."

9 Auger-Domínguez, Daisy. *Inclusion Revolution: The Essential Guide to Dismantling Racial Inequity in the Workplace*, 176. New York: John Wiley & Sons, 2024.

10 Tittle, Chris. "The People Who Don't Go to Law School, Part 3: Growing The Farm Workers' Movement." Like Lincoln, August 12, 2014. *https://like lincoln.org/the-people-who-dont-go-to-law-school-part-3-growing-the-farm-workers -movement/*.

Chapter 4: Cultivating a Culture of Care

1 Lorde, Audre. *Sister Outsider: Essays and Speeches*. Berkeley, CA: Crossing Press, 2012.

2 Ablaza Wills, Sammie. "Right-Sized Belonging: Six Practices for Organizers." *Convergence*, February 13, 2024. *https://convergencemag.com/articles/right-sized -belonging-six-practices-for-organizers/*.

3 Wikipedia contributors, "Bani Adam," *Wikipedia, The Free Encyclopedia,* https:// en.wikipedia.org/w/index.php?title=Bani_Adam&oldid=1277297391 (accessed April 2, 2025).

4 Tawwab, Nedra Glover. *Set Boundaries, Find Peace: A Guide to Reclaiming Yourself,* 222. New York: Penguin, 2021.

5 Woods-Giscombe, Cheryl, Millicent Nicolle Robinson, Dana Carthon, Stephanie Devane-Johnson, and Giselle Corbie-Smith. "Superwoman Schema, Stigma, Spirituality, and Culturally Sensitive Providers: Factors Influencing African American Women's Use of Mental Health Services." *Journal of Best Practices in Health Professions Diversity* 9, no. 1 (2016): 1124.

6 *APA Dictionary of Psychology*. "Boundary." Updated April 19, 2018. *https://dictionary .apa.org/boundary*.

7 Tawwab, *Set Boundaries*, 222.

8 Dinesh, Shradha. "More Than 4 in 10 U.S. Workers Don't Take All Their Paid Time Off." Pew Research Center, August 10, 2023. *https://www.pewresearch.org /short-reads/2023/08/10/more-than-4-in-10-u-s-workers-dont-take-all-their-paid -time-off/*.

9 Hemphill, Prentis. "A Reminder. Boundaries Are the Distance at Which I Can Love You and Me Simultaneously.'" Instagram. Accessed October 28, 2024. *https://www.instagram.com/prentishemphill/p/CNSzFO1A21C/?hl=en*.

10 Penn State Workplace Emotional Labor and Diversity Lab. "What Is Emotional Labor?" Accessed January 19, 2025. *https://weld.la.psu.edu/what-is-emotional -labor/*.

11 Garcia Zacarius, Irani. "Opinion: I Walked Through the Desert to Make It to America. Then They Took Me to the Icebox." *BuzzFeed News*, August 17, 2019. *https://www.buzzfeednews.com/article/iranizacarias/first-desert-then-ice -box-hielara*.

12 Gionta, Dana. "The Win-Win of Healthy Workplace Boundaries." *Psychology Today*, March 4, 2023. *https://www.psychologytoday.com/intl/blog/living-better-with -boundaries/202303/the-win-win-of-healthy-workplace-boundaries*.

13 Denhem Smith, Dina, and Alicia A. Grandey. "The Emotional Labor of Being a Leader." *Harvard Business Review*, November 2, 2022. *https://hbr.org/2022/11/the -emotional-labor-of-being-a-leader*.

Chapter 5: A Structure for Our Culture

1 Mitchell, Maurice. "Building Resilient Organizations." The Forge, November 29, 2022. *https://forgeorganizing.org/article/building-resilient-organizations*.

2 Pangea Legal Services. "Horizontal Structure." Accessed December 9, 2024. *https://www.pangealegal.org/horizontal-structure.*

3 brown, adrienne maree. *Emergent Strategy: Shaping Change, Changing Worlds.* Chico, CA: AK Press, 2017.

4 brown, *Emergent Strategy*, 24.

5 Kalli, Bitter. "Good Mud: A Conversation with Vivien Sansour, on Seeds and Liberation." Groundwater, November 21, 2023. *https://groundwater.substack.com/p /good-mud-a-conversation-with-vivien.*

6 brown, *Emergent Strategy*, 13.

7 Endenburg, Gerard. *Sociocracy: The Organization of Decision-Making.* Delft: Eburon, 1998.

8 Bower, Bruce. "Indigenous Americans Ruled Democratically Long before the U.S. Did." *Science News*, September 6, 2022. *https://www.sciencenews.org/article /democracy-indigenous-americans-people-rule-muscogee.*

9 Baldwin, Christina, and Ann Linnea. "The Circle Way by Christina Baldwin and Ann Linnea (BK Business Book)." Posted March 16, 2010, by Berrett Koehler Publishers. YouTube, 3:11. *https://youtu.be/vfQGUJjEduY?si=Db9NwNKpTZJExaow.*

10 Kaminski, June. "Theory: Talking Circles." First Nations Pedagogy, 2011. *https:// firstnationspedagogy.com/talkingcircles.html.*

11 Kaminski, "Theory: Talking Circles."

12 Pangea Legal Services. "Horizontal Structure."

13 Laloux, Frédéric, and Ken Wilber. *Reinventing Organizations: A Guide to Creating Organizations Inspired by the Next Stage of Human Consciousness.* Brussels: Nelson Parker, 2014.

Chapter 6: Collective Care Through Policy

1 AORTA. Client Spotlight: Proinspire, second slide. Instagram, May 9, 2024. *https://www.instagram.com/p/C6wb7nZBtDU/?utm_source=ig_web_copy _link&igsh=MzRlODBiNWFlZA==.*

2 Bernstein, Ethan, Tatiana Sandino, Joost Minnaar, and Annelena Lobb. "Buurtzorg." Boston, MA: Harvard Business School Publishing, 2022. *https://www .buurtzorg.com/wp-content/uploads/2022/11/Buurtzorg-Case-Final.pdf.*

Chapter 7: Onboarding

1 Mitchell, Maurice. "Building Resilient Organizations." The Forge, November 29, 2022. *https://forgeorganizing.org/article/building-resilient-organizations.*

Chapter 8: Offboarding

1 Green, Alison, and Jerry Hauser. *Managing to Change the World: The Nonprofit Manager's Guide to Getting Results.* New York: John Wiley & Sons, 2012.

2 Green and Hauser, *Managing to Change the World*, 174.
3 Green and Hauser, *Managing to Change the World*, 171.
4 Green and Hauser, *Managing to Change the World*, 168.

Chapter 9: Cycling Out of Executive Titles

1 Khonsari, Niloufar. "Why My Nonprofit Has No Executive Director." *Nonprofit Quarterly*, January 2, 2024. *https://nonprofitquarterly.org/why-my-nonprofit-has-no-executive-director/*.
2 Khonsari, "No Executive Director."
3 Bell, Jeanne, Paola Cubías, and Byron Johnson. "Five Insights from Directors Sharing Power." *Nonprofit Quarterly*, March 28, 2017. *https://nonprofitquarterly.org/directors-sharing-power-leadership/*.

Chapter 10: Conflict

1 Rumi, Jalal al-Din. *The Masnavi: Book One*. Translated by Jawid Mojaddedi. Oxford: Oxford University Press, 2004, 25–30.
2 Thom, Kai Cheng. "Trauma-Informed Conflict Resolution." arise embodiment, accessed January 19, 2025. *https://ariseembodiment.org/conflict-resolution/*.
3 Gallo, Amy. "Why We Should Be Disagreeing More at Work." *Harvard Business Review*, January 3, 2018. *https://hbr.org/2018/01/why-we-should-be-disagreeing-more-at-work*.
4 Auburn Seminary. "Nurturing Relationships, Navigating Conflict." Accessed October 28, 2024. *https://auburnseminary.org/wp-content/uploads/2020/10/114-Nurturing-Relationships-Navigating-Conflict.pdf*.
5 brown, adrienne maree. *Emergent Strategy: Shaping Change, Changing Worlds*. Chico, CA: AK Press, 2017, 52.
6 Schatzow, Emily, and Judith Herman. "In It for the Long Haul: Trauma-Informed Practices for Sustaining Liberatory Work." Webinar from Visions, Inc. Spring Summit, virtual, April 11, 2024.
7 brown, adrienne maree. "Murmurations: Accountability Begins Within." *Yes!*, May 31, 2022. *https://www.yesmagazine.org/opinion/2022/05/31/accountability-adrienne-maree-brown*.
8 Building Accountable Communities. "Everyday Practices of Transformative Justice." October 13, 2020. *https://www.accountablecommunities.org/videos/everyday-transformative-justice*.
9 Building Accountable Communities, "Everyday Practices."
10 Barnard Center for Research on Women. "What Is Transformative Justice?" Posted March 11, 2020. YouTube, 10:29. *https://youtu.be/U-_BOFz5TXo?si=OhgvN8lhIu0W-TDQ*.
11 Building Accountable Communities, "Everyday Practices."

12 Building Accountable Communities, "Everyday Practices."

13 "The Four Parts of Accountability & How to Give a Genuine Apology." Leaving Evidence, August 15, 2023. *https://leavingevidence.wordpress.com/2019/12/18/how-to-give-a-good-apology-part-1-the-four-parts-of-accountability/*.

Chapter 11: Funding Abundance

1 Gregory, Ann Goggins, Don Howard, and Ann Goggins. "The Nonprofit Starvation Cycle." *Stanford Social Innovation Review*. Accessed October 28, 2024. *https://ssir.org/articles/entry/the_nonprofit_starvation_cycle*.

2 Mananzala, Rickke, and Dean Spade. "The Nonprofit Industrial Complex and Trans Resistance." *Sexuality Research & Social Policy* 5 (2008): 53–71.

3 California Coalition for Universal Representation. "California's Due Process Crisis: Access to Legal Counsel." Accessed October 28, 2024. *https://www.nilc.org/wp-content/uploads/2016/06/access-to-counsel-Calif-coalition-report-2016-06.pdf*.

4 Forestieri, Kevin. "County Kicks in $3.5m for Immigrant Support." *Palo Alto Online*, March 16, 2017. *https://www.paloaltoonline.com/news/2017/03/16/santa-clara-county-kicks-in-35m-for-immigrant-support/*.

5 Shin, Heidi. "Two Fearless Nuns Are Determined to Help Detained Immigrants." *The Spiritual Edge*, November 11, 2021. *https://spiritualedge.org/s1-sacred-steps/sacred-steps-two-fearless-nuns-are-determined-to-help-detained-immigrants*.

6 Homer, Ron. "3 Lessons Learned from Impact Investing Collaborations." *Philanthropy News Digest*, December 27, 2022. *https://philanthropynewsdigest.org/features/commentary-and-opinion/3-lessons-learned-from-impact-investing-collaborations*.

7 Gibson, Cynthia M., Lisa Pilar Cowen, and Jocelynne Rainey. "Philanthropy Needs to Trust the Real Experts—The People It Supports." *Nonprofit Quarterly*, February 8, 2024. *https://nonprofitquarterly.org/philanthropy-needs-to-trust-the-real-experts/*.

8 Gibson, Cynthia. "The Historical Case for Participatory Grantmaking." *HistPhil*, August 15, 2019. *https://histphil.org/2019/08/15/the-historical-case-for-participatory-grantmaking*.

9 Kawaoka-Chen, Dana. "If We Are Not Prepared to Govern, We Are Not Prepared to Win." Medium, June 24, 2021. *https://medium.com/justice-funders/if-we-are-not-prepared-to-govern-we-are-not-prepared-to-win-8990605dcc49*.

10 Mananzala and Spade, "The Nonprofit Industrial Complex."

11 Pangea Legal Services. "Fees FAQ." July 22, 2016. *https://www.pangealegal.org/fees-faqs*.

12 Mananzala and Spade, "The Nonprofit Industrial Complex."

13 Quiroz, Julie, Weyam Ghadbian, and Miriam Cuevas Enciso. "Leading with 100 Year Vision: Transforming Ourselves, Transforming the Future." Movement Strategy Center. Accessed December 9, 2024. *https://movementstrategy.org/wp-content/uploads/2020/08/Leading-with-100-Year-Vision.pdf*.

Conclusion

1 Shierholz, Heidi, Margaret Poydock, and Celine McNicholas. "Unionization Increased by 200,000 in 2022." Economic Policy Institute, January 19, 2023. *https://www.epi.org/publication/unionization-2022/*.

2 Lorde, Audre. "The Master's Tools Will Never Dismantle the Master's House." In *Sister Outsider: Essays and Speeches*, 110–13. Berkeley, CA: Crossing Press, 2012.

3 Watkinson, Allan, and Rohit Kar. "Organizational Culture: What Leaders Need to Know." Gallup.com, September 20, 2024. *https://www.gallup.com/workplace /471968/culture-transformation-leaders-need-know.aspx*.

INDEX

A

AAN (African Advocacy Network), 8
abundance mindset, 163–165, 187
accountability
    addressing accountability issues, 128
    balancing with compassion and fairness,
        130–131
    building systems of accountability, 36
    coaching out, 127–130
    co-creating clear expectations, 74–77
    mandatory parties, 76
    prioritizing, 156
    pyramid power structures, 12
    shared responsibility, 75–76, 79
    showcasing for funders, 168
advice process decision-making, 96–97
African Advocacy Network (AAN), 8
Ahimsa Collective, 146
aligning salaries with shared values, 34–36
American Association of University
    Women, 40
American Immigration Lawyers
    Association, 14
Anderson, M. Kat, 33
AORTA (Anti-Oppression Resource and
    Training Alliance), 61, 103, 119, 138,
    155, 228
API Chaya, 150–151
Argentina worker cooperatives, 13, 26–28
Arizmendi Association, 155

Arizmendiarrieta, Jose Maria, 32
Asian Pacific Islander Equality, 56
Auger-Dominguez, Daisy, 45
authority
    defining term *authority*, 98
    hiring process, 228
authority table, 202–203

B

Baker, Ella, 31–32
balancing care and boundaries, 58–59
Baldwin, James, 43
benefits
    health insurance, 42–43
    job posting, 220
    undocumented parents, 106–108
Billoo, Zahra, 178–179
BIPOC (Black, Indigenous, and people of
    color), 5
    competitive conditioning, 35
    history of oppression of marginalized
        communities, 40–41
    lack of leadership grooming, 45
    Levi Strauss Pioneers in Justice
        Fellowship, 178–179
    roots of collective governance, 31–32
    social justice organization leaders, 13
    superwoman schema, 60
    wealth gap, 41–42

BIPOC *(continued)*
    wealth trends, 42–43
    work ethic, 12
Bird's-Eye View and Project Coordinator,
    223–224
    performance evaluation, 238
Black Lives Matter, 15
Black Panther Party, 191
Black, Indigenous, and people of color
    (BIPOC). *See* BIPOC
Board Resolution for Worker Self-Direction
    and Distributed Authority, 17, 195–196
boards, 13–24
    building, 13–16
    deferring authority to staff, 17–18
    diversity, 23
    flexibility in governance, 18–19, 24
    including staff on, 17–18, 23
    key points, 22
    models, 14–18
    owls, 16–17
    Resist, 17–18
    Robert's Rules of Order, 19
    Sustainable Economies Law Center,
        16–17
    values, 19–23
Boeke, Kees, 33
Bonus Bucket Experiment, 47
bottleneck effect, pyramid power
    structures, 29
boundaries, 58–59, 62–67
    as acts of care, 64–65
    balancing care and boundaries, 58–59
    celebrating, 66, 78
    definition of, 62
    developing well-boundaried organization,
        65–66
    Points of Unity, 61–62
    reassessing, 66
    setting and holding, 62–67, 77–78
    survey of work-life balance and
        boundaries, 61, 78
    Task Redistribution Chart, 62, 73, 78,
        199–200
Braiding Sweetgrass (Kimmerer), 33
brown, adrienne maree, 88–90, 136, 141,
    143, 149
budgeting. *See also* funding
    benefits for undocumented parents,
        106–108
    Income Hub, 92
    Pangea payroll challenge, 184–185
    transparently and collectively, 184–185
    with values, 178–182
burnout
    compensation categories, 47
    high turnover rate, 87
    proactive staffing, 186
    reducing through distributed decision-
        making, 168
    role-mapping, 64
    scarcity mindset, 161–163
    social justice nonprofit sector, 5
    vacation days, 66–67
Butler, Octavia, 88
Buurtzorg home-care nursing case study,
    109–111
BuzzFeed, Irani Garcia Zacarius op-ed,
    69, 70

C

California Dignity for Families Fund
    (CDFF), 171
campaigns, 174–175
candidacy period for new hires,
    119–120, 124
    additional benefits of, 123
    offboarding, 125–127, 131
    Pangea Candidacy Period Policy,
        225–228
    performance evaluations, 121–123, 226
CDFF (California Dignity for Families
    Fund), 171
Celebrating boundaries, 66, 78
chain-of-command systems, 28–29
Cheese Board Collective, 60
    conflict transformation, 154–156
    onboarding, 119–120
    paying for job applicants' time, 186
The Circle Way: A Leader in Every Chair
    (Baldwin and Linnea), 90
circle-based hub system, 88–89
    considerations for decision-making
        system, 98–99

decision-making and voting, 91–97
    Pangea hubs, 204
circles in governance, 90
coaching out, 127–130
coalitions, funding, 165–166
co-directors
    candidacy period, 225–228
    cycling out of executive titles, 133–138
    performance evaluations, 231–244
Collective Courage: A History of African
    American Cooperative Economic Thought
    and Practice (Nembhard), 13, 32
collective governance, 13, 30–34
    board structure, 14–18
    centered on shared values, 19–23
    Indigenous wisdom, 33–34
    key points, 22
    pay equity. *See* pay equity
    roots of, 31–33
    Teal Revolution, 33
collective leadership, 11–13, 31. *See also*
    collective governance
collectives. *See* cooperatives/collectives
collectivism, 31. *See also* collective governance
commitment, 189
communication
    boundaries, 65
    compensation, 48
    transparency in. *See* transparency
Communications Hub, 92, 204
Community Empowerment and Policy
    Advocacy Hub, 92, 204
Community Foundations Leading
    Change, 170
Community Resource Initiative, 20, 46
compassion, balancing with fairness and
    accountability, 130–131
compensation, 39–43
    acknowledging applicant socioeconomic
        barriers, 52
    aligning salaries with shared values,
        34–36
    benefits. *See* benefits
    categories of compensation, 47
    considering salary equity, 37
    creating equitable salary structures, 47
    defining limits, 52–53
    educational roadblocks, 44–45

evolving salary needs, 45–47
four-day workweek, 104
history and staistics, 39–43
learning from social justice
    organizations, 53
one-time founders' compensation,
    133–134
pathways and practice, 50–52
questioning beliefs about money, 52
redefining merit/value of lived
    experience, 47, 48–50, 53
transparency and trust, 48, 53, 116
competitive conditioning, 35
conflict, 139–140
    acknowledging and addressing harm,
        147–149, 155
    addressing proactively, 146
    designating leader for relational work,
        73–74, 78–79
    external pressures, 141–142
    giving feedback, 151–153, 157
    incorporating transformative justice,
        149–150
    letting employees go, 154. *See also*
        offboarding
    principled struggle, 140
    receiving feedback, 153–154, 157
    reflection, consent, and regularity,
        150–151
    securing external support, 154–156
    small cuts/interpersonal issues,
        145–147
    transformative justice, 147–149
    types of, 140–147
    unresolved wounds and enmeshment,
        142–145
consensus decision-making, 95, 97, 207
consent
    decision-making, 95–97
    incorporating into feedback, 150–151
Convergence, 56
cooperatives/collectives, 13
    African Americans, 32
    AORTA (Anti-Oppression Resource and
        Training Alliance), 61, 103, 119, 138,
        155, 228
    Argentina, 26–28
    Arizmendi Association, 155

cooperatives/collectives *(continued)*
    Cheese Board Collective, 60, 119–120,
       154–156, 186
    Mondragon, Spain, 32
    Movement Generation, 73, 146–147, 157
    Other Avenues Grocery Collective, 155
    Rainbow Grocery Cooperative, 155
corporate sponsorships and partnerships, 175
crisis, and opportunity, 13, 84
Cuautle, Esperanza, 49–50, 114–116, 129
culture of care, 55
    balancing care and boundaries, 58–59
    building team and trust, 56–58, 77
    co-creating clear expectations, 74–77
    living values daily, 55–56
    setting and holding boundaries, 62–67,
       77–78
    structure to support culture. *See* structure
    urgency trap, 59–62
    valuing emotional labor, 68–74, 78
Currie, Sylvia, 90
cybernetics, 33
cycling out of executive titles, 133–138

D

DACA (Deferred Action for Childhood
    Arrivals) program, 10–11
    San Francisco DACA internship
       program, 49
Dallaire, Rachelle, 19
DARCI, 91
Dean Spade, 171
decision-making, 91–97
    authority table, 202–203
    common decision-making methods, 95–97
    communicating for funders, 168
    considerations for developing, 98–99
    consensus, 207
    deferring authority and decision-making
       to staff, 17–18
    delegating with clarity, 36
    email feedback/voting, 207–209
    Email Proposal Template, 211–212
    encouraging diverse feedback, 100
    flowchart, 201

    large-scale decisions, 209–210
    offboarding, 132
    Pangea decision-making policy, 205–210
    policy developing and voting,
       104–105, 110
    pyramid power structures, 12
    quorum, 205–206
Deferred Action for Childhood Arrivals
    (DACA) program, 10–11
    San Francisco DACA internship
       program, 49
deportations. *See also* immigrant
    representation
    double punishment of immigrants, 179
    fear of, 141
    Jesus Ruiz Diego, 10
    legal system roadblocks, 171
    Obama administration, 8
    Pangea's mission, 14
    Rosa, 85
    Universal Representation campaign, 82
    valuing emotional labor, 68
Diego, Jesus Ruiz, 8–11, 21–23, 49–50, 63,
    84, 115, 164, 166, 171
director of culture and people, 73–74, 78–79
diversity, boards, 23
DreamRider Productions, 19
due process, offboarding, 132

E

earned income, 175–176, 183
ED (executive director), 15
    hiring of, 18
    Pangea, 25
    salary, 51
    transitioning from conventional
       leadership titles, 133–138
education
    redefining merit/value of lived
       experience, 47, 48–50, 53
    roadblocks, 44–45
Ella Baker Black Studies Reader (Mueller), 31
email
    feedback/voting, 207–209
    proposal template, 211–212

emotional labor, 68–74, 78

employee "life cycle", 113

Endenburg, Gerard, 33

enmeshment, 142–145

equity-based salaries. *See* salaries

Esquivel, Adolfo Pérez, 27

evaluations

candidacy period, 121–123, 226

co-directors, 231–244

execution, defining, 98

executive director (ED), 15

hiring of, 18

Pangea, 25

salary, 51

transitioning from conventional
leadership titles, 133–138

executive titles, cycling out of, 133–138

exit interviews, 129–130, 132

expectations, 74–77

external pressures, 141–142

external support for conflict resolution,
154–156

F

fairness, balancing with compassion and
accountability, 130–131

Faith in Action Bay Area, 170

fear

fear-based decision-making, 162

of ICE, 141

fee-based revenue, 175–176, 183

feedback, 157

email, 207–209

encouraging diverse feedback, 100

giving, 151–153

incorporating reflection, consent, and
regularity, 150–151

incorporating transformative justice
principles, 149–150

policy development, 104, 107, 110

preference chart, 245

providing ongoing support, 131

receiving, 153–154

Finance Committee, one-time founders'
compensation, 134

Finance Hub, 92, 204

firing. *See also* offboarding

top-down decision-making, 15

voting, 93, 97, 132

First Nations Pedagogy Online, 90

"Five Insights from Directors Sharing
Power", 138

five-year strategic plan, 82–83, 105

inclusion of wellness, 61

flat salary structure, 36, 43, 45–46, 51–52,
81, 113–114, 160

flexibility in governance, 18–19, 24

flocking, 89–90

Floyd, George, 4

foundation grants, 173

four-day workweek, 104–105

Free Breakfast for Children program, 191

FREE SF (Full Rights, Equality, and
Empowerment Coalition of San
Francisco), 9–10, 14

Freedom for Immigrants, 166

Fulbright Fellowship, 2, 11

Full Picture Justice, 20, 46

Full Rights, Equality, and Empowerment
Coalition of San Francisco (FREE SF),
9–10, 14

Function Junction Hub, 92, 204

funding, 159–160

abundance mindset, 163–165, 187

after Donald Trump election, 82–83

balancing organizational needs,
182–184

benefits and challenges of different
funding sources, 172–177

breaking scarcity mindset, 161–163

budgeting transparently and collectively,
184–185

budgeting with values, 178–182

coalitions and compromise, 165–166

collaborating rather than competing, 186

corporate sponsorships and
partnerships, 175

cost of repair, 160–161

earned income, 175–176, 183

fee-based revenue, 183

forging new paths in philanthropy,
170–172

funding *(continued)*
    foundation grants, 173
    fundraising, 174–175
    government, 174
    highlighting victories, 187
    individual donations, 172–173
    membership revenue, 176
    planned giving, 176–177
    planning for visionary growth, 186
    rethinking "investment", 185
    scarcity-driven funding, 162
    sharing the vision, 166–168
    social media fundraising, 177
    strings attached, 160–161
    trust-based and participatory,
        169–170
    Yield Giving grant, 159–160
fundraising, 159, 174–175, 184. *See also*
    funding
    long-term relational work, 187
    social media platforms, 177

G

Gallo, Amy, 140
gaps, acknowledging/addressing, 87–88, 108,
    110–111
Garcia Zacarius, Irani, 69–72, 166
Gaudet, Michelle, 19
Gibson, Cynthia, 169–170
giving feedback, 151–153
goals, performance evaluations, 232
Good Mud, 89
Gordon Nembhard, Jessica, 13, 19, 32
governance
    evaluating, 239
    "indigenized" governance tools, 19
Governance Hub, 91, 204
government funding, 174
gradient voting, 96–97, 206
grants
    foundations, 173
    government, 174
    highlighting victories in applications and
        reports, 187
Great Resignation, 5

Green, Alison, 128–129
Grove Foundation, 172

H

harm, acknowledging and addressing, 147–
    149, 155
Harmonize, 40, 47, 155
Harvard Business Review, 140
Harvard Business School Buurtzorg case
    study, 109–111
Hauser, Jerry, 128–129
health insurance, 42–43
Hicks, Kendra, 17
hiring. *See also* onboarding
    executive director (ED), 18
    reference checks, 117–118, 229–230
    top-down decision-making, 15
    voting, 93, 97
"The Historical Case for Participatory
    Grantmaking" (Gibson), 169
history of oppression of marginalized
    communities, 40–41
Honorable Harvest, 33
Hormachea, Nancy, 8
household income statistics, 41
HR Hub, 92, 102, 204
    benefits for undocumented parents,
        106–108
    employee "life cycle", 113
    four-day workweek, 105
    Life Happens policy, 102–103, 110,
        215–216
    one-time founders' compensation,
        133–134
hub system, 88–89
    circles in governance, 90
    considerations for decision-making
        system, 98–99
    decision-making and voting, 91–97
    list of Pangea hubs, 204
human resources
    Human Resources Hub. *See* HR Hub
    Life Happens policy, 102–103, 110,
        215–216
Hussein, Saddam, 72

I

ICE (Immigration and Customs
     Enforcement), 8
     action against Rosa, 84–85
     closing of Yuba detention center, 115
     detention of Irani Garcia Zacarius, 69–70
     detention of Jesus Ruiz Diego, 9–11
     fear of, 141
     Migra Watch, 84
     recovering bond money from, 49–50
     Secure Communities, 8
"If We Are Not Prepared to Govern, We Are
     Not Prepared to Win" (Kawaoka-Chen),
     170
Illegal Immigration Reform and Immigrant
     Responsibility Act of 1996, 8
immigrant representation, 8
     African Advocacy Network (AAN), 8
     double punishment of immigrants, 179
     emotional labor of advocating, 72
     Irani Garcia Zacarius, 69–71
     Jesus Ruiz Diego, 8–11
     legal defense attorneys, 163–164
     Pangea mission, 14
     publicly funded legal representation
          programs, 166
     Rosa, 84–86
     Universal Representation campaign, 82
immigrants
     competitive conditioning, 35
     work ethic, 12
Immigration and Customs Enforcement.
     See ICE
implementation, defining, 98
"In Indigenous Nonprofit Governance,
     Values Matter More Than Tools"
     (Dallaire), 19
*Inclusion Revolution: The Essential Guide
     to Dismantling Racial Inequity in the
     Workplace* (Auger-Dominguez), 45
Income Hub, 92, 159, 204
     fundraising, 184
"indigenized" values and governance tools, 19
Indigenous cultures
     Black, Indigenous, and people of color
          (BIPOC). *See* BIPOC
     collective governance, 33–34
     First Nations Pedagogy Online, 90
     Muscogee Nation, 90
individual donations, 172–173
Insight Collaborative, 125–126
insurance (health insurance), 42–43
integrity, 101–102
Interfaith Movement for Human Integrity, 85
interviews, 116–117, 123–124
     exit interviews, 129–130, 132
Iran, 72
Irani. *See* Garcia Zacarius, Irani
Iranian diaspora, 1
Iran-Iraq War, 1, 72
IRS, 18
Islamic Republic, 72

J

Jesus. See Diego, Jesus Ruiz
job descriptions
     performance evaluation, 243–244
     Bird's-Eye View and Project Coordinator,
          223–224
job postings, 113–114
     Removal Defense Attorney, 217–221
Justice Funders, 170

K

Kaminski, June, 90
Kawaoka-Chen, Dana, 170
Kimmerer, Robin Wall, 33
Kwawer, Rek, 57, 66

L

Laloux, Frédéric, 33
large-scale decisions, 209–210
Lavender Phoenix, 56
Law Center (Sustainable Economies Law
     Center), 16–18, 50, 138
lawyers, overreliance on, 20
Le, Vu, 15–16, 18–19

leadership
  BIPOC social justice organizations, 13
  boards. *See* boards
  chain-of-command systems, 28–29
  collective governance. *See* collective
      governance
  collective leadership, 11–13
  pyramid power structures, 12, 29–30
LeBlanc, Judith, 186
LeBourdais, Vanessa, 19
Lee, Deborah, 85
Lee, N'Tanya, 140
legal defense attorneys for immigrants, 163–164
Legal Services Hub, 76, 92, 204
legislation
  history of oppression of marginalized
      communities, 40–41
  Illegal Immigration Reform and
      Immigrant Responsibility Act of
      1996, 8
  legal defense attorneys representation,
      163–164
letting employees go. *See* offboarding
Levi Strauss Pioneers in Justice Fellowship,
    178–179
"life cycle" of employees, 113
Life Happens policy, 102–103, 110, 215–216
Linnea, Ann, 90
Long, Clara, 82
Lorde, Audre, 56

M

majority voting, 96–97
"Making Economic Democracy Work: How
    to Practice Shared Leadership" (Wires), 13
Managing to Change the World (Green and
    Hauser), 128–129
Mananzala, Rickke, 44, 171
mandatory parties, 76
Maru, Vivek, 128
Maté, Gabor, 142–143
membership revenue, 176
mentorship, 50
  candidacy periods, 119, 124
  PIPs, 131
merit, redefining, 47–50, 53

Migra Watch, 84
mindset
  abundance, 163–165, 187
  scarcity, 161–163
Mingus, Mia, 145–147, 156
missions, 14
Mitchell, Maurice, 86–87, 119
MOCHA, 91
modeling boundaries, 66
moments of crisis, 84
Mondragon, Spain worker cooperative, 32
Moraga, Jessica Yamane, 120
Mossadegh, Mohammad, 72
"The Most Dangerous Notion in 'Reinventing
    Organizations'" (Prentice), 33
Movement Generation, 73, 146–147, 157
Mueller, Carol, 31
Muscogee Nation, 90

N

Namati, 128
NASCO (North American Students of
    Cooperation), 57, 66
National Immigrant Youth Alliance (NIYA),
    9–10
Native Organizers Alliance, 186
New York University (NYU) Immigrant
    Rights Clinic, 49
New Yorker, 32
nigam, kiran, 60–61, 82, 87–88, 90–93, 113,
    116, 119, 122, 228
Nobody Knows My Name (Baldwin), 43
Nonprofit AF, 15
Nonprofit Democracy Network, 138
"The Nonprofit Industrial Complex and
    Trans Resistance" (Mananzala and Spade),
    44–45, 171
nonprofit organizations
  Great Resignation, 5
  Public Service Loan Forgiveness, 11
  statistics, 5
Nonprofit Quarterly, 13, 135, 138, 169
nonprofit starvation cycle, 162
North American Students of Cooperation
    (NASCO), 57
Nube, Mateo, 147

O

Obama, Barack, 8, 11
offboarding, 125–132
    balancing compassion, fairness, and
      accountability, 130–131
    candidacy periods, 125–127, 131
    coaching out, 127–130
    exit interviews, 129–130, 132
    maintaining clear policies, 124
    proactive structures and culture for
      conducting transitions, 154
    severance packages, 129, 132
Omid Advocates for Human Rights, 8
onboarding, 113–124
    candidacy periods, 119–124. *See also*
      candidacy period for new hires
    designing, 120–121
    job posting, 217–221
    maintaining clear policies, 124
    performance evaluations, 121–123, 226
    recruiting, 114–116, 138. *See also*
      recruiting
    reference checks, 117–118, 229–230
    transparency and interviews, 116–117,
      123–124
One Justice, 182
one-time founders' compensation,
    133–134
Operations Hub (Function Junction),
    92, 204
organizational integrity, 101–102
organizers, working with, 8–11
Orsi, Janelle, 16, 50
Other Avenues Grocery Collective, 155
owl model, boards, 16–17, 24
ownership, defining, 98

P

PACT (People Acting in Community
    Together), 21, 49
Palestine Heirloom Seed Library, 89
Pangea Legal Services, 2–4
    authority table, 202–203
    benefits for undocumented parents,
      106–108

board structure, 16–18
Candidacy Period Policy, 225–228.
    See also candidacy period for new
    hires
collective governance and leadership,
    11–13
decision-making and voting, 91–97, 201,
    205–210
early leadership, 25
Email Proposal Template, 211–212
employee "life cycle", 113
executive directors, 25, 135–137
fee-based revenue, 183
first employee, 25
first law fellow, 39, 45, 55, 113
five-year strategic plan, 82–83, 105
flat salary structure, 36, 43, 45–46,
    51–52, 81, 113–114, 160
formation of board, 13–16
founding of, 2, 7, 11
four-day workweek, 104–105
fundraising, 184
growing pains, 82
HR Hub, 102, 113
hub system. *See* hub system
Income Hub, 184
job descriptions, 223–224, 243–244
job posting, 217–221
Life Happens policy, 102–103, 110,
    215–216
mandatory parties, 76
mission, 14
open salary conversations, 48
overreliance on lawyers, 20
pay equity, 34–36
pay gaps, 34–36, 39, 51–52
payroll challenge, 184–185
Points of Unity. *See* Points of Unity
recruiting practices and standards, 114
relationship-building, 21
retreats, 61, 87–88, 91, 105, 137
risk aversion, 20
rooted in community and shared values,
    19–23
salary systems, 46
sharing leadership, 25. *See also* sharing
    leadership
supervisors, 75–76

Pangea Legal Services *(continued)*
  survey of work-life balance and
      boundaries, 61
  Task Redistribution Chart, 62,
      199–200
  team structure, 108–111
  Universal Representation campaign, 82
  value of lived experience, 47, 48–50, 53
parents, benefits for, 106
participatory democracy, 31. *See also*
  collective governance
participatory philanthropy, 169–170
pay equity. *See also* salaries
  acknowledging applicant socioeconomic
      barriers, 52
  aligning salaries with shared values,
      34–36
  categories of compensation, 47
  compensation history and staistics,
      39–43
  compensation pathways and practice,
      50–52
  considering salary equity, 37, 39
  creating equitable salary structures, 47
  defining limits, 52–53
  educational roadblocks, 44–45
  evolving salary needs, 45–47
  learning from social justice
      organizations, 53
  questioning beliefs about money, 52
  redefining merit/value of lived
      experience, 47, 48–50, 53
  transparency and trust, 48, 53
pay gaps, 34–36, 39, 51–52
Penn State Workplace Emotional Labor and
    Diversity Lab, 68
People Acting in Community Together
    (PACT), 21, 49
People's Organization, 83–84
performance evaluations
  candidacy period, 121–123, 226
  co-directors, 231–244
performance improvement plans. *See* PIPs
philanthropic funding
  forging new paths in, 170–172
  scarcity mindset, 161–163
  strings attached, 160–161
  trust-based, 169–170

"Philanthropy Needs to Trust the Real
    Experts", 169
Picton, Cory, 70
PIPs (performance improvement plans),
    76–77
  avoiding drawn-out PIPs, 129
  incorporating mentorship and peer
      support, 131
planned giving, 176–177
Points of Unity, 61–62, 66, 85–86, 103,
    119–120, 123, 127–128, 181, 195,
    197–198, 225
  alignment with, 209
  Communications Hub, 92
  job posting, 219–220
  performance evaluation, 241–242
  recruiting practices and standards, 114
policy, 101
  acknowledging gaps, 108, 110–111
  benefits for undocumented parents,
      106–108
  Candidacy Period Policy, 225–228
  decision-making, 205–210
  developing and voting, 104–105, 110
  handling newly passed policies, 213
  Life Happens policy, 102–103, 110,
      215–216
  onboarding policies and candidacy
      periods, 120–121, 124
  organizational integrity, 101–102
  reflection of values, 102–105
  teams of twelve, 108–111
position announcement, 113–114,
    217–221
Potawatomi, 33–34
power
  collective governance, 13
  collective leadership, 11–13
  deferring authority and decision-making
      to staff, 17–18
  pyramid power structures, 12, 29–30
  recognizing inherited systems, 36
Prentice, Jessica, 33
principled struggle, 140
principles, statement of, 197–198
Public Service Loan Forgiveness, 11
Pukhraj, Ambri, 60, 120
pyramid power structures, 12, 29–30

Q

quorum for decision-making, 205–206

R

Rai, Priya, 150–151
Rainbow Grocery Cooperative, 155
receiving feedback, 153–154
recruiting, 114–116
  diverse strengths, 36
  experienced collective leaders, 138
  job postings, 113–114, 217–221
  nine-month candidacy period for new
    hires, 119–124, 225–228
  reference checks, 117–118, 229–230
  scarcity mentality, 163
  transparency and interviews, 114,
    116–117, 123–124
reference checks, 117–118, 229–230
reflection
  incorporating into feedback,
    150–151, 153
  prioritizing self-reflection, 156
regularity, incorporating into feedback,
  150–151
Reinventing Organizations (Laloux), 33
relationship-building, 21, 23
  building team and trust, 56–58
  cultivating culture of care. *See* culture
    of care
  designating leader for relational work,
    73–74, 78–79
reliability, evaluating, 241
remote work, 103
reparation, and compensation, 47
Resist, 17–18
"Resist as a Worker Self-Directed Nonprofit"
  (Hicks), 17
responsibility
  defining term *responsibility*, 98
  performance evaluation, 240
  pyramid power structures, 12
  taking, 153
retreats, 61, 87–88, 91, 105, 137
  planning for visionary growth, 186
revolution, 7

"Right-Sized Belonging: Six Practices for
  Organizers" (Wills), 56
risk aversion, 20
Robert's Rules of Order, 19
Robertson, Brian, 32
Rodney, Jon, 10
role-mapping, 64, 79
Rooted in Vibrant Communities (RVC), 15,
  63–64
Rosa (immigrant client), 84–86, 164, 166
Ruiz, Grisel, 82
Rumi, 139
RVC (Rooted in Vibrant Communities), 15,
  63–64

S

Saadi, 59
salaries
  acknowledging applicant socioeconomic
    barriers, 52
  aligning with shared values, 34–36
  categories of compensation, 47
  compensation history and staistics,
    39–43
  compensation pathways and practice,
    50–52
  considering salary equity, 37
  creating equitable salary structures, 47
  defining limits, 52–53
  educational roadblocks, 44–45
  evolving needs, 45–47
  flat salary structure, 36, 43, 45–46,
    51–52, 81, 113–114, 160
  four-day workweek, 104
  learning from social justice
    organizations, 53
  pay gaps, 34–36, 39, 51–52
  questioning beliefs about money, 52
  redefining merit/value of lived
    experience, 47, 48–50, 53
  transparency and trust, 48, 53, 114, 116
Sampath, Roshni, 63–64, 73
San Francisco Foundation, 166
San Francisco, California, 7–10, 14
  DACA internship program, 49
  drafting proposals for, 165

San Francisco, California *(continued)*
  living wage, 51
  new Pangea office, 36
  publicly funded removal defense
    programs, 166
  representation for detained
    immigrants, 166
Sansour, Vivien, 89
Santa Clara County, California, 163–165
  exclusionary funding offer, 179–180
  publicly funded removal defense
    programs, 166
  representation for detained
    immigrants, 166
Savage-Sangwan, Kiran, 10
Savalza, Luis Angel Reyes, 49–50
scarcity mindset, breaking, 161–163
scarcity-driven funding, 162
Secure Communities, 8
SEEDS Community Resolution
  Center, 154
Set Boundaries, Find Peace (Tawwab), 59
setting boundaries, 62–67, 77–78
severance packages, 129, 132
shah of Iran, 72
Shah, Sonya, 146–147
shared accountability, 75–76, 79
shared values, 19–23
sharing leadership, 25
  Argentina worker cooperatives,
    26–28
  challenges of pyramid power, 29–30
  challenging traditional chain of
    command, 28–29
  collective governance, 30–34. *See also*
    collective governance
  pay equity. *See* pay equity
Silicon Valley Community
  Foundation, 172
small cuts, 145–147
social justice organizations
  BIPOC leaders, 13
  salary systems, 53
social media fundraising, 177
*Sociocracy: The Organization of Decision-
  Making* (Endenburg), 33
Spade, Dean, 44

SRLP (Sylvia Rivera Law Project),
  162–163, 183
staff
  conflict (small cuts), 145–147
  deferring authority and decision-making
    to staff, 17–18
  feedback preference chart, 245
  including on boards, 17–18, 23
  nine-month candidacy period for new
    hires, 119–124, 225–228
  onboarding. *See* onboarding
  overstretching, 162
  recruiting diverse strengths, 36
  retreats. *See* retreats
  turnover rate, 87
statement of values and principles, 61,
  197–198
Stephens, Sara, 18
strategic plan, 82–83, 105, 138
  alignment with, 209
  wellness, 61
structure, 81–87
  addressing gaps, 87–88
  challenges without an organizational
    structure, 86–87
  circle-based hub system, 88–89, 204
  circles in governance, 90
  considerations for decision-making
    system, 98–99
  DARCI and MOCHA, 91
  decision-making and voting, 91–97
  flocking, 89–90
  onboarding policies and candidacy
    periods, 120–121, 124
  strategic plan, 82–83, 105, 138
student loans, 44
Student Nonviolent Coordinating
  Committee, 32
supermajority voting, 96–97
supervisors, 75–76, 79
superwoman schema, 60
surveys
  work-life balance and boundaries,
    61, 78
  workweek policy, 105
Sustainable Economies Law Center, 16–18,
  50, 138

Sylvia Rivera Law Project (SRLP),
162–163, 183
"Systemic Racism and the Gender Pay
Gap: A Supplement to the Simple
Truth", 40

T

taking responsibility, 153
Task Redistribution Chart, 62, 73, 78, 199–200
Tawwab, Nedra Glover, 59
Taylor, Breonna, 4
Teal Revolution, 33
teams
building, 56–58, 77
conflict (small cuts), 145–147
recruiting, 114–116
structuring, 108–111
survey of work-life balance and
boundaries, 61, 78
Tending the Wild (Anderson), 33
termination. See offboarding
Thom, Kai Cheng, 139–140
titles, cycling out of executive titles, 133–138
Tittle, Chris, 50
transformation, 190
transformative justice, 147–149
incorporating into daily practice, 149–150
transparency
accountability, 75, 77
budgeting, 184–185
compensation, 48, 53
decision-making, 91
interviews, 116–117, 123–124
lack of, 87
recruiting, 114, 116
showcasing for funders, 168
trauma
unresolved wounds and enmeshment,
142–145
valuing emotional labor, 68–74, 78
Trouverol-Callejo, Tessa, 166
Trump, Donald, 82, 141
trust
building, 56–58, 77
compensation, 48

trust-based philanthropy, 169–170
turnover rate, 87
twelve-member teams, 108–111

U

undocumented parents, benefits for,
106–108
union organizing, 190
Universal Representation campaign, 82
urgency trap, 59–62

V

vacation days
celebrating time away, 66
using, 67
values. See also culture of care
aligning salaries with, 34–36
articulating, 166–168
benefits for undocumented
parents, 108
budgeting with, 178–182
collective governance centered on shared
values, 19–23
"indigenized", 19
living daily, 55–56
Points of Unity. See Points of Unity
policies reflect values, 102–105
statement of values and principles, 61,
197–198
valuing emotional labor, 68–74, 78
Vincent, Marie, 2, 25, 34, 36, 133
additional compensation, 134
pay gap, 34–36, 51–52
visionary growth, planning for, 186
volunteers, overreliance on, 162
voting, 93–97
Candidacy Period Policy,
226–227
email, 207–209, 211–212
gradient voting, 206
hiring/firing, 93, 97, 132
policies, 104–105, 110
quorum, 205–206

W

Wadhawan, Sheena, 66, 76, 127, 150–153, 155
Warren, Elizabeth, 44
wealth gap, 41–42
wealth trends, 42
wellness, 61
"Who Got Rich off the Student Debt Crisis?", 44
"Why My Nonprofit Has No Executive Director" (Khonsari), 135
"Why We Should Be Disagreeing More at Work" (Gallo), 140
Wills, Ablaza, 56
Wills, Sammie Ablaza, 56
Wires, Nicole, 13
women
    lack of leadership grooming, 45
    Levi Strauss Pioneers in Justice Fellowship, 178–179
    superwoman schema, 60
work ethic of immigrants and BIPOC workers, 12
worker collectives/cooperatives, 13
    African Americans, 32
    AORTA (Anti-Oppression Resource and Training Alliance), 61, 103, 119, 138, 155, 228
    Argentina, 26–28
    Arizmendi Association, 155

    Cheese Board Collective, 60, 119–120, 154–156, 186
    Mondragon, Spain, 32
    Movement Generation, 73, 146–147, 157
    Other Avenues Grocery Collective, 155
    Rainbow Grocery Cooperative, 155
worker self-directed nonprofit organizations, 170
workforce
    Great Resignation, 5
    statistics, 5
working remotely, 103
work-life balance, 66–67
    four-day workweek, 104–105
    survey of, 61, 78
    vacation days, 66, 67
workload
    performance evaluation, 243–244
    using proactive staffing to stay below full workload, 186
Workplace Emotional Labor and Diversity Lab (Penn State), 68
workweek, 104–105

Y

Yield Giving grant, 160
Yuba, California
    closing of ICE detention center, 115
    detention of Jesus Ruiz Diego, 10

ABOUT THE AUTHOR

Niloufar Khonsari (she/they) is a dedicated leader in collective governance, with over twenty years of experience in social justice advocacy, movement lawyering, and shaping values-driven organizations. Their approach is rooted in extensive training from activists, undocumented organizers, and community leaders focused on creating more just and equitable systems.

As co-founder of Pangea Legal Services, Nilou helped build a high-functioning, collaboratively run nonprofit that supported over fifty thousand immigrants, led efforts to close three immigration detention facilities in Northern California, and secured $50 million for immigrant legal representation.

Now, as a consultant, coach, and facilitator, Nilou partners with social justice organizations to strengthen team dynamics, build supportive structures, and cultivate cultures of care where both people and missions thrive.

Nilou's expertise has been recognized with multiple awards, including the BIPOC Pioneers in Justice Award from the Levi Strauss Foundation and the Innovative Leader in Struggles for Justice Distinguished Fellowship by the Squire Patton Boggs Foundation. They are a graduate of Georgetown University's School of Foreign Service and Georgetown Law.

Nilou lives on the unceded Ohlone land Huichin (Berkeley, California), where she enjoys dancing, hiking, poetry gatherings, and parenting her joyful young daughter.

ABOUT
NORTH ATLANTIC BOOKS

North Atlantic Books (NAB) is an independent, nonprofit publisher committed to a bold exploration of the relationships between mind, body, spirit, and nature. Founded in 1974, NAB aims to nurture a holistic view of the arts, sciences, humanities, and healing. To make a donation or to learn more about our books, authors, events, and newsletter, please visit *www.northatlanticbooks.com*.